MW01126824

To Bill & Peg,
The best couple ,

Keep Swinging

Eddie Mitchell

Baseball Rowdies of the 19th Century

*Brawlers, Drinkers, Pranksters
and Cheats in the Early Days
of the Major Leagues*

EDDIE MITCHELL

McFarland & Company, Inc., Publishers
Jefferson, North Carolina

LIBRARY OF CONGRESS CATALOGUING-IN-PUBLICATION DATA

Names: Mitchell, Eddie, 1945– author.
Title: Baseball rowdies of the 19th century : brawlers, drinkers, pranksters and cheats in the early days of the major leagues / Eddie Mitchell.
Other titles: Baseball rowdies of the nineteenth century
Description: Jefferson, North Carolina : McFarland & Company, Inc., Publishers, 2018 | Includes bibliographical references and index.
Identifiers: LCCN 2018026963 | ISBN 9781476664873 (softcover : acid free paper) ∞
Subjects: LCSH: Baseball—United States—Anecdotes. | Baseball—United States—History—19th century. | Baseball players—United States—Biography. | Baseball managers—United States—Biography. | Baseball umpires—United States—Biography. | Baseball team owners—United States—Biography.
Classification: LCC GV873 .M54 2018 | DDC 796.3570973/09034—dc23
LC record available at https://lccn.loc.gov/2018026963

BRITISH LIBRARY CATALOGUING DATA ARE AVAILABLE

ISBN (print) 978-1-4766-6487-3
ISBN (ebook) 978-1-4766-2962-9

Front cover: 1887 Tobin lithograph baseball card depicting Dan Brouthers (Wood River Gallery)

Printed in the United States of America

McFarland & Company, Inc., Publishers
Box 611, Jefferson, North Carolina 28640
www.mcfarlandpub.com

To Sandra, my beloved wife,
who has learned to love baseball,
and to my son, Coach David Mitchell,
who taught me the game

ACKNOWLEDGMENTS

Special thanks are due the Society for American Baseball Research, which has published extensively on the 19th century over the decades, and to its members, for their careful good work not only in researching but in documenting their sources. Many SABR articles were not only highly useful in themselves but led me to other, primary sources.

Thank you, as well, to my typist, Beverly McGhghy.

Finally, the Portsmouth Library and the National Baseball Hall of Fame Library provided access to a variety of sources, including the many historical newspapers consulted in the research for this book. I offer my thanks to these institutions and their staff members.

books to digitized newspapers and magazines. In short, I spent the two years looking at every nineteenth-century player I could find, consulting as many books and articles on the period as I could get my hands on. None was more helpful to me than David Nemec's fine reference work *The Great Encyclopedia of 19th Century Major League Baseball.*

A Note on the Organization and Sources

The book is organized first into four main categories: players, managers, owners, and umpires. Players, representing the largest of these groups, are subdivided into pitchers, infielders and outfielders, primarily because these subdivisions allowed for chapters more nearly equal in length. A fifth category, which appears under the admittedly vague title "Other Rowdies," is devoted to the more interesting people and stories that fit none of the other chapters but were too fascinating to leave out.

The reader should note that a few individuals (e.g., King Kelly) appear in more than one chapter, and that others appear in chapters (again, King Kelly) that the reader might not think to look for them. In both instances, placement is based entirely on the role these individuals played in the story cited.

Within each chapter, entries are alphabetical by player surname, and sources are generally identified within the text rather than in notes.

1

UNMANAGEABLE MANAGERS

Tom Burns, Chicago Orphans, Pittsburg

Tom Burns took Cap Anson's place in 1898. The Chicago Orphans players objected to his awarding of "Captain" to Jimmy Ryan over Bill Lange. This caused the players not to take the field on Opening Day. Right away, Burns wrote to league president Nick Young, "Whatever is the reason: I am sure we do not get what is coming to us when Tom Lynch is umpiring. When outfielder Jim Ryan injured his hamstring, Ryan told Manager Burns he could not play, but the Manager told him either he play or be released."

His pitching policy was to let the pitcher take a beating rather than bring in a substitute. He had the same philosophy for his fielders, saying "there is no one to take their place."

Burns would joke with his players about erroneous play. He did not mind his players drinking as long as they made curfew and practice. However, a player must come to the game sober. Shortstop Gene De Montreville came intoxicated, and Burns made him sit in the grandstand and fined him $25. Only a couple of days later, pitcher Bill Phyle had been drinking and did not arrive on time. Burns was lax on other matters, such as allowing Bill Lange's attendance at a horse race while using the excuse of being best man for a wedding. Yet later, Burns fined Lange $100 for faking an injury.

An early-season conversation, Chicago's Cap Anson and Tom Burns, the Pittsburg manager, was recorded in the *Chicago Daily News* (May 25, 1892):

TOM: You're in luck, Anson. The rain is a good thing. If you go east, you'll be 20 points lower. You can't hope to win against my team.

CAP: Certainly, Tom. If it was any other club. I didn't want to go against your people.

TOM: That's right, Cap. I like to see a man be frank and own up in a case of this kind.

CAP: You see, Tom. I didn't want to hurt your feelings. A defeat would reduce your popularity you enjoy in the "Smokey City."

TOM: Meanest remark I heard you make, and I'll quit you right there.

Charlie "Commy" Comiskey (St. Louis)

He was the most hated manager in early baseball. Owner Chris Von der Ahe released Ted Sullivan, and selected 24-year-old Charlie Comiskey to manage, captain and play with 19 games left in the 1883 season. After a loss in late season to Philadelphia Athletics, Comiskey allowed each player to fight third baseman Arlie Latham.

In 1884, Comiskey released Pat Deasley, who continually wanted to fight Comiskey. Comiskey believed in having players who were willing to use tricks such as hidden ice balls, throwing at batters, blocking runners, and knocking down fielders. The tricks brought with them the title "Bad Boys." Comiskey coached third base and continually insulted the umpire by calling "You're a peach."

The *Missouri Republican* (June 18, 1885) reported that Comiskey stated

> All is fair in love and war, and the same way may be said in base ball. A player acquires the reputation of being a gentleman both on and off the field.... I go on the field to win a game of ball by hook or crook. It is the game we are after, not reputation as society dudes. I do not endorse leg-breakers, brutes, and ruffians, who expect to win by injuring someone or indulging in profanity.... The St. Louis team never yet sent any players to the hospital. I do not endorse work of that kind.... I believe that kickin' is half the game.

Comiskey was a lousy loser and took it out on the players. He would not let up on scoring when he had a big lead.

In Philadelphia, on May 27, 1886, Comiskey complained about the sand around the bases. The game was stopped while Comiskey grabbed a shovel and went to removing the excess sand, to the howling of the A's cranks.

When Comiskey learned that Von der Ahe had sold half the starting lineup, he was ready to explode with anger. However, the newspapers blamed Comiskey, saying that he didn't want players who ignored his orders. Comiskey picked up replacements, including eventual Hall of Famer Tommy McCarthy. This gave Comiskey the ability to be even tougher on his players. If Comiskey gave a bunt signal and the player ignored or missed the signal, Comiskey would walk to home plate and punch the player in the mouth.

Comiskey remarked on kicking with an umpire, "I do not protest an umpire's decision but simply for the effect it will have on him in succeeding games." Comiskey in 1889 was suspicious of poor play by players Arlie Latham, Yank Robinson and Silver King. Latham told Comiskey he had a sore arm. Comiskey alerted Von der Ahe about the players. Von der Ahe's reaction was to hire a detective.

On August 1, 1889, Comiskey would not allow his team to take a wet field in Philadelphia. Umpire Byrne awarded a forfeit. The Philadelphia newspapers blasted Comiskey for his rowdy play and for cursing in front of ladies.

Comiskey told about Brooklyn owner Charlie Byrne, saying "Byrne is a shoe string gambler, a con man and ought to be thrown out of base ball." Also, he criticized American Association umpires Bob Ferguson and Fred Goldsmith as "being tools of Byrne." Comiskey was brought before the Association Board due to a forfeited game. Comiskey complained that his team could not see the ball. The Board overturned the Browns' forfeiture as unfair. The game reverted to the previous inning. Umpire Goldsmith was dismissed.

Comiskey organized a 10,000-mile tour at the season's end to earn additional money. He brought his son as a mascot on the trip. His son was arrested in Mexico for riding a donkey across a church graveyard.

Von der Ahe attempted to sell Comiskey at the season's conclusion. Comiskey arranged for Browns players to go to other teams in retaliation. Comiskey was constantly arguing with the St. Louis owner. The last straw was when Comiskey gave a rookie, Jim Wild, a tryout as a player. Even after he was not signed, Wild sent Comiskey a pig and sheep which Von der Ahe did not want on his beautiful field.

Bob Ferguson (Chicago)

He had an explosive temper as a manager who was stubborn and was disliked by his players for his dictatorial methods. He confronted gamblers and said, "they would steal a penny from their mother" and "I'll warm the ground with your carcass."

In 1876 he chastised catcher Bill Harbridge for missing a ball. He cursed players he thought were out of position. The *Philadelphia Item* (May 7, 1876) said, "We can't see how the men work as well as they do, if this is the kind of treatment they received."

The *Troy Press* (September 9, 1979) said, "They would not play worse. Ferguson over-managed. He doesn't treat his players fairly." He shouted under all circumstances. Ferguson struck Sadie Houck beside his head. The umpire reported that he did not see the collision, rather than deal with Ferguson.

Ferguson referred to his team's games as exhibition contests. While losing, 28–0, his catcher Emil Gross threw a bunt to the center fielder. Ferguson's players were afraid of their manager.

The *New York Tribune* (August 25, 1882) stated, "Ferguson is so strict with his men the audience enjoys seeing him make errors."

Ned "Foxy" Hanlon (HOF) (Baltimore)

Ned Hanlon was a dirty player and an even dirtier manager. He was a Hall of Fame manager who invented what was then termed "scientific baseball."

In reality, it was simply "rowdy ball." His Baltimore Orioles team won three consecutive pennants in the 1890s using this style of play. It did not hurt that five of his everyday players were Hall of Famers.

Hanlon was aggressive in disputing umpire calls to create a distraction and to fire up his own players. This is a technique still employed by managers. Another technique was to "hit down" on the pitch, creating a high bounce and a single. It was dubbed the "Baltimore Chop." The bounce was aided by the groundskeeper burying a cinderblock in front of home plate to make the ground harder.

Hanlon's players were known for circumventing the rules with "dirty tactics." The Orioles kept metal files hanging in the dugout to sharpen their cleats. When the opposing team came out on the field to warm up, they were intimidated by the Orioles players, who could be seen in the dugout sharpening their cleats. Extra balls were hidden in the high outfield grass to be used to make a play. Their pitcher would throw the original ball out of the stadium to get a new one. At that time, only one ball was supposed to be used for the game.

The Orioles fielders would kick runners who were running the bases. The lone umpire could not see everything. "Foxy Ned" relied on his groundskeeper, i.e., he would not water the dirt on the infield. Ned froze the ball before the game to deaden it. His players would try to get hit by a pitch. Bigger players would run over fielders.

National League President John Heydler stated, "Hanlon's Orioles are mean, vicious and ready to maim a rival player to help their cause. The opposing team would have to bathe their feet for hours after being spiked."

The results were wins and full stands. Hanlon was responsible

GOODWIN & CO. New York.

Ned Hanlon

for changing the team colors to black and orange to match the bird whose name they bore.

Comments on Hanlon:

> How can the umpire tell that the player deliberately tried to injure a player while in the act of casting his bat aside? There are batsmen in this League, notably Mike Grady and "Cy" Seymour, who have a dangerous and careless habit of casting their bat behind them after hitting the ball. But they are simply careless [*Washington Post* (March 5, 1899)].

> It is impossible to prevent expression of impatience indicating dissent with the umpire's decisions when a player in the hot heat of a game thinks he has been unjustly treated. The public don't look for that and don't want it. They like to see a little scrappiness in the game, and would be very much dissatisfied, I believe, to see the players slinking away like whipped schoolboys to their benches, afraid to turn their heads for fear of a heavy fine from some swelled umpire [*Baltimore Herald* (April 30, 1895)].

> As Manager of the Baltimore team I have been criticized a good deal because my players have kicked and indulged in hoodlumism to some degree. Other teams are winning games by rowdy ball playing and they would not stop kicking less if we wanted them to rumble down and lose. As a result, I'll admit that I winked at the evil because the players were headstrong and determined to win. It is a fact that we made them pay all of their fines themselves. The mere fact that all teams kicked made it a difficult matter for us to make reforms, and as nobody seemed inclined to make such a move up to last fall we stood pat [*New York Sun* (February 22, 1898)].

Arthur Irwin (Boston)

Arthur Irwin became manager of the Boston Reds of the American Association in 1891. However, when he hired his brother John, a poor player, he was accused of nepotism by the *Boston Globe*. By July 16, his tenure as manager was over. He would go on to being a scout for several teams.

It was learned at his death that he had two wives: Elizabeth in Boston with three children, and May in New York with a 27-year-old son named Harold. When he developed cancer, he apparently committed suicide by jumping off the boat vessel *Calvin Austin* on July 16, 1921.

John F. Kelly (Louisville)

A manager who lost control!

In 1887, Louisville manager John "Kick" Kelly had four players live at his hotel so he could watch them. Tom "Toad" Ramsey was caught drinking with women in the late-night hours. He told Ramsey he had insulted him as well as the team. Kelly suspended and fined him.

A month later, Ramsey was suspended and fined again. Kelly's remarks were recorded in the *Louisville Courier-Journal* (May 16, 1887): "Night after night he has come to the hotel in an intoxicated state, but I always forgave him on his solemn promise to do better, thinking that kindness and a few liberties would do more than harshness to make him a willing and obedient ball-player. But I am mistaken in the man, he is without principles."

Kelly had the same problem with the prodigious drinking of Pete Browning. Browning was drunk and was pulled from the game. The next day, he got five hits.

Ramsey got back into trouble three days later when he was so drunk it resulted in a three-day suspension. Manager Bill Watkins brought in a temperance preacher, Francis Murphy, to speak to his club.

Ramsey just did as he pleased and two months later he was so drunk he passed out. He was even arrested by saloon owners for debt. Kelly could not control his drinkers and resigned.

John J. McCloskey (Louisville)

His voice was so bad that the *Baltimore Saturday Telegram* (June 11, 1895) reported that he rattled his own team. He coached from the field (not allowed), so umpire Fred Jevne asked him to sit on the bench. He called Jevne a "horse thief," "bum" and "robber." Amazingly, Jevne did not eject him. Finally, McCloskey grabbed the umpire's coat and pulled him backward. The cranks from the stands jumped on the field to protect the umpire from McCloskey. Two weeks later, McCloskey was kicked out by "Watch" Burnham and he attempted to fight him, but was held back by Louisville outfielder Tom Gettinger. The *Pittsburg Dispatch* (August 11, 1895) reported that McCloskey "used the vilest epithets at Umpire Stump Weidman that had ever been heard on local grounds."

Bill McGunnigle (Brooklyn)

In 1888, he became manager of the Brooklyn Trolley Dodgers. He quickly promised "he would jump off the Brooklyn Bridge if his team lost the pennant." McGunnigle used unusual signals for plays. He would take his hat and turn it sideways, which was comical to the cranks. Another signal was to wear two hats at once. Other clubs made fun of McGunnigle and imitated him.

On August 12, 1889, St. Louis defeated Brooklyn, 11–0. After the game, McGunnigle was so devastated he wept on the bench. Playing the Browns later in August with a 2–0 lead, McGunnigle ordered his players to use stalling tactics, to no avail as the visitors gained a 3–2 lead. McGunningle was going to win at all costs, using ace pitcher Bob Caruthers every other game.

In 19th-century baseball, the team captain directed the play of the game rather than the manager. The manager was just supposed to sit on the bench. McGunnigle was the exception, which continually brought controversy. In 1888, when McGunnigle wanted an appeal play, umpire Bob Ferguson ruled the runner out. Philadelphia captain Harry Stovey objected feverishly to the umpire, to no avail. Brooklyn president Charlie Byrne would not permit McGunnigle to sit on the bench.

When he was hired to manage in Pittsburg, he moved the home benches close to the batter's box. During the game, he would go to the press box and bet a cigar on the outcome of the game.

McGunnigle required his players to report to the park at 10 a.m. for two hours of calisthenics. After lunch, an hour was spent cycling. This resulted in falls which caused cuts and bruises. This was followed by throwing. By game time, players were glad to play so they could rest on the bench. He was criticized for not allowing his pitchers adequate warm-up throws. He did not believe in rules for his players to obey, which made him popular. His pre-game practice was only 15 minutes without any batting practice, which was questioned. He got the nickname of "Gunner."

He coached the bases wearing a suit, purple pants and high-dollar shoes. He blew a whistle while managing to get the players' attention.

Jim "Truthful" Mutrie (New York)

In 1884, after managing the New York Metropolitans of the American Association, Jim Mutrie, along with players Dude Esterbrook and Tim Keefe were given a trip to Bermuda by their owner, John Day. The league had a day-to-day signing rule. So Mutrie waited until the day was up and signed the two players to the National League New York Giants, which Day also owned.

In the tight NL pennant race of 1885, a crucial four-game series at Chicago loomed. According to the *New York Times* (August 31, 1885), Mutrie remarked, "The Chicagos are quitters and afraid to meet my men." The White Stockings won the first three games with the Giants winning only the final game. Mutrie's comment was "they are lucky, wonderfully lucky, and luck goes a long way in a ball game."

When the 1886 season began, the Giants seemed the likely champion. However, after a sluggish season, Mutrie kept using his same excuse of bad luck. During the 1887 season, he brought in new, young players who did not

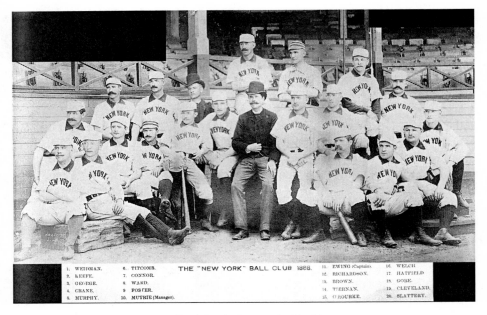

1. WEIDMAN.	6. TITCOMB.	THE "NEW YORK" BALL CLUB 1888.	11. EWING (Captain).	16. WELCH
2. KEEFE.	7. CONNOR.		12. RICHARDSON.	17. HATFIELD
3. GEORGE.	8. WARD.		13. BROWN.	18. GORE.
4. CRANE.	9. FOSTER.		14. TIERNAN.	19. CLEVELAND.
5. MURPHY.	10. MUTRIE (Manager).		15. O'ROURKE.	20. SLATTERY.

Jim Mutrie (center, in black)

fare any better. The newspapers were vocal. The *New York Times* (May 11, 1887) said, "It could not be said that the New York team played even a fairly decent game." *The Daily Tribune* (May 15, 1887) blamed Mutrie for his "lukewarmness."

The 1888 season finally brought success after Mutrie picked up a mascot (a street kid from Chicago named Fred Boldt) who brought the team the luck Mutrie had sought. (It did not hurt that Chicago's A. G. Spalding had sold his best players.) Mutrie walked down the sidelines exhorting the crowd to cheer "We are the People! We are the people!" as they won the pennant. Another pennant was achieved in 1889. Mutrie celebrated with his players at Nick Engel's Home Plate Saloon.

Mutrie was accused by Chicago of throwing games to allow Boston to win the 1891 pennant. Mutrie did not use his three future Hall of Famers: pitcher Amos Rusie, catcher "Buck" Ewing and first baseman Roger Connor. Also, two games scheduled in New York were played in Boston. The team made double their normal number of errors.

The poor attendance during the season resulted in Mutrie's release as manager. The top hat, cut-away coat and chants were gone.

In 1886, manager Mutrie fined Pat Deasley the large sum of $100 for being late for a game. This was more than five percent of his total pay.

After his new first baseman, future Hall of Famer Roger Conner, made an error, Mutrie said, "It's damn funny: we pay a lot of dumb players large salaries to play ball and they play like kids. They ought to be driving a truck pulled by a horse or mule or shoveling coal."

In 1888, Chicago's Silver Flint told Mutrie, "You never made a dollar in your life out of base ball, and of all the rotten managers you take the cake. You make me sick."

In 1892, to prevent players and managers from bench coaching, he nailed the visitors' bench to the wood floor. When questioned about his working players too hard, in the *Detroit Free Press* (September 12, 1882) Mutrie stated, "Nonsense! Aside from the pitchers and catcher, it is impossible to work players too hard. I played ball. I know that the more work men have to do upon the diamond, the better the game they will play."

Lou Phelan (St. Louis)

Phelan can only be described as a low-life. His first brush with the law landed him in jail for six months. After his release from jail, he hooked up with a prostitute, Kate Wadsworth. The two opened a bookmaking enterprise.

In August 1895, St. Louis owner Chris Von der Ahe hired his lady friend's relative, Lou Phelan, to manage the Browns, who were going nowhere in the standings. The *St. Louis Dispatch* (August 11, 1895) said, "Fancy a team whose manager knows nothing about baseball," which sums up the selection. Pitcher Ted Breitenstein said Phelan's only trait was that he "Prides himself on bluffing the umpire." The Browns finished 11–30, in last place during his tenure. At the conclusion of the season, Phelan was released. He opened a poolroom in St. Louis. However, his love, Kate, moved back to Chicago. He went to Chicago to track her down. Upon locating her at the Palace Hotel, he shot and killed her, and then himself.

Horace "Hustling" Phillips (Pittsburg)

As a player, he skipped out on his team in mid-season and had to pay back his advanced salary. This was not the man you wanted leading your team.

In 1889 he gave the following reason for a player's illness to the *Pittsburg Chronicle Telegraph* (July 12, 1889): "The Johnstown Penn water is the reason that explains it all. Pittsburg gets its water from Conemaugh River which was filled with bodies of the victims of the Johnstown flood. My men drink the water and get boils and carbuncles." He had a lackadaisical attitude, and the players did as they pleased. He did suspend Ed Morris for drinking. On July

25, Phillips was given his release from the team. Six days later, he had a mental breakdown and was placed in an asylum.

Oliver W. "Patsy" Tebeau (Cleveland)

"Patsy" Tebeau got his nickname because he played like the Irish players. Tebeau was a brawler. He had a foul mouth whose every adjective was a curse word. As a manager, he promoted a confrontational style of play. Patsy stated that "a good player can't wear a Cleveland uniform. Show me a team of fighters and I'll show you a team that has a chance." *Cleveland Plains Dealer* (May 6, 1893)

Tebeau was often ejected by the umpire. The National League imposed a $200 fine for his "intolerable behavior and diamond rowdiness." *Cleveland Press* (August 10, 1895) He got so mad at future Hall of Fame pitcher Cy Young that he replaced him in the ninth inning and promptly gave up the game-winning hit.

"Tebeau warned Umpire Hurst that if any close calls went against the Spiders, he would cut the ropes, releasing the cranks." Hurst called Tebeau out at third. He told Tebeau, "You may have beat the throw, but I called you out. Cut the ropes and I'll kill you dead where you stand." *Chicago Tribune* (July 11, 1895)

Patsy hired his brother, George, for the Spiders with the idea of confusing the other team. He would later release George, saying "He isn't much good anyway."

Patsy Tebeau yelled at everyone. When Cupid Childs, his second baseman, received flowers from friends in Baltimore, he merely grumbled. But after two errors by Childs, Tebeau tore the floral display apart with his hands and threw the rest into the stands. "There's your flowers and the next bunch of S.O.B.'s that give flowers to one of my players, I'll fire the player off my club and his damn friends can keep them if they like him so well." *Sporting News* (May 23, 1918)

In a game on August 4, 1897, Tebeau refused to replace Jesse Burkett, who had been ejected, so umpire "Chicken" Wolf threatened a forfeit. Tebeau said, "Go ahead. We don't need it." Wolf counted off five minutes. Tebeau didn't relent, and the game was forfeited with a 9–0 score.

In 1899 in St. Louis, Tebeau released Jake Stenzel, a crank favorite. The cranks yelled, "Why did you release Stenzel?" Tebeau replied, "Because he can't think fast enough and was Dutch." The cranks exploded in anger.

Tebeau got into a vicious argument with a crank in Baltimore. The fan had him arrested, but he was soon released. Tebeau pushed umpire Arlie Latham, resulting in a near riot.

John "Monte" Ward (New York)

He was too smart to manage.

Ward explained his theory on kicking with the umpire as "I know many players who would submit to an erroneous call without kicking, but if they do so they would be accused of not playing for the best interest of the team." *New York Sun* (January 30, 1898)

The *New York Herald* (June 25, 1893) said, "Hardly a game passes without Ward leaving his position to argue with the umpire to pull down the home crowds down upon him." Ward's problem was his hot temper, which resulted in poor judgment. He was accused of not having common sense. Ward had a law degree but you would not know it by his kicking methods.

The *Cincinnati Times Star* (August 27, 1897) reported that "Ward argues with all his ball players. If they wanted a drink, he didn't mind our drinking, if we would only keep away from the bars. Order what you want and charge it to the Club, but have the drinks sent to the room. The bill for the Bass ale didn't come in bottles and tasted like cocktails." Ward himself drank with his meals. He felt it helped the nerves after a big game. Ward's book, "Simply Base Ball Notebook," was sold in the stands by his players.

Ward married the Broadway actress Helen Dauvray in 1886, with New York newspapers recording every date. The marriage was short-lived when he was caught in an adulterous affair with Mrs. Jesse McDermott.

He was responsible for establishing the first baseball union, which had its own league in 1890. The Players' League, which had the best players, failed because of poor financial support rather than poor attendance.

In 1891, Ward was ejected by umpire Tim Hurst. He sought approval from owner Charles Byrne, who chided him, "If I had my way, you wouldn't play at all." After a lopsided loss in Chicago, Ward found 18 empty beer bottles in one room. Ward fined four players $100 each for drinking and breaking curfew and said, "Several of the men forgot themselves in Chicago." He never named the players he fined. Two players stayed in Washington instead of traveling to Baltimore. King Kelly was suspended by Ward for being AWOL. He did not mention his friend was back on the alcohol.

Bill Watkins (Detroit)

Bill Watkins won the pennant and World Series in 1887. But!

The *Chicago Daily News* (August 25, 1888) had these comments by Detroit Wolverines manager Bill Watkins:

Do you think these big health duffers from Detroit could play such a snide on me? I have men playing every day who are just as badly crippled up as they are. Williamson has a boil, but he's playing shortstop. Duffy hurt his knee in Boston, yet you see him going after fly balls. Then take Old "Silver" Flint for instance. Look at the game he caught and he has a finger out of place. His hand is the size of two hands. It doesn't follow that a man must go to the hospital every time the ball hits him on the end of a finger.

"Manager Watkins left the bench in the seventh inning to count up, not runs but receipts," reported the *Pittsburg Chronicle Telegraph* (April 23, 1888). "Pittsburg's Manager Watkins purchased bedroom slippers for his players to wear while in uniform in hotels," it reported on March 23, 1898.

While in spring training in 1888, Watkins discovered that the train's sleeper car could lay over for a later train. Watkins threatened the railroad agent with bodily harm, and the sleeper car would be on the overnight train. However, Watkins discovered that the train was going in the opposite direction. Pushing and shoving between Watkins and the agent ensued. They missed their train. Watkins convinced the railroad bosses to run a special

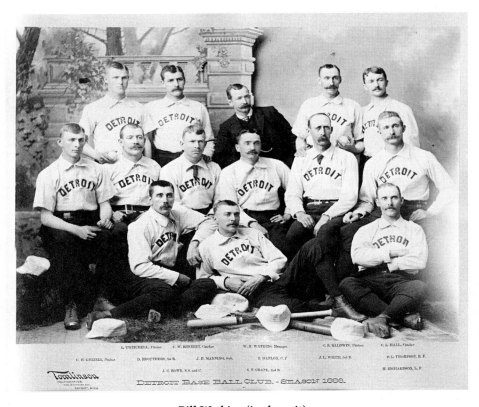

Bill Watkins (in the suit)

train. When he informed his players, they grabbed sandwiches and took off for the train. Two players were no-shows. They were later found napping in the shade. The train was moving faster than any train the players had been on. Owner Scheibeck became sick, and the others were woozie. The train came to an abrupt halt. The trains were backed up. When the mess got untangled they went on their way and arrived at 2:00 a.m.

Watkins had the following conversation with Chicago manager/captain "Cap" Anson that was recorded by the *Chicago Daily News* (August 13, 1887):

WATKINS: We are here, now what are you going to do with us?

ANSON: Well, we are going to do our best to *knock* both your eyes out!

WATKINS: I understand that Clarkson's arm is failing and very sore.

ANSON: Maybe.

WATKINS: I also hear Phenomenal Van Haltren has exploded.

ANSON: Time enough yet to see.

WATKINS: Well be honest, and admit that Baldwin cannot pitch.

ANSON: I don't admit a thing. We do not give any odds and we do not take any.

Watkins was disliked by his players for fining them for what he called "indifference." He suspended Fatty Briody and Stump Weidman for drunkenness. Pitcher Charles "Lady" Baldwin objected and asked to be released, which Watkins did. The Detroit press took the players' side and said the team was over-managed.

Charlie Getzien was pitching in the box in July 1886 when Watkins started yelling at him about his poor pitching. Getzien merrily fired back insults at Watkins. When the game ended, Watkins handed Getzien $100 in fines.

Watkins was on the bench when he heard Anson, who was coaching first, say Jimmy Ryan would hit a home run. Watkins replied that if he did, "I'll fall on my face." It did not happen.

He suspended Bill Smith and Lady Baldwin for careless play. Charles Getzien was suspended for backtalk. Harry Porter was suspended for poor work. John McCarty was fined $100 for playing poker and drinking. Heinie Reitz was suspended for "indiscretions." It's a wonder Watkins had a team left.

Watkins was hired to lead the 1893 St. Louis Browns. However, players spending time at saloons resulted in a bad season. Pitcher Ted Breitenstein simply left the club. Watkins blamed injuries for the poor season. The injuries came from lifting beer mugs.

2

UNCONTROLLABLE OWNERS

Frank Bancroft (Providence)

Frank Bancroft was a gentleman manager whose players were rowdy. Bancroft was a trickster. He would avoid expected losses by ordering the groundskeeper to use a fire hose on the field to make it unplayable.

Bancroft oversaw his boozers by tying a string to their doors to determine arrivals. On a season-ending trip to Cuba in 1879, he had "Hop Bitters" marked on their uniforms. Hop Bitters was a 40 percent alcohol product that was a cure for any ailment.

Bancroft's ace pitcher, Hoss Radbourn had pitched 20 straight games to claim the pennant and 56 wins to date. He rested him for three days, then used Radbourn to pitch the final three home games to obtain larger gate receipts. This same pitcher was suspended by Bancroft for complaining.

Charlie Byrne, Owner/Manager (Brooklyn)

Charlie Byrne was described as a "nervous little man." He was a hard-nosed owner and manager who fined his nine players $50 each for an eight-error loss to the St. Louis Browns. He called St. Louis owner Chris Von der Ahe a "mentally small man who is arbitrary in his methods and language."

When Yank Robinson scored the winning run by cutting third base short, Byrne went to sit on the St. Louis bench and lectured Robinson on cheating. This action was from a man who financed his team from his gambling interests. He used every advantage, even playing Louisville in August 1889 in four inches of mud, saying he did not want to disappoint the Brooklyn cranks.

He hated St. Louis so much that he attempted to have the Browns expelled from the American Association. The Brooklyn cranks would regularly throw objects at the St. Louis players. Byrne would not provide police protection, saying the stadium was in Ridgewood, outside of Brooklyn. Charles Comiskey, the St. Louis Browns' manager/captain, said, "Byrne is a shoe string gambler, a con man and ought to be thrown out of baseball."

In 1886, Byrne fined Germany Smith $200 for not leaving the hotel promptly to meet the train.

Sporting Life (June 19, 1889) reported that "Byrne had picked a monkey as the Brown's team mascot." Byrne was a manipulator trying to secure umpires who favored Brooklyn. He had offered higher salaries to St. Louis' best players. He was seen in Louisville talking to Browns star Arlie Latham. This was a fact Latham did not deny. Yet, he called Latham "thoroughly obnoxious."

He allowed his players to bet on games. The Brooklyn Trolley Dodgers were notorious for using stalling tactics with a late-inning lead, hoping for a darkness call. His friendship with umpire Bob Ferguson became a point of dissension and calls of favoritism.

Charlie Byrne established the first "Ladies Day" in an attempt to reduce rowdy behavior among the cranks.

Mordecai Davidson, Owner/Manager (Louisville)

Mordecai Davidson was an owner of a furniture business who became a majority owner of the Louisville Colonels in 1888. After 39 games, he relieved manager John Kelly. He had never seen the game before 1887. Davidson completed the season with a 34–52 record. His primary technique was to fine his players for what he deemed as infractions.

Davidson brought in Dude Esterbrook in 1889 but released him after ten games. The players had endured enough, and six players went on baseball's first strike on June 14 in Baltimore. The American Association voted for Davidson to relinquish control. Barney Dreyfuss bought him out. Louisville had four managers and a 27–111 record, one of the worst records in baseball history.

Andrew Freedman (New York)

Andrew Freedman was part of the ugly politics of the era. "Tammany Andy" was the nickname that was used behind his back. On January 24, 1895, Andrew Freedman purchased the New York Giants for $53,600, which was a controlling interest of the team. Freedman changed managers three times in the first year, starting with rookie George Davis (3B), then "Dirty Jack" Doyle (1B), and concluding with Harvey Watkins (financial secretary).

"Reporters were an irritation to Freedman because he did not take criticism." Sam Crane, a reporter for the *New York Press,* was a constant critic. On August 18, 1895, Freedman banned Crane from the Polo Grounds. Crane purchased a ticket to get into the game. Freedman had security usher Crane from the stands. Crane hired ex–Giant John Ward as his lawyer and sued Freedman. All the New York sportswriters, and even cranks, supported Crane, who won the suit.

The 1896 season series began with a series of losses. The *New York Daily Tribune* (April 21, 1896) reported, "The glaring mismanagement has been repeated this season, has disgusted the intelligence of followers of the Club, and there isn't enough confidence in the City to blow up a balloon."

The Giants' top pitcher, Amos Rusie, sat out the entire 1896 season when Freedman fined him $200 at the end of the 1895 season for "failure to give his best." The cranks and newspapers were furious at the treatment of their eventual Hall of Fame player. Freedman's method of rebuttal was to attack the sportswriters (literally). "He punched sportswriter Ed Hurst." The *Evening World* (April 22, 1896)

The period of revolving managers began when Arthur Irwin was replaced by "Scrappy Bill" Joyce. The Giants improved drastically to 28–14 under Joyce. However, Freedman blamed the Spanish-American War for the poor attendance in spite of winning at the season's end.

The 1897 season was one of promise with the play of the last month of 1896 and the return of ace pitcher Amos Rusie. The Giants expected a pennant. In August, the Giants had moved into third place. The year-end push did not come, and they finished third at 83–48, 9.5 games behind. Freedman had finally made the right choice with Joyce. The winning season did not stop the press from calling Freedman "an arrogant grudge holder with inordinate ego, and just plain evil."

The 1898 season went downhill quickly, which resulted in a 77–73 record (seventh place), the firing of Joyce, and his replacement with Cap Anson. "The official verdict that the war was the culprit was obviously preposterous. The war did not similarly affect other sports, and there was no discernable reason why base ball alone should have suffered, unless one looked at the management problems and lack of competition with the game." *New York Press* (November 11, 1898)

The *New York Press* (August 20, 1898), declared that the Players Association resulted from "Freedman's spirit of impatience, arrogance and prejudice toward players. A spirit inimical to the best interest of the game."

Freeman began the 1899 season by issuing pay cuts to all the players. Rusie refused to sign, as well as Cy Seymour, the ace pitcher from the previous year who had recorded 25 wins. The Giants were terrible with a 60–90 record and a last-place finish.

The 1900 season started with the hiring of Buck Ewing as manager. The Giants still had Jack Doyle, outfielder George van Haltren, and the league's best shortstop in George Davis. The team won the same number of games with a reduced schedule which limited the losses to 78, but still finished in the cellar. Freedman helped reorganize the National League with him ruling the League as a Trust. The entire National League was now syndicated.

Charlie Mason (Philadelphia)

Why is this owner rowdy? He wasn't, but the event was. The Athletics' catcher, Jack O'Brien, blacked out due to heat stroke on July 8, 1883. The Athletics did not have a substitute. Second baseman Cub Stricker went behind the plate. This meant right field was without a player. Co-owner Charlie Mason was sitting in the stands. Mason, who had pitched in college, threw his silk hat down, removed his coat and tie, and rolled up his pants.

Only in the 19th century would you see this picture. Charlie Mason actually caught a fly ball bare-handed and got one hit in two plate appearances. He had lived every crank's dream.

Arthur Soden (Boston)

Was he a spendthrift or a miser?

The owner of the Boston Beaneaters was a millionaire, yet the cheapest owner in the National League. The players paid $20 annually for their uniforms and were required to collect tickets on game days. They mowed the grass with push mowers. They were allowed only one set of shoelaces. The players paid their own fare to the games on the road. The players' wives had to pay to get into the games. Soden was responsible for the "Reserve Clause," which kept players tied to the same team. Also, he eliminated the "free press box."

This same man spent $10,000 to purchase King Kelly and then had an enlargement of the check posted in the window of his office. As President of the National League, he eliminated lower-income teams.

He was not friendly with his players. Boileryard Clarke stated that he was on the team for two years and never spoke to Soden. In his own words, "When a player ceases to be useful, I will release him." He would put players on a "blacklist" so other teams could not hire them. When Charlie Jones attempted to get back pay of $378, he was suspended for two years.

A. G. Spalding (Chicago)

Spalding was one of two men who started the National League. But like many owners, he saw his time and money in baseball as an investment. In Spalding's own words, "ownership of a great ball club involved man-killing experiences" and "the man whose soul is absorbed in the business of playing ball has no soul left for other business."

In 1887, Spalding made the most questionable move of the 19th century when he sold the top hitter of 1886 and number one drawing card, King Kelly, to Boston. (This was the equivalent of Boston selling Babe Ruth to the Yankees.) The response of the Boston cranks appeared in *The Sporting News* (February 16, 1887):

> Of his presence he bereft us,
> Kelly of the diamond bold,
> He's deserted us for Boston.
> Although Albert laid the cost on,
> Ten thousand and clear in Puritan gold
> We surely have the pity of every sister city,
> In our loss of Kelly, the tricky and the bold.

> But we've entered for the pennant,
> And we'll win—depend on it,
> Notwithstanding Mike has left us in the cold.
> Just hear those bank notes rustle,
> Ten thousand, crisp and clean.
> True Boston's got Mike Kelly,
> But Spalding's got the lengthy green.

He eventually hired detectives to follow players and relate any infractions of their contracts. Spalding even stooped to providing gossip to the newspapers to help attendance.

His ballpark, which held 10,000, was the best in the league. Cranks received free scorecards and were allowed to rent seat cushions. The stadium had 18 private boxes with curtains and expensive armchairs. Spalding's box had a direct telephone line to the dugout to give advice to Cap Anson.

Spalding was a prejudiced individual and insisted in an exhibition game with Toledo that Toledo's black player, Moses Fleetwood Walker, not play that day. He produced a yearly "Base Ball Guide" which sold 50,000 copies; the Guide was filled with his advertisements, and the advertisements of others who had paid $50 each for the privilege.

Spalding's accomplishments included a World Tour in 1888–1889. However, even this had a negative tone when he took along Clarence Duval, Chicago's young black mascot, to create publicity.

Spalding normally left running the team to Anson, but in 1879 he went on the field to question the positioning of second baseman Fred Pfeffer. Anson had umpire Phil Powers remove Spalding from the field. Spalding didn't believe Anson did this, announcing, "I'd have told him to go to Hades."

He had a running argument with Providence captain Arthur Irwin. When Anson and Irwin were in a dispute, Spalding jumped onto the field and yelled he would protest any call against his team. Irwin was not subject to Spalding's demands. Spalding violated Rule 17 for coming on the field and Rule 47 for being responsible for stopping play. Spalding was not fined because he was the second-most powerful man in the National League.

A.G. Spalding

He continued to overlook the drinking of his players, saying, "I am sure that drinking never injured the playing of Mike Kelly." *Chicago Herald* (July 10, 1887) He arranged for spring training in New Orleans, which turned out to be a financial disaster as well as the worst place for drinking players. He was against his team playing on Sunday, yet he would sell his bats, balls and gloves to teams that did play on Sunday.

He felt small fines would be enough to discipline players. However, in 1887, he stated, "Anson was right and I was wrong. I put those $25 fines on the boys last summer just to show them I was onto them. But they were worse, if anything, than before." *Chicago Herald* (January 9, 1887)

Spalding wrote a letter to Tom Burns after he requested a $100 advance on his pay, which read in part: "I am never in a very good mood when demands are made on me by players. I am not better natured by demands from my frugal players like yourself who I supposed had saved enough money to run your next engagement."

Frederick Stearns (Detroit)

In 1888, Stearns was given an opportunity to switch from the National League to the American Association. He elected to stay in the National League, and they dropped Detroit at the season's end.

He was most noted for establishing the schedule for the 1887 World Series against the St. Louis Browns. It was to be a 15-game series which resembled a carnival at the following locations:

Detroit (2 games)
Brooklyn
New York
Philadelphia
Washington
Baltimore
Brooklyn
Detroit
Chicago
St. Louis (5 games)

Detroit won the fiasco, ten games to five.

After winning the pennant, one would think attendance the following year would be good; but 1888 attendance was so poor they played the last half of the season on the road, where they received a portion of the gate receipts.

Chris Von der Ahe (St. Louis)

The "Boss President" would rather be a dictator.

Von der Ahe was a rich tavern owner who got into baseball to be famous and sell beer. Beer and whiskey could both be sold at the ballpark. Set on making the park into an early version of Disneyland, he had lawn bowling, a handball court and fireworks. There was even a beer garden in right field. The beer garden was in the ball game play area, and balls hit into the beer garden had to be retrieved from the area and thrown to the pitcher before being thrown to a base.

On May 2, 1882, Von der Ahe led the team with a band from the tavern to the park. The opposing team received hurled vegetables and cursing. After the game, the team marched back to the tavern to consume his products. The players got mugs of beer and Von der Ahe's salute, "Money dot ist to spend."

When the cranks complained to Von der Ahe about umpire John Kelly, he sent for a new umpire. Umpire Charlie Daniels missed his train, and Von der Ahe paid $300 for him to ride a special train to St. Louis. His team still lost the game. When speaking with his manager, Ted Sullivan, he said, "A rolling moss never catches a stone." What?! He continually gave orders to the manager during the game. With improved play, Von der Ahe invited Congressman

John O'Neil and the governor to his private box to see his team lose, 9–2.

A new season brought new hope and printed score sheets. Von der Ahe requested from Comiskey a telegram on road games. Von der Ahe received a telegram costing $27 with a play-by-play account. Von der Ahe went to the telegraph office and wired, "For God's sake, don't send any more telegrams."

Von der Ahe was having trouble with alcoholic Yank Robinson. He hired a detective to monitor his travels. Robinson got out of a $100 fine by saying he had "hydrophobia." Von der Ahe actually advanced him $25. He enjoyed rowdy play and gladly paid any player's fines, which were often.

Von der Ahe led the team into Sportsman's Park in 1886 dressed in striped spats with a silk top hat, Prince Albert coat, gold cane, and accompanied by his two greyhound dogs.

He quickly paid American Association President Wychoff $260 for the previous year's fines for Comiskey and Latham. He would blast his players on losses in the local newspapers. He fined his players for drinking or disobedience. Von der Ahe's life-sized statue donned the front of Sportsman's Park. He was a heavy drinker and a lady's man.

Chris Von der Ahe

Von der Ahe attempted to sack League President Wheeler C. Wyckoff for his handling of umpires. The move failed by one vote. Von der Ahe gained victory when he tried to play on Sunday. The Court proceedings ruled that baseball was sport and recreation, and allowed games on Sunday. This was an important decision to continue profits for the Browns.

Von der Ahe cost his team the 1887 Dauvrap Cup Series against Detroit. He cursed his players, resulting in sloppy play and drinking at night. Further, he refused to give the players any portion of the profits. After the season, the player's clubhouse burned down, and the fire engulfed Von der Ahe's Gold Lion Saloon. In November, he sold his top two pitchers, Bobby Caruthers and Dave Foutz, catcher Doc Bushong, shortstop Bill Gleason, and outfielder Curt Welch, for a total of $23,000. Von der Ahe promised that players would now get a percentage of the gate receipts.

Von der Ahe arranged a Cannon Ball Train for the team's exhibition games in 1888.

Von der Ahe spared no expense for the 1888 World Series. He purchased a special train with giant banners, special crank cars, buffets and hotel accommodations costing $30,000. He could not be called cheap. He had spent money like water and then blasted his players for losing. He purchased suits, hats, shoes and banquets, yet the players were not satisfied with his personal treatment, resulting in annual holdouts.

On May 2, 1889, a little thing became a disaster. Comiskey told Yank Robinson his pants were too small. Robinson sent a boy after another pair in his room. The boy retrieved the pants but was not allowed back into the park without a ticket. Robinson blasted the ticket taker, and Von der Ahe responded by going to the bench, chastising Robinson and fining him $25. The episode was not over because the team stayed at the train station to support their teammate. When they did arrive in Kansas City, the Browns lost four games with poor play. The first strike in baseball was real. Von der Ahe eliminated the fine and reinstated Robinson.

Von der Ahe claimed he wasn't making a profit, yet he was making improvements such as providing free seat cushions.

Von der Ahe fined Arlie Latham $200 for his suspect play. He fined Silver King for poor pitching. Pitcher Ice Box Chamberlain was fined $100. Yank Robinson only drew a slap on the wrist for heavy drinking. Von der Ahe remarked in the *St Louis Globe-Democrat* (October 30, 1889), "We have lost but it was scheming and not ball playing which beat us. The Browns won every series including Brooklyn ... the Club which got the pennant did not earn it."

Comiskey had arranged for an exhibition game but was short a player. Seeing Von der Ahe in the stadium, Comiskey asked Von der Ahe to play. Von der Ahe replied, "You know Charlie, I never had a uniform in my life." Comiskey told Von der Ahe to go to center field. "I'll tell the pitcher not to pitch the centerfield ball and you won't have anything to do." Von der Ahe even practiced. However, all of a sudden, balls went flying to center field. The Browns owner said, "I quit." But Comiskey would not let him and he actually caught a ball. Von der Ahe said, "If dey can effort to pay $500 to see me play," Von der Ahe treated all that evening to reward his play.

On March 12, 1895, he showed his prejudiced side by attacking a black man, George Stevenson, on a street corner. He hit the poor man in the face and then took out his pistol and fired at his feet, with a bullet striking Stevenson in the heel. Stevenson filed a lawsuit, and Von der Ahe was arrested for assault. The St. Louis Court of Criminal Correction Judge ruled that Stevenson had not committed a crime. Von der Ahe's bogus defense was that "Negroes had repeatedly robbed his saloons to steal alcohol." Von der Ahe's son Eddie testified that his father sent cases of liquor to his mistresses and then wrote them off as robbery. Von der Ahe won his case when Stevenson failed to pay court costs.

Von der Horst Family (Baltimore)

Baseball was simply a means for selling his beer. Henry Von der Horst owned a large brewery in Baltimore. In order to increase sales, he purchased the Baltimore Orioles. The brewery was always his first interest. He became the first owner to introduce beer sales at the game. Also, he built a restaurant in the stadium that served his products.

The Orioles were one of the only two teams which played on Sundays. Soon, Henry's son, Harry, a baseball enthusiast, was given authority over the Orioles. His first move was to hire manager "Foxy Ned" Hanlon to take over the Orioles. Hanlon turned a poor team into a dynasty and won pennants three years in a row.

The Horst beer, "Eagle Brew," was brought to Union Park in large kegs. Harry Von der Horst turned any holiday into an all-day affair at the park. The cranks would leave drunk, but fortunately there were trolleys or horse-drawn carriages to take them home.

He loved to beat the New York Giants over other teams. The *Baltimore Morning Herald* (August 28, 1896) reported that he entertained Giants treasurer Eddie Talcott at dinner, using serenading cranks as they sang the following ditty to the tune of "Tit-willow":

> A man from New York, silently sat at his plate
> Sighing, Orioles, Orioles, Orioles
> Why am I consigned to this awful fate?
> Oh! Orioles, Orioles, Orioles
> Is it weakness of pitching or muffs, he cried
> Or a great run of base hits all on the wrong side?
> Then he swallowed his napkin and slowly he died.

In 1898, after three pennants, the team still did not show a profit. Harry Von der Horst accused the cranks of getting fed up with winning. The *Morning Herald* (June 29, 1898) blamed the attendance problem on the fact that "the rowdiness on the diamond is driving the cranks away."

Von der Horst's answer was to move to another city. He purchased the Brooklyn Americans, thus owning two teams in the same league. He wanted to shift the whole team to Brooklyn. However, the plan backfired when John McGraw and catcher Wilbert Robinson refused to go to Brooklyn. They did not want to leave their business interest in Baltimore. McGraw became the manager, and with the addition of top rookie pitcher Joe McGinnity, managed to post an 86–62 record. The Brooklyn Superbas won the 1899 pennant under Hanlon with a 101–47 record.

The Brooklyn team doubled its attendance, registering 270,000 cranks. Brooklyn duplicated this feat in 1900. But the Orioles were gone. "A bitter pill for any Baltimorian." *Morning Herald* (December 9, 1899)

3

WILD PITCHERS

George "Grin" Bradley (St. Louis)

Bradley was a pitcher who "would use violence to win," said the *Chicago Tribune* (July 24, 1893).

Bradley and his catcher would hit the game balls with a bat against a stone slab to dull the ball before the game. The ball was like hitting a clump of mud. Eventually, the umpire realized that the ball was a dud and started taking it directly out of the box. The evolution took George Bradley from the pitcher's box to third base.

He was constantly bickering with the umpire. He was one of the most disliked players in the league. A picture of Jesse James was a substitute for Bradley in the newspaper. Bradley smashed Cincinnati Reds first baseman Charles Comiskey in the mouth as he ran the bases.

Ted Breitenstein (St. Louis)

Breitenstein was part of the "pretzel battery," a name he got at the Golden Lion Saloon (beer pretzels).

His first game as a starting pitcher was the last game of the 1891 season against Louisville, which was a no-hitter that he didn't realize until congratulated by teammates. In 1893, he spent spring training in Arkansas drinking at a local tavern. He failed to make the train in Chicago after being intoxicated.

Von der Ahe hired a detective to spy on the players. He caught Breitenstein drinking four beers during a game he wasn't pitching. Breitenstein claimed it was soda water. Also, the detective reported Breitenstein was betting on the horses.

In 1896, Breitenstein and new manager Harry Diddlebock did not get along. In an early-season game against New York, Breitenstein walked six men in two innings, then walked off the field. He remarked, "That's all right, blank, blank, blank, I'll try these fellows again tomorrow and show you."

When he held out the next year, Von der Ahe ordered Breitenstein to report to him and he would judge if the pitcher was in proper condition. As soon as he reported, he was sold to Cincinnati.

Elton "Ice Box" Chamberlain (Cincinnati)

Chamberlain was the "coolest pitcher in base ball"; therefore, the name "Ice Box." Chamberlain was suspended 30 days by Cincinnati's Manager Charles Comiskey for insubordination. He was a boxer in the off-season and was arrested for an illegal prize fight in Mayville, New York, in February 1891.

Chamberlain sweated so badly that his uniform was always soaked. This was a source of ribbing from the cranks.

Chamberlain owned two horses that also took up his concentration. On his reason for leaving Cincinnati, he stated, "It was the bum atmosphere coupled with the rankest water in the universe." *Cincinnati Commercial* (November 11, 1894)

John Clarkson (Chicago) (HOF)

John Clarkson, who was superstitious, was the first to believe that the seventh inning was lucky. He carried a silk handkerchief in his pocket for luck. Clarkson's manager had to continually stroke Clarkson's ego since Clarkson's sulking affected his pitching performance. There were instances when he would not pitch because he thought he had been offended. Cap Anson said, "Clarkson was peculiar in that in order to get his best work, you had to keep spurring him along. Otherwise, he was apt to let up; this being especially true when the ball club was ahead and he saw what he thought was a chance to save himself." His own teammates called him "Black Jack" because he disliked any criticism.

John Clarkson Hall of Fame plaque

John Clarkson began drinking with fellow Chicago White Stockings pitcher Jim McCormick. McCormick was released because of his drinking. Then Clarkson started drinking at local bars by himself. Anson blamed their loss of the 1887 World Series on Clarkson, saying "If he had taken care of himself, it would have been a different tale." *Sporting Life* (December 14, 1887). Clarkson was supposed to pitch Game Five of the World Series, but was unable to perform due to a hangover. Clarkson found a new drinking cohort in Mike "King" Kelly, who caught for him in Chicago and Boston.

He was a member of the Brotherhood of Players. In December 1889, Clarkson was expelled from the Union and called a "turncoat." His friend, King Kelly, who had earlier turned down a similar offer, publicly censored Clarkson and ended the friendship.

The bad feelings with his friends and fellow players resulted in increased sulking and more moodiness. His "gentleman" side had turned into a demanding player who wanted everything his way. New manager Frank Selee went to a three-man rotation, which gave Clarkson more time to feel sorry for himself.

On October 5, 1889, with the pennant on the line, Clarkson sent a telegram offering Cleveland pitcher Henry Gruber $500 to win his game. (He lost.) Clarkson wore a shiny belt buckle to distract the batter. Normally, the umpire would make him remove it. While playing for Cleveland in 1893, Clarkson's tirades with players had so incensed his teammates that they refused to field balls in an attempt to make him lose. Clarkson called out future Hall of Famer Jesse Burkett for his poor fielding, which resulted in a tussle in the clubhouse. Manager Patsy Tebeau had enough of Clarkson and released one of the top five pitchers of the era.

His temperamental attitude showed in the way he played the game. Often, he would throw to the wrong base or not run out pop flies, even though there was no such thing as an automatic out with players catching the ball barehanded. He got into a fight after a game with third baseman Ed Williamson.

Clarkson was tutoring Mark Baldwin on how to pitch to certain batters. When Baldwin asked about pitching to home run-hitting Dan Brouthers, the conversation went like this:

BALDWIN: Can Brouthers hit a low ball?

CLARKSON: No, he doesn't hit it; he kills it.

BALDWIN: Where is a good place to put them, John?

CLARKSON: Curve them high and close to his breast and he won't find them.

When Clarkson wanted a trade to Boston, the following 1887 conversation occurred between owner A. G. Spalding and Clarkson:

SPALDING: Hello, John. What's the trouble?

CLARKSON: Nothing. Only I don't want to play in Chicago.

SPALDING: Well, me and "Cap" want you.

CLARKSON: I can't help that. I won't play here, whether you want me or not.

He was sold for $10,000 to Boston, where he joined King Kelly. Clarkson was fined $25 by captain Morrill of Boston for "painting the town red" in Pittsburg.

On May 13, 1905, Clarkson had a nervous breakdown and was taken to a sanitarium for his mental problems.

Ed "Cannonball" Crane (New York)

His nickname told what he looked like. After years of overeating and excessive saloon time, Crane had a tremendous arm and would sometimes get into throwing contests with opponent players. He had the record at 406 feet.

In 1886, he consumed a dozen soft-boiled eggs followed by two dozen clams. He was known for his well-dressed attire. He toured with a team around the world and started drinking wine nightly aboard the ship. By the time of the team's arrival in San Francisco, he was absent without leave (AWOL) on several pitching turns. On the ship, he had become someone to avoid, a heavy drinker who irritated any manager. By 1890, he was an alcoholic.

He got unruly in a Harlem saloon where he was arrested by New York police. He was fined $10 for resisting arrest. "Ed Crane did skip a few games without permission and showed up at work drunk more than once. Also it doesn't help that he walked many batters." *New York Sun* (September 29, 1890)

In 1891, Crane played for King Kelly's team when the *Sioux County Herald* reported that "Big Ed" Crane had been a disorganizing element in Kelly's team, which released him. In 1893, Crane was released by the Giants for being out of shape. His drinking only got worse. He overdosed on sedatives at age 34.

George "Nig" Cuppy (Cleveland)

His name resulted from his dark skin. Cuppy had a German heritage. He had a dark complexion and became known by the nickname "Nig." The name demonstrates the racism of the era.

Cuppy employed the tricks advocated by the Cleveland Spiders. He ran to cover first base by running in the base line, causing the runners to reduce their speed. The *Brooklyn Eagle* (September 13, 1882) called "Cuppy's play a dirty trick."

Cuppy used every trick to gain an advantage since the pitching distance had been increased to 60'6". He even used his spikes to cut the ball to give movement to it. While pitching against Louisville, he used his spikes on the ball. The Louisville players pleaded with umpire Weidman. Louisville's catcher pulled a new ball from the umpire's coat pocket. Cuppy's other trickery was applying tobacco juice mixed with sand to gain an advantage.

Hugh Ignatius "One Arm" Daily (New York)

Daily's biggest handicap was not his arm, but his mouth. He had an uncontrollable temper which resulted in vile cursing at the umpire, opponents or his teammates. This resulted in his not playing for the same team two years in a row. He had a harness strapped to his non-pitching arm and could catch the ball with what he called "the hollow." Fly balls were very difficult for him to catch.

In a game on May 10, 1878, Daily surrendered six runs on six errors in the ninth inning, resulting in a 17–16 loss. Daily lost control over the team's collapse and let loose a cuss-laden tirade that stunned the fans into shocked silence. He was suspended for one month the next day. His teammates despised him. While playing for Rochester, catcher Pat Deasley kept firing the ball back to Daily so that he could not catch it. He motioned for his catcher and as the catcher leaned in, Daily swung his stump and cracked Deasley in the jaw. Deasley did not fight back, but simply allowed passed balls, causing the team to lose the game.

On October 11, 1880, Daily was playing with the New York Metropolitans when a fan insulted his handicap. He walked off the mound and did not play again that year.

Daily cursed at each batter to throw them off. A tirade against umpire Ormond Butler on May 26, 1881, led to an ejection. Butler got even later with horrendous calls, costing Daily the game. The same year, Daily threatened a reporter if his error was reported. The *New York Herald* called Daily "The Growler." He was sent back to the minor leagues.

While playing with Cleveland in 1883, he got into a fight with Fred Dunlap, Jack Glasscock and Lemi Hunter on a train. Many cranks blamed Daily for losing the pennant.

In 1884, he hit Hoss Radbourn in the chest with a pitch in order to get him out of the game. In 1885, Daily was suspended for his continual cursing. He paid a $500 fine and was reinstated to play for the St. Louis Maroons. He was so irritable that his teammates were accused of trying to lose when he pitched.

In 1886, he lost every game he pitched, and allegations surfaced that he was drinking. King Kelly called Daily's bat a "pencil," which almost resulted in a donnybrook. Even the cranks had turned on Daily and called him "Cripple, Cripple." His career was now relegated to the minor leagues.

Pete Dowling (Louisville)

Pete Dowling was an Irish pitcher known for what *Sporting Life* (October 12, 1899) called "Dowling's Escapades." Pete Dowling got drunk in Paducah. When he was placed in jail, he kicked over a stove, setting fire to the jail. Later, he went before the police judge, who gave him one hour to get out of town.

His contract contained a sobriety clause. After an episode of heavy drinking on July 4, 1905, he was walking down a railroad track when he fell asleep on the track and was killed.

William Charles "Cherokee" Fisher (Philadelphia)

"Cherokee" Fisher was the first pitcher in baseball to be released, by the Philadelphia White Stockings in 1875 for drinking. He was known for his fastball and heavy drinking. He played for eight teams in eight years. This resulted from his losing his welcome due to his heavy drinking and missing starts due to hangovers.

Fisher missed the entire pitching year of 1877 due to his alcohol problem. He did manage to surrender the first National League homer to Ross Barnes in 1876.

Frank "Monkey" Foreman (Cincinnati)

Frank Foreman was an "icy" pitcher.

In 1895, Cincinnati pitcher Frank Foreman discovered a trick called "icing the ball." He would set a chest of balls on ice for three days, then let it dry on the outside. The balls would be wet inside and when hit would die without traveling much distance.

Foreman was playing for Baltimore when Pittsburg Pirates first baseman Jack Beckley, adept at blocking runners, gave Foreman his hip, causing Foreman to fly into the air. Falling to the ground, Foreman was knocked unconscious. Foreman got up and continued pitching. Foreman later got even by hitting Beckley in the side.

Foreman was fined $25 by manager Billy Barnie for playing while intoxicated.

Danny Friend (Chicago)

Danny Friend was a mediocre pitcher for the Colts. While losing 1–6 to Cleveland on July 1, 1896, he asked Cap Anson to bring in another pitcher. Anson refused and even told the other pitchers (Clark Griffith and Bert Briggs) to go to the clubhouse. Finally, in the eighth inning with the score now 19–7, Friend walked off the mound, tossed the ball to Anson and left for the clubhouse. Anson's response was, "I don't know what's the matter with the boy. He seems to have lost his nerve."

Friend showed his temper again on August 29, 1897, as reported by the *Chicago Record*. "Chicago pitcher Danny Friend was so upset at the calls of Umpire Hank O'Day that he went to pieces. Friend was fined $10. 'Cap' Anson said 'I'll not collect even if they pull the umpire's nose. All I want to see is the umpire get a good licking. I'll pay the fines of any one of my men who licks the umpire when occasion presents itself.'"

Anson did fine Friend $10 for missing practice.

Charlie "Pretzels" Getzien (Detroit)

Charlie Getzien was a "moody" player, which affected his pitching performance. The *Detroit Free Press* (1885) described his performance: "The Washington Nationals batted him all over the field until Getzien said he was ill. A doctor was called from the stands to examine Getzien. Dr. Bond announced he didn't consider Getzien sick, only discouraged by the pounding he received."

In describing Getzien's pitching motion, the *Grand Rapids World* (1886) reported, "Getzien's antics may deceive the batter, so that they are unable to discover the exact course of the ball in time for it to be a strike. He cannot throw a ball so as to make a curve on the horizontal plane."

His curve ball was later defined as a pretzel pitch, which Getzien claimed was a curve which broke twice. This pitch would be called a knuckle-curve today.

In 1888, Getzien was accused of intentionally throwing a game against Boston. Getzien answered that his performance was intended to provide humor to the Boston cranks. *Sporting Life* (June 20, 1888) said, "It is time for Getzien to get over his childish humor and do the best he knows how whenever called on."

William "Kid" Gleason (Philadelphia/St. Louis)

Kid Gleason actually ran onto the field to urge a teammate around the bases on a long-hit ball. If you are wondering why this was allowed, the answer is probably because there was no rule to prevent it.

Gleason often slammed into fielders, such as catcher Jack O'Brien, as he ran the bases, even when it slowed him down. While playing second base, he would give a runner the knee to impede his stride. *Sporting Life* (August 1, 1885) reported, "If he should someday break a limb or his neck, not a ball player would feel the slightest regret."

He would straddle the foul line as his teammates ran on the field to start the game for luck.

When Gleason found he had his pay cut short by Chris Von de Ahe, he stormed into the office and yelled, "Look here, you big fat Dutch slop. If you don't open the safe and give me the $100 you fined me, I'll knock your block off." *St Louis Dispatch* (November 1, 1894)

Gleason was an aggressive base runner who believed the bases belonged to him. Manager Charlie Comiskey, who roomed with Gleason, said, "he wouldn't go to sleep until he figured out how to win the game the next day." While on base, Gleason constantly cursed insults directed at fielders.

CLEASON, P. Phila

COPYRIGHTED BY GOODWIN & CO. 1888

OLD JUDGE
CICARETTES.
GOODWIN & CO., New York.

Kid Gleason

Gleason served as Comiskey's base coach, and he continually berated the catcher's ancestry, personal habits, and lack of skills, which resulted in passed balls. Gleason would over-react to any umpire call, resulting in the cranks screaming and throwing objects.

"Kid" Gleason was a man when it came to rough stuff. He is not to be confused with Bill Gleason, who played shortstop (1882 to 1889) for the St. Louis Browns. He was a second baseman and sometime pitcher.

Kid Gleason's first encounter with rowdy ball was when the New York Giants' Sam Crane attempted to spike him, and Gleason gave him a knee to the nose. He also had an encounter with the dirty Noisy Tucker, who ticked a ball away from him while he was covering second base. Tucker also grabbed his arm on a double play attempt, which umpire John Hunt ruled interference.

However, when Gleason drank, he got ugly. In 1895, Gleason struck a black boy in the face. When a policeman named Officer Lerp arrived on the scene, Kid cursed the policeman and punched him. When the policeman attempted to draw his firearm, Gleason's drinking buddy, John Murphy, hit Officer Lerp beside his head. Things got worse as Gleason, Murphy and now Sadie McMahon all jumped on the officer and beat him badly. The three players ran from the incident and hid in the Baltimore hotel room of boxer Jake Kilrain. The only player caught was McMahon, who gave up Murphy and Gleason. The night cost Gleason a half-year of salary but no jail time. He promised he would not get into any more trouble.

He was caught using a block on Boston runner Bobby Lowe. He was nabbed by umpire Hunt, and Lowe was awarded third base. In 1895, as a pitcher for the Baltimore Orioles, he was involved in the "hidden ball trick," which was attempted during almost every game in that era. He rolled the ball to John McGraw at third base. When the St. Louis runner, Joe Sugden, took his lead, McGraw fired the ball to first baseman Dan Brouthers, who made the tag on Sugden. This was all legal. When outfielder Steve Brodie used his foot rather than his glove to stop a ball, Gleason called Brodie a "dub," and the scuffling was on.

In 1898, while playing for the New York Giants, he threw the ball out of the stadium in order to get a new one. He was much rowdier than Bill Gleason.

Fred "Goldy" Goldsmith (Chicago)

Fred Goldsmith was considered by sports writers to be a "flake." He was chubby and rarely covered first base on throws. On dropping an easy pop-up, his remark to Cap Anson was, "Why Cap! Didn't you see? I made it hit my glove." He hit a home run and was so shocked he laughed all the way around the bases. He hit a second home run his next at-bat. This time, he just dropped to home plate and howled with laughter. Anson had to plead with him to run the bases. When he did run the bases, "it was like a staggering drunk."

When an opposing player hit a home run, Goldsmith would whistle "Over the Guard Wall." The *Chicago Tribune* (July 11, 1884) called him "fat and lazy." He was released on August 7, 1884, by Anson.

Fred Goldsmith carried a clipping from the *New York Tribune* in his back pocket that stated he was the first pitcher to throw a curve ball. The test was made in drawing a chalk line a distance of 45 feet, with a pole set at each end. Goldsmith was on the left side of the chalk line. He delivered the curve with the ball traveling around the opposite pole. He completed this exercise six times, proving it was not an optical illusion, but an established fact."

Clark Griffith (Chicago)

Griffith was a very superstitious pitcher who thought throwing a shutout was bad luck. When it got to the ninth inning and he had a shutout, he would tell his teammates to make errors so the opponent could score a run. This would prevent "a special curse descending upon him."

He would gouge a ball with his spikes to throw his trick pitch. The Detroit Club presented him a bill for $5 for 11 baseballs he damaged. He later threw a spitball, which was legal. He claimed to have invented the screwball. As a manager, he used baseball clowns to coach first base and entertain the cranks.

Early in 1898, an umpire fined Griffith $50 for his "kicking" and ejected him from the game. What was worse, club president Jim Hart fined him another $25, and said, "It may seem as a hardship, but we saw the results of men being put out of the game." Griffith's reply was, "Well, what can I do? Take the fine off, I'll be a good boy, but if it stands well I might be a bad boy. It's like the story of the boy who was whipped at school, and then whipped at home for being whipped at school. It's a bad thing. The umpire knows we are afraid of kickin'. So, he bullies us all he pleases." *Chicago Record* (April 28, 1899)

Charlie "Bumpus" Jones (Boston)

Charlie Jones was a colorful player and was called a "dandy" by the cranks. He had an expensive wardrobe, which resulted in his also being referred to as "The Knight of the Limitless Linen." He enjoyed his alcohol and came to the ballpark inebriated. Boston owner Soden claimed his "conduct was aggravating beyond the patience of most people." Soden refused to pay Jones the remainder of his salary. When Jones blew up at Soden, he was blacklisted from the National League in 1880.

The reason for being blacklisted was given as "poor play and insubordination." He played for Cincinnati of the American Association in 1882 until he was dismissed for drinking. He was reinstated in 1883 and played for the Reds until 1887.

Daniel "Jumping Jack" Jones (Philadelphia)

Daniel Albion Jones was a one-year wonder in baseball. He had pitched for Yale and was signed and released by Detroit (NL). After a dozen games, he was picked up by Philadelphia to assist arm-troubled Bobby Mathews.

What made him unusual was his pitching style. With two strikes, he would leap into the air, flinging his arms and legs out, which resembled the jumping jack exercise. He would do this while singing and whistling on the mound. Even the opposing team cranks would break out in laughter. The *Philadelphia Press* (September 15, 1883) described his pitching by saying, "His antics in the pitching box, by jumping up and cracking his heels on every other ball pitched, was very amusing to the crowd."

The *National Police Gazette* (August 11, 1893) said, "Again and again they tried to make a pitcher out of this big soap-bubble, but they might just as well have tried to train a pet poodle dog."

"Jumping Jack" was named after the exercise. His own teammates mimicked his motion. He actually had a winning record but was dumped by Detroit and Philadelphia because he was not taken seriously.

William "Brickyard" Kennedy (Brooklyn)

"Brickyard" Kennedy was a non-stop "chatter box." When pitching, he carried on conversations with base coaches. He especially enjoyed hollering at the fiery John McGraw. Kennedy would get in the last word when he won the game.

The *Brooklyn Eagle* (May 21, 1893) said, "Kennedy laid down a sacrifice, but somebody yelled 'foul' and 'Brickyard' stopped running so that he was put out at first base."

The *Baltimore American and Commercial Advertiser* (October 1, 1899) said, "Brooklyn Brickyard Kennedy fell for a John McGraw trick. 'Brickyard' was pitching and McGraw asked Kennedy to toss him the ball. McGraw jumped out of the way and the Baltimore runner trotted to second base." (Time had not been called.)

On August 31, 1897, Brickyard Kennedy got angry at umpire Hank O'Day's calls and threw the ball at him. The ball missed O'Day and allowed the New York Giants' George Davis to score the winning run.

Frank "Lefty" Killen (Pittsburg)

Frank Killen was one of the first pitchers to plunk batters on purpose. The *Baltimore American and Commercial Advertiser* (May 26, 1897) reported, "Pittsburg's pitcher Frank Killen hit Baltimore's Hughie Jennings. Jennings made some threatening remarks but Umpire Tim Hurst got between the two players to prevent a fight."

The *Cleveland Leader* (July 20, 1893) reported, "Pittsburg's pitcher Frank Killen deliberately threw the ball striking Cleveland's 'Patsy' Tebeau in the back. In the last six years of baseball experience in the city, a more rascally play was never made on the ball field. Killen is a coward of the lowest grade. Tebeau said nothing and ran to first base."

On July 31, 1896, Pittsburg's pitcher threw a ball which hit umpire Daniel Lally in the face. The Pittsburg cranks stormed the field with disgust that their own pitcher would do such a deed. Killen was arrested by the police and charged with disorderly conduct.

Killen's delivery was questioned as being illegal. The *Pittsburg Dispatch* (June 21, 1898) reported that "'Cap' Anson agued the entire game that Killen's style of pitching was illegal. Anson got red in the face and the old man attempted to give an imitation of Killen's act to cinch the argument. His effort was about as graceful as an elephant eating." His claim was that Killen was an inch away from the rubber. The left-hander was not rattled and did not change his style of pitching.

In 1894, Pittsburg manager Al Buckenberger suspended Frank Killen for ten days for poor play.

Terry Larkin (Chicago)

Larkin was a talented pitcher but had many losses attributed to intoxication. After a comeback attempt on April 24, 1884, he went home and took it out on his wife by shooting her with a pistol. After realizing what he had done, he slit his throat in a presumed suicide attempt. He was hospitalized, jailed and released, because his wife did not press charges. He was released by the Virginians Base Ball Club.

He was arrested on February 18, 1884, for trying to shoot his father. His drinking got worse, with no more baseball in his life. In 1886 he got into an argument with a saloon owner. He took two pistols to the saloon and proposed a duel. The saloon owner marched off the paces out of the saloon and locked the front door. The saloon owner got the police, and Larkin was arrested again. The *Brooklyn Eagle* (August 9, 1886) reported, "he was adjourned for a week, so that he could get the liquor out of him."

Larkin was put into an insane asylum in Brooklyn. He committed suicide by slitting his throat with a razor on September 16, 1894.

Robert "Little" Bobby Mathews (New York)

Bobby Mathews was expelled from the minor leagues for being drunk in 1873. He was a dominating pitcher of early baseball. In August 1874, he left a game early while playing for the New York Mutuals. The game was won by the Chicago White Stockings. However, the *Chicago Tribune* accused the Mutuals of "fixing the game."

Mathews left no doubt where his allegiance was when he turned over a telegram from a gambler to the *New York Herald* to prevent any more accusations. A New York police sting provided more gamblers' telegrams and prompted arrests.

Mathews would "throw the first ball to each striker over the batsmen [*sic*] head," according to the *New York Clipper* (August 9, 1885). "'Little' Bobby would turn his back to the striker with the ball tucked in his armpit. It was like the ball disappeared and a feat to be remembered," said *Sporting Life* (August 15, 1886).

Mathews called his curve "a good and chute." Mathews was given credit for throwing the first spitball by Hall of Fame umpire Hank O'Day, per *Sporting Magazine* (May 1912), said "There is no doubt it was employed by such a veteran as Bobby Mathews. He would spit on the palm of his hand and rub the ball in the moisture. In the course of two or three innings, the ball would be perfectly black in the spot it should be white." The pitch was legal.

Jim McCormick

Jim "Mac" McCormick (Chicago)

Jim McCormick owned a saloon. Jim McCormick and Silver Flint had left the hotel and were seen drinking at "Rath's Keller." His drinking had gotten so bad that a detective was following him. In 1886, McCormick went to the detective on the train platform. When the train reached the depot, McCormick grabbed the detective by the throat, hit him in the eye, and jumped onto the moving train. He was fined $350.

In 1887, although McCormick had signed an abstinence vow with the White Stockings, he drank worse than ever. His drinking led to Al Spalding selling him to Pittsburg. In Pittsburg, McCormick said, "Detectives are funny fellows. They were tracking me in Philadelphia to find if I was drinking and I was in New Jersey all the time." *New York World* (July 14, 1887)

Jim McCormick was King Kelly's best friend and sometime drinking buddy. They were in a play together where McCormick was to pretend to be hanged. However, when the block was kicked aside, he was really hanging and his father came on stage to cut him down. He was left "blue in the face."

He missed the entire 1886 World Series due to a questionable rheumatism. Spalding stated, "Almost from the first of last season just past McCormick began drinking, if he disputes it, I have proof in my possession." *Chicago Daily News* (November 10, 1886)

In 1884, Jim McCormick had jumped to the Union Association with the hope of higher salaries. However, the league only lasted one year. McCormick came crying and begging for Anson to reinstate him. He promised Anson that his drinking had stopped. In 1883, he drank so much that he could not be endured.

McCormick wrote the words for the following poem on detectives that was recited at Kelly's house in 1886.

> Chicago has a ball club
> The finest in the land.
> A detective brought news
> And Burns with a smoke in his hand
> Twenty-five it was the damage
> The Club house suffered the pain.
> The directors had ball
> But when we played ball
> We get there just the same.
> Sweet violets, only a pansy blossom,
> When the Robins not again, Rats!

William "Wee Willie" McGill (St. Louis)

At 16 years old, he became the youngest pitcher of the era when he played for the Cleveland Infants of the Players' League in 1890. However, his youth succumbed to the late-night activities of road ball players. He was friendly and would talk with cranks after games. Because of his personality, he was continually invited to parties.

McGill lacked discipline in 1891 and missed games due to what the newspapers called "high living." He would have late-night escapades with his cohort Curt Welch. After being insulted by cranks he entered the stands with fists flying.

Joe McGinnity (HOF) (Baltimore)

Joe McGinnity was rude to the umpires. He made friends with John McGraw, who instructed him on baiting an umpire. He learned quickly. McGinnity spit in the face of umpire Tom Connolly and was later arrested and suspended for the remainder of the year. McGinnity apologized, which resulted in American League president Ban Johnson reducing the suspension to 12 games.

McGinnity got into a fight with Pittsburg Pirates catcher Heinie Reitz, and McGinnity was suspended for ten games. National League president Harry Pulliam accused McGinnity of "attempting to make the ball park a slaughterhouse."

John J. "Sadie" McMahon (Baltimore)

"Sadie" McMahon was a member of an Irish youth gang which picked fights. When he teamed up with catcher Wilbert Robinson, they were called "the Dumpling Battery." McMahon was known as a hell-raiser.

In 1892, McMahon's drinking resulted in a five-day suspension. However, when he cursed manager Ned Hanlon and owner Harry Von der Horst, it was increased to a one-month suspension and a large fine.

George B. "Win" Mercer (Washington)

His nickname was "Win," yet he lost more games than he won. He played for one of the worst teams in baseball, the Washington Nationals. He was good-looking. All the ladies loved him, and he loved all of them. He also loved gambling on the horses. *Sporting News* (July 30, 1896) suggested, "Win had gambling debts that were unpayable." He would continually get advances on his pay. He attacked umpire Bill Carpenter and was ejected on "Ladies Day," creating a riot.

During a barnstorming trip after the 1902 season, he ran a tube from a gas jet to his mouth and committed suicide at the Occidental Hotel in San Francisco. According to the *New York Times* (January 14, 1903), his suicide note warned about "the evils of womanizing and gambling."

Ed "Cannonball" Morris (Pittsburg)

Ed Morris was a poor fielder who had a fiery temper. He was the recipient of the Allegheny cranks' rowdy comments. He retaliated by jumping in the stands to face the cranks. He was a prominent gambler. His heavy drinking resulted in his suspension in 1889.

As a drinker, he was known for loud and obnoxious behavior which resulted in his being thrown out of saloons. After he quit baseball, he opened a bar so he could stay with his favorite pastime.

Anthony "Tony" Mullane (St. Louis)

Tony Mullane and second baseman Sam Barkley were teammates. However, they both liked the same woman. This resulted in jealousy and feuding between them. Mullane and Barkley became mortal enemies. In a pre-season exhibition game, Mullane almost hit Barkley in the head. Barkley thought Mullane did it on purpose. Barkley took off after Mullane with his bat, but he was subdued by other teammates before any real damage occurred.

Mullane was a hard-nosed pitcher who would maim batters who

Ed Morris   **Tony Mullane**

crowded the plate. He disliked his black catcher, saying "I disliked a Negro and whenever I pitch to him I used to pitch anything I wanted without a signal."

He enjoyed hitting people (with the ball). In 1889, he threw a pitch at the head of Cleveland's Bob Gilks. Gilks responded with a few choice words and walked straight to the pitcher's box. The umpire got between the two. Gilks, instead of leaving with his teammates, got dressed in the Cleveland club house. When Mullane came into the dressing room, the two players had words, and then the fists flew. There was no report of injury to either player.

In 1893, there were three episodes while Mullane was pitching for the Orioles. Arlie Latham was teasing Mullane, who had been singing at the Highland House at night. Umpire Bob Emslie had enough and ejected Latham. Latham, now in the grandstand, had the cranks yelling in unison, which rattled Mullane so bad that he surrendered three runs in the ninth inning and lost, 3–2. The next day, a Cincinnati crank attacked Mullane outside the park. Mullane fended him off, then fired a stone which hit the crank in the back. On the third day, Mullane was back in the pitching box and while warming up threw four pitches close to Latham, who was outside the batter's box. Later, Mullane slid with spikes high into third baseman Latham. Latham simply stepped on Mullane's foot with his spikes. Latham called Mullane "a thickheaded Dago" and "told him to go to the bench. You don't have backbone to stay in the game." *Cincinnati Commercial Gazette* (July 12, 1893)

Jimmy Murphy (Tryout) (Providence)

Jimmy Murphy was from Providence, Rhode Island, and tried out for the Grays on June 27, 1883, as a pitcher. Joker Cliff Carroll sneaked up behind him in the pitcher's box with a garden hose and soaked him with cold water. All the Grays players laughed unmercifully. Murphy just walked out of the stadium. When the players were leaving the ball grounds after defeating Philadelphia, 8–4, Murphy jumped out to confront Carroll. He held a pistol to the side of Carroll's head and fired. The bullet hit utility player Joe Mulvey. Fortunately, Mulvey was only wounded. Jack Farrell chased after Murphy.

At his trial, Murphy was still outraged and yelled to Carroll, "I'll break your head if I ever get out again." *Providence Evening Press* (June 29, 1883)

Edward "The Only" Nolan (Pittsburg)

His nickname came from his claim to being the only pitcher on any team. Nolan began his career by pitching for the Indianapolis Blues in 1878.

On August 14 he claimed he was going to a funeral, but instead got drunk. Manager John Clapp promptly kicked Nolan off the team. Nolan played for the Cleveland Blues in 1881 but continued his drinking escapades. In September, Nolan and eight other players were put on the blacklist, banning them from the National League.

Several days later, the *Chicago Tribune* (May 18, 1878) declared, "Nolan hit four batters and is keeping up his little game of laming and bruising batsmen. He pitches in a cruel and needless manner." Three days later, he hit John Cassidy on the head, knocking him unconscious. After the game, several Chicago players had an impromptu talk with Nolan.

In Indianapolis, Nolan hit Lip Pike, who threw down his bat and cursed at Nolan. Umpire Bill McLean only warned Pike. Teammate Cal McVey challenged Nolan to a fight after being plunked. Nolan slowly went to hitting batters at random so it would not be as detectable.

In 1883, while playing for Pittsburgh Allegheny of the American Association, Nolan was fined $10. Later, while on a drinking spree, "The Only" Nolan put the bill for his drinking on the team's account. This resulted in a suspension.

Later in 1883, after an evening of drinking, Nolan told his manager that his brother was ill. It was later learned that his brother had died years before. He was expelled and blacklisted. Nolan went to Paterson, New Jersey, and opened a saloon.

Nolan also pitched for the Wilmington Quicksteps in the Union Association in 1884. Nolan once yelled at the opposing Boston outfielder to look out for the fence, causing him to drop the ball. (There was no fence.) This resulted in a brawl, and the umpire fined Nolan $10. "'The Only' lit into the umpire with all his fury resulting in a $150 fine." *Boston Globe* (April 3, 1884)

In 1885, back in the National League Nolan pitched for the Philadelphia Phillies, but got in a fight with manager Harry Wright and was suspended. Believe it or not, Nolan later became a member of a police department.

James E. "Tip" O'Neill (St. Louis)

O'Neill was the team enforcer. He corrected wayward teammates with his fists. His claim to shame was writing the following note about proposed exhibition games against Cuban Giants:

Dear Sir:
    We, the undersigned members of the St. Louis Base Ball Club, do not agree to play against Negroes tomorrow. We will cheerfully play against white people at any time, and think by refusing to play we are only doing what is right, taking everything into consideration and the shape the team is in right now.

Signed: J. E. O'Neill, W. A. Loatham, John Boyle, R. L. Caruthers, W. Gleason, W. H. Robinson, Charles King and Curt Welch.

O'Neill threw a bat at Curt Welch, who was standing in the on-deck circle, and the bat hit Welch in the face. This was a message to Welch to mend his boozing ways.

The later years for O'Neill, who had become a notorious drunk, were unproductive. "He was a drunken and immoral ball player deserving no cloak." *Sporting Life* (April 14, 1892)

Tom "Tacky" Parrott (St. Louis)

Tom Parrott would be described in baseball today as a "flake." His pitching motion looked like a windmill. He did not take care of his uniform and always looked sloppy, therefore, the nickname "Tacky" was applied to him. He had long sideburns and a long, thick beard.

One pitching event in spring training set Parrott apart. The *Sporting News* (April 10, 1896) recorded that "Tom Parrott looked like a circus impresario, but not a good ball player. In an exhibition against Belleview with the score tied in the eighth inning with Parrott pitching, a batter hit a ball that caught Tom in the chin, making the stop with his beard. Parrott stuck his fingers into the tangle to retrieve the ball" to throw to the base. Unfortunately, the ball would not come loose, so Parrott ran to first base. The runner beat Parrott "by a 'hair.' The Boss President Von der Ahe fined Parrott $25 and made him shave."

Von der Ahe stated, "Everybody knows 'Tacky' as some kind of pumpkin."

Charlie "Hoss" Radbourn (Providence) (HOF)

"Hoss" Radbourn could drink his weight in beer. On September 1, 1884, *The Pentagraph* accused him of throwing the game by making five errors. He admitted he was approached by gambler Jim Connors but was too drunk to remember the conversation.

When a photographer was taking a team photo, Radbourn lifted his hand high and thrust out his middle finger. The photographer did not notice Radbourn's trick. He even did the same act on his "Old Judge" Tobacco card.

Two gamblers approached a drunken Radbourn and offered him $25 to throw a game. When he sobered up, he told the gamblers, Ed Stahl and Jim Connors, that he wanted nothing to do with selling out his teammates. Radbourn called whiskey medicinal and took a shot before games. Radbourn was known to drink the whole season. His brother stated that he drank a quart of whiskey every day of his career.

Radbourn was resentful that he had to pitch ever day with no additional pay as a reward. On July 16, 1884, he changed his delivery to hit Barney Gilligan, his catcher. Radbourn would give the wrong sign, crossing up Gilligan, who had no protection. When brought before the Providence owners for his temper tantrum, he said he had no intention of hurting Gilligan, but was angry at umpire Stewart Decker. He received a three-game suspension.

Radbourn became a Hall of Fame pitcher who doctored the ball with a foreign substance. He sometimes cut the ball with his spikes to get a better grip on his "drop ball." He was the only pitcher to give the catcher the sign for his pitch. He actually motioned for the curve so even the batter knew it was coming. He pitched around better hitters and walked them on purpose. He warmed up by tossing an iron ball. Radbourn and the other pitcher in the rotation, Charlie Sweeney, had a running feud.

In the winter of 1883, Radbourn issued a $1,000 bird shooting challenge in the *Bloomington Pentagraph* (January 13, 1883). A W. D. Pearce from Missouri responded and won the event. Radbourn married Caroline "Carrie" Stanhope, who owned a prostitution house in Providence. It was reported that he drank whiskey like water.

The great 1884 season did witness a problem when Radbourn was seen drinking before a loss. The *Boston Globe* (July 1884) said, "Radbourn was in no condition physically or mentally to pitch. He snapped in the eighth inning in a dispute with the umpire and catcher Barney Gilligan. He pitched the ball so wildly that no man could hold it."

Radbourn, with Sweeney out, was pitching every day without any extra compensation. He was unhappy. The *Sunday Morning Telegram* (July 13, 1884) reported, "Radbourn was cranky and has been hitting the bottle and it is ugly."

On July 1884, Radbourn's temper took over after several bad umpire calls. He took out his anger on his poor catcher, Barney Gilligan. Radbourn threw a different pitch from what he signaled. Gilligan's fingers were bruised and bloodied. Radbourn commented, that he was "forced to strike out 27 men in a game, as his men would not back him up." *Evening Telegram* (July 17, 1884) This resulted in the Grays suspending Radbourn.

With Sweeney gone, Radbourn's suspension ended and he was well rested. He drank sulfur and molasses, which he called "brimstone and treacle," to make his blood thinner. Radbourn, with all the bickering about a higher salary, stayed with Providence so he could be close to his love, Caroline Stanhope.

During the 1885 season, Radbourn was accused of throwing games to Chicago late in the season and was suspended for the rest of the season. Many believed this was a financially motivated suspension, since he had the highest salary in the league at $4,800 and Providence was not going to win the pennant.

In 1887, he was again suspended by owner Arthur Soden (Boston) for "careless and slovenly play." Radbourn was never in the best condition as a pitcher. During his entire career, he lived with his girlfriend Carrie Stanhope, and this was frowned upon by the cranks. However, he married her right before he died.

In 1888, the *Daily Inner Ocean* reported, "his days of usefulness are about at an end."

Thomas H. "Toad" Ramsey (Louisville)

"He is not to be pitied. A man upon whom fortune thrusts success and but repulses it or abuses it. Fortune does not deserve the compassion of his fellow man. When he gets down in the gutter completely and finds no one who extends a friendly hand or gives him a look of recognition, them he will be able to think of what might have been had he known the manhood to withstand the temptation of a life of debauchery." *Cincinnati Enquirer* (September 21, 1886)

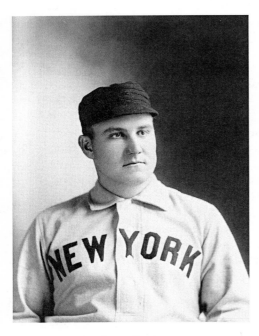

Amos Rusie

Amos Rusie (New York) (HOF)

For a brief period, pitcher Amos Rusie used "elixir," which was supposed to give him strength. The elixir was actually mashed-up ox brains. It was really a placebo, which he didn't use again. He used the elixir during the Temple Cup. This was an early attempted use of performance enhancing drugs.

He enjoyed the nightlife of New York. Everyone wanted to buy him a drink. Rusie's hard partying did not affect his pitching. He drank more at home games than on the road, which almost cost him his marriage.

Rusie staged two famous holdouts, one of which lasted the entire 1896 season.

Fred "Crazy" Schmit (Baltimore)

During a 12-year period, Fred Schmit played for five teams and sat out seven years. He kept a notebook on batters in his back pocket. During a game against the Chicago Colts, he pulled out the notebook and read aloud his notes on Cap Anson: "He has no weaknesses." Schmit walked Anson on five pitches. *Cleveland Plain Dealer* (August 8, 1899)

"Crazy" Schmit was a heavy drinker and came to games intoxicated. After what he deemed an erroneous call, he would lie down on the grass and spread his legs, resulting in an ejection. His teammates threw his suitcase (with his notebook) off the train while traveling to the next stop.

James B. "Cy" Seymour (New York)

The *New York Times* (September 5, 1897) reported that "Cy" Seymour was "the youngster with a $10,000 arm and $.00 head." He was a heavy drinker. During his rookie year, "he suddenly got wild, his cheeks turned red, he threw his hat off, and then threw his glove away. He then ran to the catcher and grabbed the ball, returned to the mound and quickly threw another pitch." He was one of the most excitable players who ever played.

Seymour was prone to alcoholic binges and once threatened a reporter until he was arrested. He insisted on being called James Bentley and said he was related to the Duke of Somerset. He got into a brawl with Lee Tannehill. He punched out teammate Henry Theilman. He planted a kiss on Arthur Shafer.

His drinking can somewhat be attributed to his migraine headaches. He beat up Arlie Latham in a hotel lobby, which resulted in his suspension from the Giants. John McGraw also fined him for leaving the team after the first game of a doubleheader.

John "Phenomenal" Smith (Philadelphia)

John Smith had the largest ego of an average talent player. He changed teams eight times in seven years. His career pitching record was 54 wins and 74 losses. He gave the nickname "Phenomenal" to himself. His teammates described him as brash and cocky. He was not liked by his teammates. "Phenomenal" stated that he did not need any help to win.

On June 17, 1885, while pitching for the Brooklyn Grays in the American Association, Smith's teammates decided to teach him a lesson by purposely committing 14 errors and losing, 18–5. Seven of the runs were earned. Manager

Charlie Hackett fined each player $500, which was about a quarter of their salary. Club president Tom Lynch released Smith the next day to assure harmony.

Jack Stivetts (Boston)

Jack Stivetts was a steady drinker, which caused him to miss pitching assignments. He and Tommy McCarthy got into a fight in a hotel dining room and caused considerable damage. Stivetts ended up with a bloody nose.

Stivetts was a believer in the high life, which resulted in his weight gain up to 225 pounds. In 1899, he finished up the Cleveland Spiders, the worst team in major league baseball history. His hard drinking and failure to keep his weight down prevented him from having an outstanding career.

After drinking before a game, he got into a fight, using a bat against Hugh Duffy and Tommy Tucker. He was then released.

Tony Suck (Buffalo)

This player didn't need a nickname. His playing ability matched his name. What is amazing is that he changed his name from "Zuck." In 52 games, he compiled a batting average of .151 without ever knocking in a run.

Charlie Sweeney (Providence)

In 1884, Charlie Sweeney did not return with the team from spring training; instead, he remained with a lady friend.

Later, Sweeney was drinking during the game. Manager Frank Bancroft switched him to right field in the eighth inning with the Grays still leading. Sweeney refused to go to the position. He left the game and changed into his street clothes. The umpire allowed a replacement for Sweeney, saying he was injured. The Grays suspended Sweeney, and the National League expelled him from the league.

After he was taken out of the game, Sweeney went to the field in street clothes. He threatened the Providence directors with bodily harm. *Sporting Life* (July 24, 1884) reported, "the foolish pitcher left the grounds in the company of two prostitutes." An hour later he was staggering on the streets of Providence.

In 1885, Sweeney's drinking was worse. The *New York Clipper* (November

21, 1885) reported, "he hit utility outfielder teammate Emmett Seery a terrific blow to the face, which sent him over the back of his chair with blood spurting from his nose and mouth." *Sporting Life* (November 22, 1885) described Sweeney as a "whiskey-guzzling cowardly nincompoop."

In 1886, he procured a gun and fired 14 rounds into a bar; fortunately, no one was hit. He got into a fight with teammate Tom Dolan while heavily intoxicated.

In 1891, Sweeney beat a train conductor senseless and left him clinging to life. In 1894, he owned a bar, got into an argument with gangster Con McManus, and killed him with a pistol shot. He went to prison for manslaughter.

Jesse Tannehill (Pittsburg)

Jesse Tannehill was a flake, a left-handed, outstanding pitcher who was a saloon owner before he turned to baseball. He was known for his superstitions:

1. Not shaving on day he was pitching
2. He played for Pittsburg which he felt was a "Jonah" club
3. Black dog (not cat)
4. Never cross a funeral procession
5. Horseshoe in glove when not wearing it

He would sometimes have a negative disposition, which resulted in a fight with teammate Jimmy Burke which dislocated his shoulder.

He continually complained about the pitcher's mound. But the worst was the wind that blew in Hilltop Park. He said "A cold wind blows over the diamond. You can't pitch against the wind. A man would have to have a cast iron arm to win in Pittsburg." He was a no-show at the beginning of the season because he did not like spring training.

Jack Taylor (Philadelphia)

Jack Taylor committed two dirty tricks on one play. He took offense when Chicago's Cap Anson wanted to see the ball with him on the mound. Taylor's temper resulted in his hurling the ball at Chicago's bench, whose players dodged the sphere. Amazingly, no one was hit by the ball.

Taylor had a run-in with Baltimore's Hughie Jennings at second base. First, he gave Jennings a shove and then a hip check. Two dirty plays at once without being caught. Finally, in 1895 a fly ball tag resulted in "Taylor slapping

Jennings in the face, bloodying his nose to give him a lesson well deserved." *Philadelphia Times* (April 19, 1895)

Taylor's dumbest trick was throwing a mud-covered ball over the fence. Umpire Tim Keefe provided a new one, which resulted in a ten-run inning and a loss.

In 1893, he was fined $25 for drunkenness by manager Harry Wright. He was suspended for not showing up for a game by Cincinnati's manager, Buck Ewing, in 1899.

John "Brewery Jack" Taylor (Philadelphia)

"Brewery Jack" Taylor was a pitcher with an uneventful career who moved from team to team. He had a propensity for arguing strike calls. The only manager who tolerated his drinking was Harry Wright, but Wright quit.

Taylor called his drinking problem "malaria" in hopes of obtaining sympathy. However, the strict disciplinarian manager, George Stallings, would have none of it. The *Sunday Item* (June 2, 1892) stated, "his illness could be cured with the stiffest fine that would prevent him from contacting it in the future." Taylor did not accept the penalty and missed just the next game.

In 1897, Taylor was not consistent in his pitching due to his drinking. *Sporting Life* (August 7, 1897) said, "Jack Taylor treats his teammates as strangers." His teammates accused him of having given up for the season. He was continually drunk and arrived late for games. On August 11, 1897, he showed up for a game intoxicated. Manager Stallings suspended Taylor for the remainder of the season. In 1899, he felt he had found a home in Cincinnati. However, the owner was John T. Brush, who endorsed the temperance movement. Taylor did not even get out of spring training before he was seen drinking the night before an exhibition game in Georgia. His performance against the Orioles was terrible. Owner Brush ordered manager Buck Ewing to check out the situation. Ewing reported that he found no evidence to support the claim.

During the 1899 season, Taylor posted a poor record. He missed his next assignment by saying "my mother is sick." He was gone the next two days with the excuse that he was stuck on a fishing vessel. Manager Ewing was furious and told Taylor that he should have swum to shore.

Taylor actually had been fishing with Steve Brodie (Orioles) and Patsy Haley (a prizefighter). Ewing suspended him for the remainder of the season. He received a heavy fine of $700 from owner Brush, along with a salary loss of $500. Taylor was still required to attend daily workouts with the hope of keeping him sober.

After the season, Brush required Taylor's contract to have a temperance clause. However, he died of Bright's Disease (kidney failure) at age 26.

Guy "Rubber-Winged" Weyhing (Philadelphia)

A mediocre pitcher who holds the record for the most hit batters. He played for nine teams in a 14-year career. The *Louisville Courier* (January 26, 1892) reported,

> Guy Weyhing was before the Police Court this morning on alleged charges of grand larceny. During the past two days, a number of pigeons have been stolen from the coops at the National Show, and last night when Weyhing started out of the building with his basket, a pair of blondinettes valued at $100 were found in his possession. He could not explain how he got the birds and was arrested.
>
> Weyhing has in the past been in trouble through indiscretion, but nothing more serious than being sociable and excessive drinking.

He got into an altercation with Curt Welch after a base path collision.

Jim "Grasshopper" Whitney (Boston)

Jim "Grasshopper" Whitney—so-called because of his long, lanky frame and unusual gait—was described as having "a head about the size of a wart." *Detroit Evening News* (August 10, 1883) He would throw over the batter's head to unnerve him. He would hit them repeatedly since "hit by pitch" did not exist. His actions often resulted in brawls. To prevent payback, he would swing at three straight pitches no matter how close to the strike zone. He was referred to as "the hoodlum from the Far West." *Buffalo Commercial Advertiser* (May 11, 1881)

In June 1883, Dick Burns hit Whitney in the leg. In his next at-bat, Whitney hit Burns in the head with his first pitch. Burns was knocked unconscious and taken to a local hospital. Whitney was not even fined.

Jim Whitney

4

Irregular Infielders

Adrian "Cap" Anson (Chicago) (HOF)

"Cap" Anson, at 6'2" and 227 pounds, could destroy an umpire with his voice. When his team was losing, he would get himself ejected just so he could get some rest. When he yelled, the whole park would get silent.

Anson demonstrated how to break up a double play by tackling second baseman "Bid" McPhee. Anson was called for interference and argued so vehemently that the umpire declared the game a forfeit.

Anson ran off the team mascot by calling him a "little coon." The worst sign of his prejudice came in 1888, when he refused to face two Negro players, George Stovey and Fleetwood Walker, in an exhibition game in Newark. Newark removed the two players.

Anson's power in the National League served to help ban Negro players from entrance into organized baseball.

He also criticized the Irish players for their mental capabilities. Hall of Famer Hugh Duffy who played with the Chicago club, said, "Cap Anson of the Chicago Club had no use for the players who had Irish blood in their veins and he never loses an opportunity to insult those men who have played with him in the past." *Sporting News* (January 18, 1898)

Anson was the "First Kicker" of umpires. He discovered that by his loud burst he would gain an advantage in a game. The *Brooklyn Eagle* (September 12, 1888) issued its opinion of Anson's kicking:

> He wants to be a kicker
> And with the kicker stand;
> Finding fault with every umpire
> And the way the pitcher stand.
> He kicks about his players
> And about the scorer, too;
> He thinks the man that never kicks

54

Cap Anson

A meek and humble fool.
For he is a kicker from kickerville
And his patron saint's a mule.
[Ran in *Chicago Sportsman's Reference*—No longer exists]

Anson used the kicking to rest his players.

Anson would bet on anything and elected to prove he was not as slow as the newspapers portrayed him. He bet on a race between himself and pitcher Fred Goldsmith. The race was from home plate to first base. Naturally, the slow-footed Anson lost $50. The *Cincinnati Enquirer* (October 9, 1882) reported, "Anson can run but so can an ice wagon or a turtle." He bet manager Jim Mutrie a suit of clothes on who would win the pennant.

While playing cards for money, he got into a fight with his player Ned Williamson, the same player, when playing for Pittsburg, he had run over when he was trying to catch a pop-up. Anson bet his teammates $500 he would not strike out during the season. He was called out only once on a bad call, and the players paid the bet.

Anson loved to shoot pool with players, and he bet on the games. In 1896, he bet his player Walt Witmot $100 that Chicago would win the pennant; he lost and paid his bet. He did bet one time against his team, to spur slumping pitcher Clark Griffith by wagering he would lose the game. The bet was $20, but he did not mind paying when he lost. At the conclusion of his career, he owned a bowling alley and would bet all comers. However, he was firmly against gambling with bookies, to the point where he punched a man who suggested that his players took a bribe. After he won a bet, he would light up a big cigar.

Anson believed in using any trick to win a game. On August 6, 1890, the Chicago Colts faced the Boston Beaneaters' sensational new pitcher, "Kid" Nichols. Anson got into the batter's box but quickly jumped to the other side as Nichols prepared to deliver the ball. Nichols stopped, and Anson quickly jumped back to the right side. Nichols began winding up again, and Anson jumped again, causing the pitcher to stop his motion. A frustrated Nichols implored the umpire to stop Anson. (There was no rule to prohibit Anson's actions.) Nichols refused to pitch to Anson, and he was awarded first base by the umpire.

Anson was hit by a Cleveland crank on the head with a seat cushion. He went after the crank with a bat, grabbed a crank, and prepared to deck him. Suddenly, he discovered he had the wrong crank and apologized.

His style while captain of the team was to issue obscenities whenever a physical or mental mistake was made. He would get nose to nose like a modern army drill sergeant. He would move players to different positions, such as King Kelly from right field to catcher to shortstop. His tolerance of drinking by players Kelly, George Gore, Silver Flint and Ned Williamson hurt the team drastically. Anson finally set a curfew that the players ignored. He fined players for loafing on the field. Also, he fined a player $100 for throwing a pillow at him.

In 1894, "Hardy" Richardson threw a ball that hit Anson on the head and bounced into the stands. It caused an egg-sized bump on Anson's head, but Anson simply jogged back to the bench.

Anson bought a new bat to be used against Boston. The expensive bat cost $5. It had ash wood strips glued together with rattan. The bat provided a 25 percent increase in distance. He got six hits in two games. He would not let anyone else use it. The National League later ruled the bat illegal.

In 1895, Anson required that all his players obtain a sleeping car pass so he could monitor the curfew. "Bad Bill" Dahlen went to his sleeping berth only to be awakened by a porter who wanted his ticket, which he had not gotten. Anson suspected Dahlen of drinking, but did not want to fine his star player. Anson asked the train porter to put Dahlen off the train. Dahlen was ejected from the train in Indiana, and the club officer suspended him.

Dahlen laughed when Anson chided him for missed plays. Anson recognized that Dahlen was an outstanding player who needed constant chiding. He fined Dahlen $50 for skipping out on a game.

The *Chicago Herald* (November 14, 1886) reported an encounter between Philadelphia owner John Rogers and Anson:

ROGERS: You don't know what you're talking about.
ANSON: I know we'd licked you out of your boots if the fight had gone on.
ROGERS: Why, in point of law, you had nothing in the world to base a case on. We had a splendid case against you.
ANSON: I don't care a damn about law. I'm talking base ball, and I can bring a dozen people to testify that the crowd was disgusted with Irwin.
ROGERS: And I can bring a hundred who are disgusted with a big baby by the name of "Cap" Anson.
ANSON: Let's see 'em.

And both walked away with their hands in the air.

Anson was not short on gall, ordering owner A. G. Spalding off the field. Anson interacted with the cranks as follows:

CRANK: You ain't in it any more, Anson, old boy.
ANSON: That's all right, my boy, we will here two more days just the same.

In 1889 while playing the Cleveland Spiders, umpire George Barnum asked Anson to judge the first base foul line. The cranks yelled at Anson because he was not in the coach's box. Anson replied, "Gentlemen, I'm put here to watch fouls." He was cheered by the cranks.

In 1892, umpire Jack McQuaid called Brooklyn's Tom Daly out on a pick-off play. Anson told McQuaid, "When you make a decision, call it loud. Not a man on the field heard your decision." McQuaid told Anson his voice was sore. A crank yelled at Anson, "You're right, pop." Anson merrily said, "I made the decision before he did."

The *Washington Post* (August 2, 1895) recorded this encounter with the cranks: "Anson jumped into the stand, falling at the feet of a lady and a man.

Will you permit me to pick up the ball? No Sir. He threw the ball to the back of the stands. I was hot, but I turned to him and said, the lady who accompanies you doubtless considers you a very great man. Your action just now was truly sportsmanlike."

He once yelled so loud on a balk call that he scared umpire Stewart Decker and even apologized. In Cleveland, when a seat cushion hit Anson in the head, he confronted the crank and wanted to fight. He threw a punch but it was blocked by another crank. Anson told umpire Henry Murphy that if he gave another close call, "I'll prevent you from umpiring again."

In 1887, Anson was accused of pitching sore-armed John Clarkson. Clarkson told Anson that his arm would be lost for the season, to which Anson replied, "I won't be fooled." Anson was roasted in local papers for threatening to dock Ned Williamson's salary for not playing due to boils on his throwing arm.

Anson, not normally one for fanfare, had his team ride to games in open, horse-drawn carriages, saying "Travelling our way raises the tone of the game. It places your club above the others and it puts the players on their good behavior." The *Chicago Mail* (September 6, 1887) described the players' trickery, saying "Anson had ordered lamb and peas at dinner. When the waiter passed Ed Williamson, he imitated Anson's voice, saying 'Never mind the lamb, just bring the peas.' When Anson got his plate of peas, the team roared with laughter."

Anson was waiting on the train platform for the team luggage when the train departed. Anson ran after the train when Tom Daly cried, "Slide, Slide." A player pulled the bell-cord and the train came to a stop. Anson boarded the train, screaming at the conductor. Anson got the conductor to wait 20 minutes for the luggage.

In 1888, "Dad" Clarke threw a ball that hit Anson in the stomach. Anson grabbed a bat and chased Clarke until he hurled himself over a fence. Anson felt he was not worth the energy and gave up. Buck Ewing prevented Anson from beating Heinie Reitz's face in.

Anson's wife, Jennie, played poker with the players for ten cents a hand.

The *Chicago Mail* (October 6, 1888) gave this account of Anson's forcefulness in dealing with the teams:

Chicago showed up late in Washington and Umpire Daniels had declared a forfeit. Their train had arrived late and the trunks did not arrive until 3:25 p.m. There was a hurried scrambling and rush for uniforms. Anson telephoned the Washington club house that he would be late. Still, Daniels called a forfeit. A cloud of dust sprang up near the Capital Building and pretty soon three carriages tore down the street. Out of the first came a red faced Anson. He jumped from his carriage and strode on the field. The gate tender mentioned playing a makeup game. This didn't suit the old man at all and he called the men from the field and went into the club house to roast the

Washington people. The result of the roast was Washington withdrew their forfeit and the scheduled game was played.

Ross Barnes (Boston)

Ross Barnes was the first player to drop a fly ball intentionally to make a double play in 1874. In 1875, he hit Chicago's Cap Anson in the middle of his back as hard as possible. Barnes fell down on the play and as Anson turned, he kicked Barnes. In 1876, Barnes caught a ball hit by Hartford's Bill Harbridge. When he looked at his hands, there was nothing but yarn. Harbridge had actually knocked the cover off the ball.

When Barnes got a hit, he doffed his hat and bowed to the cranks. Barnes showed up late for a game, saying he "had overslept himself." Ross Barnes did not get along with teammate and first baseman Charlie Gould, saying they "never spoke to one another and met with fierce glares." His 1879 contract had a 50-cent deduction for personal expenses. Evidently, management was counting their pennies. Another $100 deduction was made when he was injured while playing.

Jake "Eagle Eye" Beckley (Cincinnati) (HOF)

"Eagle Eye" Beckley was a schemer whose goal was to circumvent the rules. When batting, he would yell "Chickazoola" at the opposing pitcher to throw him off his game.

He tripped "Cupid" Childs, causing him to break his collarbone.

Beckley was notorious for running from first base to third base, totally skipping second base. He even attempted to run from second base directly to home. Umpire Tim Hurst called him out, saying, "You big son of a bitch, you got here too fast."

While playing first base, Beckley would try the hidden ball trick that was commonly used in this era. His primary ploy was to hide an extra ball in a hole that he had dug out at first base. He used this trick play in each home series. Another of Beckley's tricks was to hide the ball under his armpit. He pulled this trick on Cleveland's Joe Kelley, which started a brawl between two players.

Beckley had a poor throwing arm and would run to tag a runner trying to score rather than throw the ball. In one close game, he ran from first to home plate to tag a Louisville runner trying to score. The runner, Tommy Leach, was tagged out, but two ribs were broken in his collision with Beckley. One of Beckley's wildest maneuvers was bunting with the handle of the bat while holding the barrel. This was legal then, but no other player used this technique.

Pittsburg Pirates first baseman Jake Beckley once fielded a ball and stood his ground as hitter Cap Anson rounded the bag. The larger Anson knocked Beckley on his rear. Beckley was later caught cutting second base short by umpire Bob Emslie, resulting in an out and costing his team a possible run. Sometimes the dirty tricks would cost the team and the pocketbook. After the season, Beckley sent a letter requesting that his uniform be mailed to him so he could practice in it during the winter. Evidently, there were no sweat suits to work out in.

In 1895, "first baseman Jake Beckley made Cleveland's Jimmy McAleer fall when he blocked the base. Umpire Fred Jevne awarded Beckley a $25 fine for his action," as reported by the *Cleveland Leader* (July 4, 1895).

During the same season, Beckley's knee was applied to "Muggsy" McGraw. McGraw responded to Beckley's dirty tactics by telling him that "he better look out." Beckley was credited with coining baseball chatter terms "getatem," "heads up," and "be alive." *Baltimore Sun* (April 15, 1895)

Beckley told Cincinnati's pitcher, Frank Foreman, "Here is where I put you against the fence." After Foreman struck Beckley out, he was ready to injure Foreman and later blocked him off first base. Foreman countered by sticking his leg out, which resulted in a tumble in the air. Foreman landed on his head and lay unconscious.

Beckley once elbowed New York Giants Bill Joyce at first base. Joyce, as a manager, had released Beckley in 1897. Another trick was to bend over to pretend to catch a low throw, causing the runner to go "full out." "Eagle Eye" was known as a "leg breaker."

In 1897, Beckley now with Cincinnati, tripped McGraw again. The *Cincinnati Enquirer* (July 5, 1897) said, "McGraw flew into the air like a balloon and fell like an injured pigeon landing on the ground."

Beckley detected a sign on the fence for W. H. Keith change colors to indicate which type of pitch the pitcher was going to throw. Umpire Tim Hurst was alerted to the tactic and made Pittsburg desist. Beckley got caught again by umpire Kick Kelly for dirtying the ball with tobacco juice, which cost him $5.

Jake Beckley

A Pittsburg player threw the game ball into the stands with the hope of getting a new one. Beckley spotted the maneuver and alerted a policeman to the crank who had the ball. The policeman confiscated the ball and arrested the crank for stealing.

Marty Bergen (Boston)

Trouble followed Marty Bergen wherever he played. In 1891, while playing for his first team in semi-pro baseball, he got into an altercation with a teammate. Unusual and rowdy behavior hampered the outstanding catcher wherever he went. Upon joining the Boston Beaneaters, he slapped pitcher Vic Willis for sitting beside him at breakfast. His teammates described

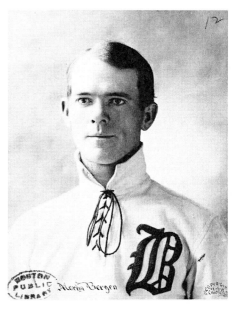

Marty Bergen

him as "trouble with a good many of the boys, so we just give him a wide berth." *Boston Globe* (April 21, 1896)

Bergen had hallucinations that other players were trying to poison him. He would walk sideways to avoid contact with others. While catching, he once missed two pitches, then said, "I was avoiding a knife." He continually missed games without giving an excuse. He would storm off the field if he felt the cranks in the stands did not applaud properly.

On July 20, 1899, Bergen jumped off the train to Cincinnati. He always chewed tobacco, which many felt was the cause of his problems.

Bergen was an unpopular teammate who was a "sullen, sarcastic chap who never associated with other players, and he always nursed a grievance." Four teammates chanted for him to strike out when he batted. "It is now considered that the Boston Nine drop off is largely due to the trouble between Bergen and the players." *Sandusky Star* (September 11, 1899)

It finally got to the point that the whole team was afraid of Bergen. In 1899, he broke his hip, ending his career. Today, it is evident that Bergen suffered from severe mental problems that lacked proper medical treatment. Manager Frank Selee said, "I knew Bergen was not in his right mind." Pitcher Ted Lewis noted, "I was always afraid of him." *Boston Globe* (February 5, 1900)

On January 19, 1900, Bergen killed his whole family with an axe and cut his own throat.

Frank Bowerman (Pittsburg)

The *Washington Post* (July 2, 1899) said, "Pittsburg's Frank Bowerman has the nasty habit of thrusting his burly anatomy in the path of base runners. His blocking is purely carelessness."

In 1897, Chicago's catcher, Bill Lange, bumped into Bowerman twice on attempts to throw out runners at second base. Umpire Tim Hurst allowed the play because he recognized "Bowerman's slowness of foot."

Catcher Bowerman once delivered a hard tag to Honus Wagner at the plate. Wagner got up and pushed Bowerman. Bowerman pushed back, and Wagner thought better of the situation and walked to the bench.

The *Baltimore Sun* (May 31, 1897) said, "Chicago's Jimmy Ryan poked the ball away with his bat when catcher Frank Bowerman dropped the third strike. When the runner took second, Umpire Tim Hurst returned him to first base."

Dennis "Big Dan" Brouthers (HOF) (Detroit/Baltimore)

"Big Dan" Brouthers was a first baseman who was slow of foot, which brought criticism. When receiving criticism, he would claim an injury, such as a toothache, and leave for his home in Wappingers Falls, New York.

Brouthers would bring his Irish setter, Kelly, to every home game, where the dog would watch from the dugout.

When you think rowdy, you don't envision Dan Brouthers. However, some of his antics speak otherwise. One episode involved his birthday. He needed to catch a 5:30 train, but an unexpected doubleheader was delaying those plans. In the second inning a ball was popped up in back of first base, Brouthers stepped back quickly, lifted his outstretched arms, and the ball hit him on the head. He fell prostrate on the ground, apparently severely injured. He was carried to the dressing room. Brouthers, suitcase

Dan Brouthers Hall of Fame plaque

in hand, made a crafty exit for the depot and his birthday party. Manager Charlie Byrne ran after him. He missed his train, but was presented a candle-laden cake.

Sporting Life (February 24, 1894) reported that "Dan's annual town painting spell is still in abeyance." He was a familiar visitor to Old Jed's Tavern. "He had sworn to not go on any more benders." *Washington Post* (March 10, 1896)

In a game against Providence, he missed the ball, but inside his shirt was another ball which he produced and used for an out. Baltimore second baseman Heinie Reitz kept joking with Brouthers one day until Brouthers knocked the ball out of his hands. The umpire made no call. In 1884, "Buffalo first baseman Dan Brouthers used the 'new' hidden ball trick on Chicago's Billy Sunday. Dan pretended to throw the ball to the pitcher. When Sunday took his lead, Brouthers tagged him out. Sunday almost lost his religion on being fooled." *Buffalo Times* (June 18, 1884)

Playing at Detroit, Brouthers experienced the most embarrassing play of his career. "Brothers [*sic*] hit a pop fly and Chicago's catcher 'King' Kelly made out like the ball was behind him. Brothers just watched Kelly with his bat at his side. Pitcher Jim McCormick misplayed the pop fly, but 'Big Dan' didn't see him. He was thrown out at first base with the entire White Stockings' players laughing hilariously." *Detroit Journal* (June 21, 1886)

Louis Rogers "Pete," "Gladiator" Browning (Louisville)

Browning could be found on any bar stool where he played. "I can't hit until I hit the bottle" were Browning's own words. He was nearly deaf and was afraid of being in surroundings other than those to which he was accustomed. His "Gladiator" nickname was due to his continued verbal battles with owners and sports writers. He was the first player to have his own custom bat made by "Hillerich and Bradsby."

He was one of the worst fielders the game has ever seen. He tried every position except catcher, without much success. He would stand on one leg while playing the infield to avoid collisions. However, he did the same thing in the outfield to avoid collisions on fly balls. He could not hear the outfielders calling for the ball. He couldn't hear the ball hitting the bat to determine a shallow hit or hard hit. He refused to slide.

In 1883, Browning was fined 13 times for $130. The rest of the team was fined $10.

Browning outsmarted John McGraw in one game by unbuckling his belt. When McGraw attempted to grab Browning by the belt, McGraw was left holding nothing but the leather belt as Browning ran home and scored.

Browning received a $200 bonus if he came to the games sober. The sobriety did not last long. "He was found drunk fishing in a gutter outside the team hotel." *Louisville Courier Journal* (June 11, 1889)

The sportswriters continually questioned his saloon time, which often resulted in tussles. One newspaper sportswriter dubbed him "Pietro Redlight District Distillery Interests Browning."

Browning was arrested while drunk when he argued over a streetcar pass. He was fined $200. "He was fined $110 for being drunk at a team picnic. He was suspended the final two months for drinking." *Louisville Courier Journal* (July 26, 1889)

He had the habit of speaking to his bat when he approached the plate, and he gave each bat a name. When he stopped using a bat, he would say, "it was retired."

Pete Browning

When arriving at a hotel, he would often shout, "Championship Batter, The Gladiator." *Louisville Courier Journal* (May 30, 1889) He was noted for frequenting prostitute establishments. He would stare at the sun with the notion that it would improve his eyesight.

John "Black Jack" Burdock (Boston)

"Black Jack" Burdock was one of the toughest players of any era.

He was a nasty player who enjoyed torturing opponents with hard slides. Opponent "Moose" Farrell started putting small rocks around the base path which split Burdock's pants. Burdock was described as a hard-drinking, cursing, irritable, bulldozer player whom cranks hated. He would grab the uniforms of runners to slow them down when the umpire was not looking. His protests to the umpires were always belligerent. In June 1884, Paul Hines gave Burdock what he had given others by knocking him out cold. Burdock got up after 15 minutes and blocked second base as Hines was picked off, to the roars of the Boston cranks.

Hoss Radbourn knocked Burdock's fingernail off, which resulted in his leaving the game. Burdock replaced John Morrill as Captain. The *New York Times* (August 9, 1884) described his action with the umpire "as worst humor possible and he pranced about the field and yelled in a manner that would lead one to believe he was a fit subject for a lunatic asylum." Umpire Tom Gunning was truly afraid of Burdock.

He was knocked unconscious by New York Giant Tim Keefe in 1886. A doctor was summoned from amongst the cranks. After a period of ten minutes, Burdock jumped to his feet and continued playing second base. He was knocked unconscious four other times during his career. He became King Kelly's roommate.

Burdock was a binge drinker and was suspended in 1887 for coming to games intoxicated. On July 21, 1888, he was arrested for assaulting a 16-year-old female store clerk, but was released due to lack of evidence. During another drinking episode, he attempted to kiss a Miss Tillie Brown at a saloon. In 1891, he served a two-day jail term for "public intoxication."

Unbelievably, he played 20 years as a player while getting into so many scrapes and having suffered so many concussions.

Thomas P. "Oyster" Burns (Baltimore)

"Oyster" Burns had an irritating voice. His teammates referred to him as a "disturber." He had a bad disposition and made it "unpleasant for any of the boys who crested him. He is what you call a bulldozer."

"Burns is the noisiest man that

Oyster Burns

ever played for Brooklyn. His voice reminds one of a buzz saw," said the *New York Clipper* (May 19, 1885).

Burns threw a ball at the opposing pitcher, hitting him in the back. "'Oyster' was suspended for five games," reported the *New York Press* (August 30, 1887).

In 1893, between the games of a doubleheader, Burns stabbed teammate Tom Daly with a penknife. Daly missed two weeks due to the injury.

Albert John "Doc" Bushong, D.D.S. (St. Louis)

"Doc" Bushong was a practicing dentist and catcher. He wore a mouth guard that he had made himself. However, in 1885, a ball bounded off his head and was caught by the pitcher, which resulted in an out. He actually lost income while playing baseball.

With Pete Browning on first base, the St. Louis infield started dancing around to confuse him. Bushong had the ball and as Browning watched, he tagged him out. During a visit to Paris, pitcher Pete Caruthers and Bushong sent a telegram saying they would not return for the 1886 season unless their salary was higher than the $2,000 minimum. Owner Chris Von der Ahe took the threat as real and offered Bushong $2,500 and Caruthers $3,200. Bushong was a poor hitter, but only "Buck" Ewing was paid more as a catcher.

In 1886, Von der Ahe released Bushong, who was picked up by the archrival Brooklyn Trolley Dodgers. The same year, the owner accused Bushong of trying to bribe "Tip" O'Neill to throw games. O'Neill was suspended for playing poorly. O'Neill stated that his poor play was due to dysentery.

Near the close of the 1889 season, Bushong split his finger and could not catch. Brooklyn manager Charlie Byrne provided the names of three catchers (who were not in attendance) to the Kansas City manager. None of the three were at the game since they resided in the graveyard. Bushong was picked as umpire, which resulted in an easy victory for Brooklyn. Bushong offered O'Neill a job with the Dodgers if he would play poorly. Browns owner Von der Ahe protested to the American Association.

Brooklyn manager Charlie Byrne even dispatched to watch the Browns play. This was the first use of a baseball scout. When Von der Ahe saw Bushong at the game, he went into an uproar and called the scouting despicable.

While playing for Brooklyn in 1889, Bushong was the first catcher to use a padded mitt.

He umpired a game when an umpire did not show up for the game. Kansas City's Manager Bill Watkins did not object. Doc Bushong, Brooklyn, offered suits, overcoats and money to Louisville and Cincinnati pitchers as incentives to beat the Browns.

George "Scoops" Carey (Baltimore)

"Scoops" Carey was a Baltimore first baseman whose method was to stand in the runner's way and then hop out of the way, resulting in collisions. When he was moved to third base, his new glove was larger than other players', causing Cleveland's manager Patsy Tebeau to use a tape measure. The game was delayed 20 minutes before umpire Ed Andrews allowed the glove.

The *Baltimore American and Commercial Advertiser* (August 14, 1895) reported that Baltimore's first baseman "pulled the hidden ball trick on New York Giants 'General' Stafford."

"'Scoops' Carey cut first base short by 15 feet and he was called out by Umpire Jim McDonald," said the *Baltimore Sun* (July 17, 1895). The smart players would cut other bases short but not first, since the umpire normally watched first.

Clarence "Cupid" Childs (Cleveland)

Childs began as the "star" of the Syracuse Stars. "While playing with St. Louis 'rowdy' Perfectos, he did not try to complete a double play but instead took swings at Cincinnati's runner Elmer Smith. Perfecto's centerfield Mike Donlin came in and pushed Smith to the ground. It took the police to restore order," reported the *St. Louis Star* (September 2, 1899).

In 1896, Childs intentionally ran into Baltimore catcher "Boileryard" Clarke on a pop fly. Clarke was not even fazed and made the catch. Umpire Tom Lynch figured "no harm, no foul." Cincinnati's Charlie Irwin attempted to block Childs from reaching third base. Childs' plunge jolted the ball loose, and he was called safe by umpire Bob Emslie.

Cupid Childs baseball card

Fred Clarke blocked Chicago's second baseman "Cupid" Childs on a throw to first. "Cupid," who didn't back down and wasn't intimidated by any player, jumped to his feet and swung at Clarke. Clarke landed a fist to "Cupid's" head. That evening Childs and Clarke pummeled each other with vengeance, rolling about on the train platform, disfiguring each other's anatomy and playing havoc to their clothes. The police arrived and stopped the altercation [*Chicago Record* (May 7, 1900)].

Childs did commit some minor violations, such as dirtying the game ball, for which umpire Bob Emslie fined him $5.

A foul ball was returned to the infield by a crank. Childs attempted to hide it by stepping on the ball forcing it into the ground. Two teammates saw his action and stood in front of him to block the view. Umpire Stump Weidman was not fooled and ordered the ball played. Cleveland Manager Patsy Tebeau told "Cupid" to "throw out the ball and don't let me catch you doing that again." Everybody laughed, even Umpire Weidman [*Cincinnati Times Star* (August 26, 1895)].

While playing with the Chicago Orphans, Childs threw a ball out of the stadium after making the third out. He was not ejected from the game.

Billy Clingman (Pittsburg)

In 1895, Pittsburg's third baseman, Billy Clingman, got in the way of Chicago's Bill Lange. Lange was tagged out in a rundown, but was awarded third base by umpire Jimmy Galvin.

The *Baltimore Herald* (August 28, 1899) reported,

Baltimore's Gene Montreville hit what looked like an inside the park home run when Billy Clingman, Pittsburg's shortstop, fired a new ball from his shirt over third base. DeMontreville trotted home only to find Pittsburg's catcher Mike Powers with the ball. Note the original ball was thrown in by left fielder Fred Clark to Clingman to Powers. Umpire Ed Swartwood ruled Montreville out at the plate and the game ended 4–4. Montreville and Swartwood were not sure what happened. St. Louis' Bill Keister, on a pickoff throw, poked his fist into the right eye of Chicago's Billy Clingman who tagged Bill out. The umpire made no ruling on the play.

Tommy Corcoran (Cincinnati)

Tommy Corcoran believed in dishing out blows to his opponents. He gave Chicago's third baseman, Bill Everitt, an elbow to the eye when running to third. The *Chicago Tribune* (May 30, 1896) reported, "blood covered Everitt's shirt collar." Umpire Tim Hurst saw the play but made no ruling. However, the cranks went wild, screaming at Corcoran.

Once he gained a reputation for administering blows, he was avoided on the base paths, to the point that Pittsburg's Bill Gray jumped completely over him. Another trick applied by Corcoran was clapping his hands to pretend he was catching the ball when it was not even near. This play fooled future Hall of Famer Willie Keeler, who ran back to second. Even notorious base path blocker Charlie Dexter got out of Corcoran's way.

On two consecutive days, Corcoran's in-the-field trickery worked. First, lured by Corcoran's pointing to third and yelling, St. Louis' future Hall of Famer, Bobby Wallace, ran on a fly ball and was easily doubled up. Then, Cleveland's Jesse Burkett was told by Corcoran to go back. Burkett was not going to be fooled, so he continued to run. When the ball was caught, Burkett was out, too. He was mad and cried, "I'll punch you in the nose." Other players falling for Corcoran's advice were Philadelphia's future Hall of Famer, Elmer Flick, and Chicago's George Bradley. The fact that Corcoran was louder than the base coach was a reason this trickery worked.

Corcoran held "Noisy Tommy" Tucker's arm to prevent him from making a throw. His bad throw caused a run. When John McGraw spiked Corcoran's foot, Corcoran went to McGraw and grabbed his collar. He punched McGraw in the face. Joe McGinnity got into the fray by grabbing Corcoran around his midsection in a death grip, causing Corcoran to give up the fight. McGraw told Corcoran "he would make him jump hurdles when he came to second." National League President Nick Young said McGraw "was to blame for the agitation."

Corcoran described Baltimore's field in the *Cincinnati Times-Star* (June 17, 1897) "as springy or what in race horse parlance would be called fast. Balls bounce on it more lively, causing ball players to do more hustling and this increases the life in the game. The grounds in Boston are slow or heavy. It takes a hard hit ball to travel any distance on the ground, and infield hits come much slower than in Baltimore."

Corcoran was able to detect when the St. Louis Browns threw an "old ball" on the field and alerted umpire Ed Swartwood to the illegal ball. The umpire threw it out, only to have the ball reappear two more times. The last time this happened, Swartwood allowed the ball to stay.

One of the more unusual ploys of Tommy Corcoran was repairing his broken bat. The *Cincinnati Enquirer* (April 18, 1898) reported, "He put the bat back together with wax thread, screws and nails. Some players would use a glue and lead to provide more power. Also, caulking of bats was legal."

Sam Crane (New York, Cincinnati, Detroit, St. Louis, Washington, Pittsburg and Buffalo)

While playing second base for the New York Giants, Crane tried to injure St. Louis Brown Kid Gleason at second base. But Gleason kneed him in the side, which caused "Crane to tumble backward. When he got up he was bleeding badly." *St. Louis Post Dispatch* (September 15, 1883)

He played for eight teams in seven years and even managed a team for two years (Buffalo Bisons in 1880 and Cincinnati Outlaws in 1884). However, it was his love life that got him in trouble. He had an affair with a fruit dealer's wife and stole $1,500 from him.

Later, Crane became a sports reporter. After he wrote an article on the New York Giants' temperamental owner, Andrew Freedman, he was excluded from the Giants' field at the Polo Grounds. He was writing for the *New York Advertiser*.

Bill Craver (Philadelphia)

In the first days of the National League, New York catcher Bill Craver used a new play when he dropped a third strike. The runner on first took off for second. Craver fired the ball to second baseman Jimmy Wood to get the out. (A dropped third strike did not require a throw to first base. It would not have mattered since the base was covered.) Craver's move was simply a method to fool the runner into attempting to gain a base.

Another trick Craver was credited with was snapping his fingers. The snap would fool the umpire into calling a foul tip a strike.

Playing for the Troy Haymakers in 1872, Craver showed the ball to umpire George Leroy, saying the yarn was exposed and asking for a new ball. The umpire agreed with Craver and put a new ball in play but the opposition Baltimore Canaries refused to use the new ball. Umpire Leroy called a forfeit for the Haymakers. The stubbornness of the players caused a 6–3 lead to end a 9–0 forfeit loss.

Lave Cross (Philadelphia)

The term a "disgruntled player" describes Lave Cross. He played for nine teams over a 21-year career. In 1893, he received a $1,800 pay cut (55 percent). Lave Cross would go along with his best friend Ed Delahanty. He often borrowed money from Delahanty, who hoped Cross wouldn't remember he needed to pay it back. Cross objected to the temperance clause in his contract even though he did not drink, saying the "contract implied he drank." So he refused to sign it.

In 1884, Delahanty, Delahanty's brother and Cross played on a barnstorming team in Ohio to make extra money. Cross was let go and promptly sued the team for $300; the lawsuit lasted a year, but he won. Cross' attitude made him popular with the cranks wherever he played. In 1896, Chris Von der Ahe fined him $50 for "indifference." In 1899, he was player-manager of the worst team in baseball history, the Cleveland Spiders, who had a 20–134 record.

William "Bad Bill" Dahlen (New York)

He got his nickname from his terrible temper, which managed to get him ejected 68 times in his career.

In 1892, while playing shortstop for Chicago, Dahlen collided with outfielder Mike Tiernan, and the Giants bench screamed "deliberate and dirty."

Umpire Edward Seward once fined Dahlen $5 for profanity. Dahlen retaliated by throwing dirt in Seward's face, which cost him another $10. *The Sporting News* (November 25, 1893) said Dahlen was "sulky and does not try to play ball with a losing team." An example was given as a game in late July with Louisville, when Dahlen changed into street clothes before the game was over. The Colts rallied in the top of the ninth, and everyone had to wait for Dahlen to put his uniform back on and return to the field.

"Bad Bill" Dahlen threw a bat at St. Louis catcher Heinie Reitz. *Chicago Dispatch* (July 9, 1893)

After a losing streak, Dahlen left the team for a trip home on May 6, 1894. He returned a week later and apologized for his mistake. *The Sporting News* (May 14, 1894) chastised Dahlen for not showing the proper spirit. Manager Cap Anson fined him $50.

The Sporting News (June 22, 1895) reported that during the sixth inning, "George Tebeau [Cleveland Spiders] blocked Bill Dahlen from first base so that Dahlen spiked him. Tebeau retaliated by kicking Dahlen who was on the ground. Bill got to his feet and connected with a right punch which sent Tebeau to the ground. Play resumed and on the next pitch Dahlen slid back into first with his spikes high. Manager Tebeau rushed to the field." (Neither Bill Dahlen nor George Tebeau were ejected. Umpire Pud Galvin was fired in August.)

The Sporting News (October 3, 1896) stated, "On the train trip home Dahlen went to bed without getting his train berth ticket. When awakened by the conductor, Dahlen refused to go to Anson to get his ticket. The train stopped at a railway crossing and Dahlen was put off. He spent the night in a deserted picnic ground. Anson's remark was the young man simply got gay."

In 1898, Dahlen was ejected a league-leading six times. The *Chicago Tribune* (July 29, 1898) called Dahlen's actions "inexcusable." *The Sporting News* (August 13, 1898) called him "the personification of pigheadedness." The *Brooklyn Eagle* (June 3, 1898) said, "In fact throughout the game Dahlen was permitted to kick unmolested." *The Sporting News* (July 2, 1898) said, "His interest is not what it should be." This was after he skipped a game against Brooklyn to go to Washington Park to bet on the horses.

Dahlen, when refused a loan by owner James Hart, took off his uniform and confronted Hart in the stands by saying he was "on strike." Hart threatened to bench Dahlen for the remainder of the season. "Dahlen for all his skills, is not a valuable man to a team owing to his peculiar temperament," said *Sporting Life* (September 24, 1898).

In 1899, Dahlen was transferred to the Brooklyn Superbas. He did not change his opinion of the umpires' calls. Hank O'Day ejected him on June 28, and Bill Smith ejected him on July 4 for profanity-laden disputes.

Dahlen came to the defense of umpire Bob Emslie when a crank came on the field. Dahlen threw the crank down.

One episode of Dahlen as a manager needs mentioning. "Dahlen went to home plate to question a fair ball call. Dahlen was screaming in Rigler's face that the ball landed foul. He was yelling and waving his arms when Rigler, thinking Dahlen was getting ready to hit him, struck first. He smashed the Brooklyn manager in the face with the punch landing under Dahlen's left eye. Dahlen retaliated with a punch of his own. The two men exchanged blows until Wilbert Robinson and Pinkerton security men broke the melee up." *Brooklyn Daily Eagle* (April 21, 1912)

Dahlen's antics with manager "Cap" Anson in 1895 were described. "You stay here until you learn to throw the ball up to me," said Anson. A batter would ground the ball to Dahlen, and he would shoot it over to Anson. Every throw was hitting the ground, and by the time Anson had stopped a few with his chins and chased after the balls that got by him, he was furious. Finally, Anson said he was going to give Dahlen the beating of his life. Away they went, with Dahlen going easily while the ponderous Anson lumbered after him. The other players were thrown into ecstasies of laughter by the chase. Dahlen would pop around a corner, dive over a bleacher wall, and Anson went tumbling after him. All the time, the old man was getting more furious.

Cornelius "Con" Daily (Brooklyn)

"Con" Daily was a rough, tough catcher.

In Boston, he was fined $50 for drinking in 1886. Now with Brooklyn, he used his glove to impede Denny Lyons' bat. Daily was bigger than Lyons, so all he received was a dirty look. The *Pittsburg Chronicle Telegraph* (June 2, 1893) reported, "Lyons faked throwing the bat at Daily."

Daily threw a wood mallet at "Pebbles" Glasscock. A smaller "Muggsy"

McGraw wanted to take on Daily, at six feet, 200 pounds. Daily had beaten several prize fighters so he was often challenged by players. Daily laughed at the thought.

Daily once took advantage of rookie umpire Charlie Snyder by putting an "old dead ball" into play. The ball was used for the rest of the game.

Conrad "Dell" "Wiener" Darling (Chicago)

Darling got the nickname "Wiener" because he ate four wiener-wurst before a game. He believed that a baseball player's diet should be wieners.

When he caught, he would tell the pitcher how many strike calls were missed by the umpire in the game. This would make Cap Anson angry, but the umpires were more upset when given a number. Darling was not an umpire's friend.

Washington's pitcher Dupee Shaw made these verbal comments to Dell Darling when Darling batted against him:

> *(Strike one)*
> SHAW: Fooled you, eh?
> *(Strike two)*
> SHAW: Can't hit 'em, eh?
> *(Strike three)*
> SHAW: Too speedy for you, eh?

(In 1887 four strikes were required for an out.) The next pitch resulted in Darling hitting a triple.

> ANSON (coaching third base): "No, he can't hit em, eh?"

Dell once grabbed the arm of Philadelphia's Charlie Bastian when he attempted to complete a double play. Umpire Herm Doscher called interference and an out at first base.

George Davis (New York)

George Davis was not considered a trickster, but he fooled people. George Davis ran into the knee of Boston's first baseman Tom Tucker. He was groggy and had to leave the game.

Cleveland's third baseman, George Davis, got tangled with John McGraw. A few pushes were the brunt of the action. Later in the season, Davis told McGraw, "What are you standing there talking for? You are delaying the game. Don't you know you are delaying the game? Don't you know that the umpire has called you out?" McGraw stepped off the base, and Davis tagged him. The umpire, Mike McLaughlin, called him out. *Baltimore American and Commercial Advertiser* (May 15, 1892)

Baltimore's Steve Brodie was going to make an out at third base and deliberately kicked New York third baseman George Davis in the side. George Davis ran into John McGraw at third base. Umpire Ed Andrews, aware of McGraw's reputation, called interference on McGraw. McGraw called to Andrews, "You're a robber, Andrews." McGraw was fined $5." *New York Sun* (April 21, 1899)

John McGraw sued George Davis for his share of the Temple Cup split. Davis had borrowed from the New York club and was basically broke. In 1897, Louisville Colonels Fred Clarke attempted to take out New York's George Davis, but Davis dodged his attack. Davis called Clarke out, and Clarke swung his fist at George's head. Davis landed a blow to Clarke's jaw. The Giants' "Kid" Gleason broke up the "bout." *New York Herald* (July 17, 1897)

George Davis

George Davis was caught in a rundown with a ball being delivered to Boston's Chippy McGarr. Davis put up his hands to push McGarr. After the collision, both players lay on the ground until suddenly McGarr kicked Davis. Davis jumped to his feet and began punching McGarr. The men were separated without either receiving a fine.

Tom Daly (Chicago)

Daly was a jokester and scuffler who once fought a hotel desk clerk at 2 a.m. Anson fined him $25 for breaking curfew, but nothing for the fight. He frequently did not wash his uniform and always looked like a "dirty bag."

Once while he was at bat, a close pitch just missed his thumb. So he grabbed his finger and put his thumb in his mouth. Umpire John Kelly laughed, "No it did not hit your thumb."

He would commonly do handstands after a great catch or do a little dance while playing center field.

He picked on rookie pitcher Willie Mains by pulling his bedding into the train aisle with him sleeping on it. He dumped him out of his bunk on another occasion. He even poured ice water on Mains while he slept. Mains retaliated by throwing a pillow and wrestling with him in the train aisle.

After the season, the team rode to California to play some exhibition games. The fun-loving Daly got behind John Clarkson on all fours, and Jimmy Fogarty pushed Clarkson so he would tumble back over Daly. The next day he put tacks in Cap Anson's cleats.

The *Cincinnati Enquirer* (November 1, 1888) revealed the following incident:

A few nights ago George Wood was bunked over "Cap" Anson's father. About midnight Daly got Jim Fogarty and George Van Halren to obtain the bat-bag (containing approximately two dozen bats) and took it to Wood's bunk. They pulled down the curtains in the sleeper car when Wood awoke and grabbed the bag. Mr. Anson woke up also and bats flew out the bat-bag landing not on Wood, but Mr. Adrian Anson. The trio of mischiefs ran out of the car chased by the 230 pound senior Anson and "Cap's" wife Virginia.

The train had stopped at a water station. The players jumped off and ran to the end of the train, jumped back on and hurried to a berth. In a few moments, the whole Anson family arrived with the conductor. The conductor told "Cap" it was a mistake because no one had left the rear car. "Cap" told his father he had been dreaming. Mr. Anson replied, "You damn fool, come look at the bat-bag, and see if it was a dream."

"Cap" went back to his father's sleeping berth but magically the bag and bats had disappeared. "There Pop, you see I was right." The father said what about the lump on my head. "Cap" laughed and went to bed only to find the bat-bag in his berth. He rushed to Daly's berth but Tom was asleep. "Cap" offered a $100 reward for the culprit but there were no takers.

Anson would secure all the berths for the train. He would put tickets in a baseball cap and the players would draw, hoping for a lower berth. Daly would take two tickets and give back the least desirable berth.

Daly was a gambler who liked to bet on the horses. He even bet $100 on Grover Cleveland to win the 1888 presidential election. He lost when Benjamin Harrison won.

Late in his career, John Morrill fined Daly $150 for drinking. Daly was not just a jokester, he also rescued umpire Bob Emslie when cranks came on the field in Brooklyn. Daly threw one crank to the ground, which caused the others to leave.

Pat Deasley (St. Louis)

The *St. Louis Globe-Democrat* (May 17, 1884) reported that "Deasley approached two women on the street. He propositioned them and when his overtures were rejected, Deasley grabbed one of them by her arm. Both women escaped to the safety of a store that sold women's hats. Deasley steadfastly pursued them. The Indianapolis police arrested him for drunkenness and insulting ladies." Deasley paid a $10 fine.

On July 2, 1884, Deasley showed up drunk at Sportsman's Park. Deasley assaulted manager Ted Sullivan while drunk and spent a night in jail. Tom Dolan was provoked into "hammering" Deasley. Deasley condemned the manager loudly to the cranks.

Gene "DeMont" DeMontreville (Chicago)

Cap Anson once slid into National's second baseman Gene DeMontreville. "DeMont" criticized Anson for his slide by saying, "Why, you readheaded old yap, if it weren't for your age, I'd get after you. You should apply for an old age home and give a young man a chance." Anson replied, "Young man, you ought to be ashamed of yourself. The idea of talking like that to me. I'm old enough to be your father." DeMontreville responded stronger than that by saying "Make it your grandfather." *Chicago Tribune* (August 7, 1897)

He would go to games drunk and would miss nightly curfews because he was out drinking. He got into a tussle with his manager, Tom Burns. In 1898, DeMontreville was relegated to the grandstands for the game. He denied being drunk but paid his fine. He played for eight teams, and everywhere he played it was the same "hard drinking" problem. He got into a bar fight in Chicago and was released.

He was criticized by his teammates for his fear of being spiked even though he was an outstanding fielder.

John Joseph "Dirty Jack" Doyle (New York)

Inflicting pain was "Dirty Jack" Doyle's game. The "Dirty Jack" nickname did not relate to the way his uniform looked. "Dirty Jack" was despised because of his attitude. "He is cold blooded," according to the *Baltimore Morning Herald* (August 18, 1896). He was an excellent hitter, yet he changed teams ten times in a 17-year career.

"He was a no-nonsense aggressive base runner who ran over any fielder in his way," reported *Sporting Life* (September 6, 1897). Most believed Doyle played dirty because he enjoyed it.

While playing for the Giants in 1892, Doyle threw his mask into the baseline, which resulted in a base runner tripping. As a runner, he would dive into the first baseman after the ball was caught, in an attempt to loosen the ball. Sometimes the umpire would eject him, but others would let him get away with it rather than face his wrath. The National League reprimanded "Dirty Jack" for dropping pebbles into the batters' cleats while catching. They would start for first base and then begin hobbling. He was suspended for three games. When questioned, his reply was, "an edge to be gained was to be taken."

Ned Hanlon, Orioles manager, traded Kid Gleason for Doyle, saying "he would fit right in with his rowdies." However, some of the Orioles held grudges against him. Willie Keeler did not get his share of Temple Cup money from Doyle. Doyle had hip-bumped "Muggsy" McGraw off first base and then tagged him out. Doyle was only with the team a few weeks when he got into a fist fight with center fielder Steve Brodie.

In 1896, while playing an exhibition game against a minor league team in Petersburg, Virginia, there was no authorized umpire for the game, which resulted in chaos. Doyle started the chaos by yelling at the Petersburg player who was umpiring. When the Petersburg second baseman tagged Jim Hughey hard in the eye, Doyle went out to defend his teammate and knocked the second baseman down. This brought the cranks from the stands onto the field. The police broke up the mob, but the situation was not over. That night at the hotel, a crowd attacked Joe Kelley and Doyle. They could hold their own in fisticuffs with anyone. The lobby furnishings were destroyed. The police came and ushered the whole team onto a train to Norfolk. The cranks followed them, still cursing as the train and team left.

On August 6, 1897, the Baltimore Orioles were playing the Boston Red Stockings. Tom Lynch ejected Orioles Joe Kelley and Arlie Pond, who were jabbering at him from the bench. Doyle called Lynch "a big stiff." Doyle commented at the conclusion of the inning that Lynch would "get trimmed" in Baltimore. Lynch ejected Doyle, who responded by head-butting Lynch, closing his left eye.

When pitcher Joe Corbett (Orioles) was having a poor outing, Doyle went to the mound, saying "let someone else try pitching" and motioned manager Hanlon to the mound. Hanlon brought in rookie Arlie Pond to hurl. Doyle told Pond, "You are no better than the other pitcher." Pond and Doyle immediately began tussling on the mound. Hanlon broke up the fight. The *Baltimore Morning Herald* (July 18, 1895) said, "Doyle was continually cutting down his teammates."

During Doyle's entire career, he had a running feud with the most rowdy player, John "Muggsy" McGraw. After games, the two players would erupt into brawls. Both were small. Hanlon traded Doyle at the end of the 1897 season to lowly Washington. Doyle stated he would get revenge on McGraw, who stated he would not play another season with Doyle.

He got even with McGraw by "hip checking him off first base and then spiking McGraw in the leg" *New York Press* (June 9, 1900). McGraw missed a week of play due to the injury. The feud continued when McGraw became manager of the New York Giants in 1902 and immediately traded Doyle for a weak-hitting Dan McGann.

Before McGraw arrived, Doyle got into fights with umpires Tom Lynch and Bob Emslie, leading to two five-game suspensions. In a 1901 game at the Polo Grounds, Doyle broke his hand in a fight with a crank who had jumped onto the field. *New York Times* (June 16, 1901).

Later in the season during a Giants visit to Baltimore, the cranks were cursing him unmercifully when Doyle jumped into the stands, swinging his broken hand. He was arrested and fined $200.

When Bill Dammann threw a ball at the head of Baltimore's Doyle, Doyle walked to the mound "shaking his finger and cursing him." Doyle asked Nig Cuppy to throw at Dammann. Another trick was to stand in front of base runners.

In 1896, Doyle threw his first baseman's mitt at umpire John Hunt, costing him $25. He was fined $10 for running into Washington's Jack Crooks. He accused married players of toning down their game, so as not to appear foolish. Doyle stuck his bat in the pathway of Washington's catcher Jimmy McGuire's throw. The umpire, Jack Sheridan, sent runner Hughie Jennings back to first. Not only was Doyle's play dirty, but so was his mouth with vile cursing at the least occurrence. Doyle threatened umpire Bill Carpenter, who was half his size. But Carpenter, a good talker, convinced Doyle to lay off.

Doyle, though not captain, would chastise players with his sharp tongue on any misplay. He was good at getting a new ball, by tossing the old ball over the right field fence. Umpire Charles Power caught Doyle and fined him $10. On another occasion, Doyle rolled the ball in the mud until it looked like coal. He was actually cheered on during one episode when he went into the grandstand and took the game ball from a small child.

Doyle Comments:

On Teammates Fighting:

　A great many people wonder how so many scrappy ball players manage to get along together. We do fight on the field and during the games, but that is due to the intense desire to win, but as soon as the game is over we walk off arm in arm.

Signals:

　We never use any signs at all, but work through our knowledge of what the man on base or bat will do. It makes us laugh to see some of the teams that play by signs. A fellow will get to first and then stand there rubbing himself on the shirt front and telegraphing to everybody that he intends to make a rush for second. That kindergarten style of play is out of date, and is not used by players who know their business. When a Baltimore player goes to bat and a man is on base, both are so familiar with each other's play that no signs are necessary. In ninety-nine cases out of one hundred, both men will do the exact thing needed to advance the runner and there will be no fuss about it. The Baltimore players pay little attention to pitchers, but we always look at the score card to see who is going to catch. A heady catcher will interfere more with us than all the pitchers together. We rehearse plays just as they do on the stage, but we don't use a play very long, but set to work and get up some new wrinkle.

William "Billy" Earle (St. Louis)

Billy Earle was nicknamed "Little Globetrotter" because he went on baseball's World Tour of 1888–1889. He was forced out of baseball because teammates believed he "had power of the evil eye." Teammates avoided him, saying he had "voodoo" power. He did take morphine and believed in spiritual healing. He studied hypnosis to use on female friends. He had piercing eyes and gave teammates a creepy look. He would blow his money gambling at poker.

On May 11, 1887, Billy Earle, Bill Barnes and John Ake were in a small boat that capsized. John Ake did not make it to shore and drowned. Earle never got over watching his friend drown.

Norman "The Tobasco Kid" Elberfeld (Philadelphia)

Elberfeld enjoyed arguing. He reached the National League in 1898, playing shortstop for Philadelphia. His confrontation with an umpire made him an instant crank favorite. He continually interfered with runners, resulting in altercations with opposing players. However, the Philadelphia press referred to him as "minor league." He was sold to the Cincinnati Reds, where he reportedly threw a clump of mud into an umpire's mouth during a heated exchange. He was ejected and fined. Elberfeld described himself as playing an aggressive style of ball.

Thomas J. "Dude" Esterbrook (New York)

"The best player to play the game according to him," said *Sporting Life* (April 5, 1889). "When there was a pretty woman in the stands, he forgets there is a game going on."

Esterbrook's owner had one team in the American Association and another in National League, so John Day switched Esterbrook Tim Keefe and manager Jim Mutrie to the New York Giants. His team-mate found a letter in which Esterbrook extolled fictitious feats. Earlier, while playing for Cleveland, his antics and ego had resulted in his walking papers.

He managed Louisville in 1889 but was let go after 11 games for his abusive language toward the players.

He developed a theory that death could be overcome by acting like a boy playing in the streets. Eventually he was put on a train to a mental hospital in Middletown, New York. "He squeezed his head through a twelve-inch window and dashed his head on a stone ballast." *Sporting Life* (April 30, 1901)

Dude Esterbrook

ESTERBROOK, 1st B Indianapolis

William "Buck" Ewing (HOF) (New York)

In 1883, "Buck" Ewing got hit on the arm by Chicago's Jim McCormick. Ewing walked to the pitcher's box and showed McCormick his arm. McCormick pretended to kiss his arm, Ewing laughed and walked back to the batter's box. (A hit batter was a dead ball.)

On September 12, 1888, New York Giants captain Ewing sent in Will Brown to replace him in the lineup. Chicago's Cap Anson argued that the substitution was illegal. Umpire Charlie Daniels agreed that the only reason could be illness for a substitution to be made. Ewing had used the ploy before to leave games early. By now, Ewing had undressed in the Club house. Daniels gave Ewing ten minutes to be on the field. Ewing shouted, "I'll take my men off the field." Daniels ruled the game a forfeit and fined Ewing $500.

In 1888, Ewing was batting with two strikes. Boston's King Kelly was catching when he yelled, "Look out 'Buck!'" Thinking the ball was coming inside, Ewing fell to the ground. He looked up to see strike three come over the plate. Umpire Daniels separated Ewing and Kelly before there was any more trouble. At another game in 1888, umpire John Kelly said, "New York Giants catcher 'Buck' Ewing is in the habit of taking a ball from way out [of the strike zone] and quickly bringing it back in with his glove as if it had come straight over the plate, and then kicking when the pitch is called a ball." Ewing was accused of leaving his mask in the base path four times in one game. The play was used to trip the runner coming home.

Ewing once requested a new ball while playing Boston in 1889. Captain King Kelly argued correctly to umpire Watch Burnham that one was not warranted. However, during the kicking, Ewing had replaced the old ball with a new one. Kelly had returned to his position in right field, not realizing that the greatest trickster had been tricked. Ewing, in the same year against the Cincinnati Reds, had put the game ball in his pocket to get a new ball.

In 1893, he was playing for the Cleveland Spiders. They were playing their arch rivals, the Baltimore Orioles. John McGraw attempted to block third base as Ewing knocked McGraw over, with his feet flying headlong over Ewing.

In 1895, in a game between Baltimore and Cincinnati, Cincinnati's captain Ewing asked umpire Bob Emslie how many captains did Baltimore have? Emslie replied "about 12, I guess." The rule stated that only the captain could argue calls, but each player on the Baltimore club would argue any close call.

Charles "Duke" Farrell (New York)

"Duke" Farrell believed in any trick to win.

Farrell was a catcher playing against Cincinnati with a late-inning lead when he pretended it was too dark to see by allowing each pitch from pitcher Amos Russie to hit his chest protector. Umpire John Gaffney would not fall for the trick. In 1888, after Farrell slid roughly into Pittsburg catcher Fred Carroll, Carroll accused him of trying to maim him. Carroll's confrontation was recorded in the *Pittsburg Dispatch* (June 30, 1888):

> CARROLL: Don't ever try that on me again. You would not have tried it that time if I had been looking for it.
>
> FARRELL: It was a mistake. I didn't intend to do it.
>
> CARROLL: Yes, you did, but don't do it again. I am playing ball as well as you are.

Playing the rough and tumble Orioles in a series in 1896, John McGraw slid into home, slapping catcher Farrell in the face. (He had removed his mask.) Later Steve Brodie attempted to body-block the ball loose when Farrell was making the tag. Farrell's tongue gave Brodie more than he could handle as he walked sheepishly back to the bench. The umpire said nothing. At the season's end, it was Farrell who was the peacemaker. In the Temple Cup, Baltimore's McGraw, the foulest mouth in the league, was cursing umpire Bob Emslie unmercifully when Farrell pulled Emslie away from McGraw.

Farrell's pitcher, Jouett Meekin, attempted to walk Cap Anson. When Farrell moved to the side, Anson jumped over the plate, so Farrell moved to the other side. Anson kept following Farrell to prevent the walk. John McQuaid motioned for Anson to go to first to prevent the game from being delayed more.

The *Chicago Herald* (August 21, 1883) reported the following chicanery by Farrell: "Farrell requested catcher Malachi Kittridge to sweep off the plate. Kittridge unsuspectingly grabbed for the broom which was beside the plate. As he turned to clean the plate, "Cub" Stricker on third dashed for home amid the laughter and cheers of the spectators."

Charley Farrell was a poker player who lost $200 in a game to Tom Burns in 1892. Farrell, who began his career with the Chicago White Stockings, described his uniform coat "as a tuxedo jacket over our uniform with blanket robes, we are the best dressed on the field." *Cincinnati Enquirer* (June 28, 1889)

He sought his release from Pittsburg when his teammates tried to make him cut off his moustache. In Farrell's words, "It may be a Jonah, but I am going to keep it." The *Boston Globe* (December 31, 1898) gave him the nickname "the Duke of Marlborough."

John A. "Moose" "Jack" Farrell (Providence)

"Moose" Farrell was described as a heavy drinker who would use his fists whenever confronted. He was irritating to his teammates and opponents. Farrell, who played second base, would place sharp stones around the base to injure the knees and legs of sliding runners.

He would swipe at any runner stealing second with two outs and run off the field, daring the umpire to not call them out. He did not take instructions from the manager. He was listed as one of the top ten drinkers in the league. He missed games, claiming he was ill, when he was really hung over from the previous night at the saloon.

Bob "Death to Flying Things" Ferguson (Troy)

Bob Ferguson's bad temper resulted in continual problems. On July 24, 1873, he got into an altercation with New York Mutuals catcher Nat Hicks. Ferguson hit Hicks with a bat and broke Hicks' arm. Hicks did not press charges.

The Sporting News (July 9, 1876) had previously reported that "Ferguson had few friends among the players. He was a man with ways that were too blunt to cultivate a friendship."

On August 13, 1876, the Brooklyn Eagle reported, "Turmoil is his middle name and he is in a scrap of some kind every game."

As a team captain, Ferguson threatened second baseman Jack Burdock by saying he would like "to ram his fist down Burdock's throat." On May 18, 1881, when Detroit base runner Sadie Houck collided with Ferguson at second base, Ferguson slapped Houck in the face.

Frank Sylvester "Silver" Flint (Chicago)

"Silver" Flint was a hard-nosed, hard-drinking, catcher without equipment, who sat behind the batter. He broke every bone in both hands and half of the bones in his face. This was due to the lack of safety equipment for catchers.

The pain he suffered is said to be one of the causes for his heavy drinking. Flint failed to pay a hotel bill in Indianapolis because he had used the money for drinking. The police boarded the train but did not find him because he had hidden in the baggage car. Manager Anson arranged for the train's schedule to omit Indianapolis on future travel plans.

In 1883, a Florida man complained to Chicago owner A. G. Spalding of a Flint debt. Flint repaid the loan but he continued to ask for advances in pay. Flint stayed broke due to fines for his saloon visits. He was an ugly drunk who broke things, which resulted in additional fines.

Silver Flint

William "Shorty" Fuller (New York)

Fuller was known for his fake tags that would sometimes cause him to miss throws. "Harry Taylor tried to steal second and Fuller used his fake tag and the ball sailed into centerfield. Taylor stood on the bag ready to argue with Umpire Charlie Snyder that he was safe. Then the ball was tossed to third base. Taylor realized he had been duped." *New York World* (July 27, 1893)

"The Chicago White Stockings were playing the New York Giants when 'Shorty' Fuller applied the hidden ball trick on Chicago's Bill Lange. Later in the same game, 'Cap' Anson got even with Fuller by grabbing him at first base." *New York World* (June 17, 1893)

Charles J. "Chick" Fulmer (Cincinnati)

On July 21, 1883, Hick Carpenter, the star third baseman for the Cincinnati Reds, missed the train to Columbus. He was able to catch a later train but the later train was not scheduled to arrive in Columbus until 4:00 p.m., which was game time. Backup pitcher Harry McCormick was sent to the train depot to meet Carpenter with a uniform and carriage, but because the rules of the day allowed for substitution only in the case of injury, the Reds needed somehow to delay the start of the game if they hoped to get their third baseman into the lineup.

It fell to shortstop Chick Fulmer to save the day, which he did by pretending to be sick. As the game was about to begin, Fulmer left the field and was later found, according to Ed Achorn in *The Summer of Beer and Whiskey*, curled up on top of a chest, "complaining of terrible cramps…. The Columbus boys at once thought of the Egyptian Plague, and several faces blanched." After tending to Fulmer awhile longer, and announcing to the crowd that the game had been delayed by Fulmer's poor health, the carriage carrying Carpenter arrived. Fulmer and his teammates promptly exited the clubhouse and took the field.

Andrew Bernard "Barney" Gilligan (Providence)

Barney Gilligan was Hoss Radbourn's catcher in 1884. He was notorious for making the other Providence pitcher, Charlie Sweeney, look bad. The *Providence Journal* (July 17, 1884) reported that Radbourn "threw with reckless haste, giving Gilligan false signs, and seemingly striving to break up the little fellow." Gilligan would get through the pain with a couple of shots of whiskey.

Gilligan used a trick play where he would walk away from the plate, which would distract the batter. Radbourn would quick-pitch, and Gilligan would dive back to knock the ball down for an out. Gilligan was fearless and would even run into the fence to catch foul pop-ups.

However, the pain he endured in his hands from catching gloveless over the years with broken bones took its toll. In 1887, he was fined $25 for binge drinking and not showing up for games.

"Pebbly" Jack Glasscock (Cleveland)

Don't be fooled by Glasscock's nickname; he was tough and rough.

He played for nine teams over a 17-year career as a shortstop. It is said that he had many enemies and few friends. He was good at breaking legs. He spiked arms, hands, and even faces.

The *Philadelphia Sunday Dispatch* (September 17, 1882) said, "Glasscock not only interferes with a base runner, but prevents a fielder from throwing the ball."

Glasscock blocked Providence's Jack Farrell by grabbing his uniform. Umpire Stewart Decker awarded Farrell the base and fined Glasscock $5. He also tripped Philadelphia's Jimmy Fogarty, but umpire John Egan awarded Fogarty third base.

In 1887, Glasscock was coaching first base and ran down the line, trying to draw a throw. Bobby Caruthers fell for the trick. There was no rule that prohibited the play.

The *St. Louis Globe Democrat* (August 29, 1898) published the following poem about Glasscock:

> With a knife in his teeth and a gun in his belt,
> With a dynamite bomb in his goodly right hand,
> With a dagger in his shoe and a sword in his side
> Tears the giant toward the spot where King Glasscock doth stand.
> And the ambulance close at his heels tears along,
> With bandages, plasters, splints, sponges, and such
> And the doctors agree as they watch the "Great steal"
> That of giant and of Glasscock, there won't be much left.

Glasscock spiked Pittsburg's "Doggie" Miller. The two players were separated by umpire Kick Kelly. A week later, he spiked the hand of New York's Mike Tiernan after Tiernan's teammate, Roger Connor, took Glasscock out at second base in revenge. Glasscock told second baseman Charley Bassett to cover his base against the Giants. Glasscock attempted to block Philadelphia's Ed

Andrews. Another trick of his was to hold out his bat when a catcher threw to third. When he batted, Philadelphia catcher Jack Clements was one of his victims. He attempted to fight Detroit's Pete Conway, who threw a ball that Glasscock did not like.

In 1889, he yelled at Cleveland pitcher Henry Gruber when he tried to catch a pop fly. Glasscock attempted to cut teammate Con Daily with his knife. He knocked down Paul Hines and later threw a ball at him. Hines walked away from the confrontation, and the Philadelphia cranks gave Hines an ovation. Glasscock used his bat to strike the fingers of Cincinnati's catcher, Jim Keenan.

In 1889, while coaching third, he ran home to confuse Cincinnati's shortstop, Ollie Beard.

In 1891, Glasscock belted Charlie Reilly (Pittsburg) when he tried to run from second to third.

In 1892, while playing for St. Louis, he stood close to the plate when he was on deck so he could irritate the pitcher. However, when a ball hit umpire Tom Lynch, Glasscock laughed out loud and told him to "cheer up." He gave Fritz Clausen a blow on the neck which resulted in a $10 fine from umpire Bob Emslie. One of his least intelligent plays was waving his hat at Pittsburg's Lou Bierbaur. Umpire Tim Hurst called a double play.

In 1894, he tried to stop St. Louis' Dick Buckley from catching a foul pop by throwing his hat at him, to no avail. Umpire Jim McDonald fined Glasscock $10.

The *Kansas City Times* (September 10, 1886) reported, "St Louis's Jack Glasscock and his best friend Kansas City's Dave Rowe fought for 10 minutes. He had called Rowe 'a pimple brain.'"

In 1887, he was fined $50 by Indianapolis manager Fred Thomas for drinking and being in a house of prostitution. Owner Chris Von der Ahe suspended Glasscock for drinking in 1892.

The *Pittsburg Commercial Gazette* (September 28, 1888) summed up Glasscock by saying "Glasscock's reputation as a dirty ball player is too well known to need further explanation."

Jack Glasscock

Mike Grady (Philadelphia)

Grady was the first bat slinger. The *Washington Post* (March 5, 1899) said, "Grady has the habit of casting his bat behind him after hitting the ball. He is simply careless."

Unfortunately, he is best known for an embarrassing play while playing third base for the Phillies. "The play began when he dropped a grounder (error one). He then threw wildly to first allowing the runner to advance to second (error two). The first baseman threw to him at third, which he missed (error three). Now, as the runner sprinted home, Grady threw the ball over the catcher's head (error four). This feat would not be duplicated." *Pittsburg Post Gazette* (August 11, 1894)

Grady was chasing a foul ball while playing first base when Pittsburg's Jake Beckley yelled, "Can't get it, Mike." Grady stopped running when he could have caught the ball. This was a "knucklehead play."

In 1897, he tripped Baltimore's Joe Quinn at second base. However, Quinn was called safe. Baltimore Hughie Jennings got Grady at home by spiking him.

While hitting for the New York Giants in 1899, Grady stepped in front of Chicago's catcher, Tim Donahue, to block his throw. Umpire Hank O'Day did not call interference, which would have been the final out of the game. Mike Grady's play allowed his team to "carry the day." *Chicago Record* (July 19, 1899)

Charles Irwin (Philadelphia)

"All you get is ill will when your nine loses" are words of Captain Irwin. His players said "he reminded them more of an old woman than a baseball general." He was not liked at all. In 1892, he asked umpire John Gaffney if he could wear a uniform. He had a player's contract but had never stepped onto the diamond. Irwin and his manager, Harry Wright, argued about where the catcher was to play. Wright wanted him close to the batter, but Irwin wanted to be 10 feet behind. It took 15 minutes before the catcher eventually settled. The other team's manager, A.G. Spalding, then walked onto the field to agree with Wright.

Irwin then said "You go where I place you" to catcher Jimmy McGuire and then to Manager Wright "Go back and sit down."

Irwin's owner, A.G. Spalding went to the field shaking his hand at Irwin saying "We'll have you disciplined for your tactics." Irwin with his hot temper would rather object than make the correct baseball play.

He had his players dress at the hotel and ride in pen carriages to the game like a parade. In 1892, Charles made this remark, "I don't understand players. They have never experienced any hard umps, and I think it would do some of them good to travel like actors. There is no money at the door, no salary only after the play do you get paid based on how well attended the game is."

Hughie Jennings (Baltimore) (HOF)

Hughie Jennings was described by manager Ned Hanlon as a loafer, drinker and carouser. Jennings was a hard-nosed, cocky player who enjoyed being hit by a pitch. He was a constant agitator and would bait the umpire to gain an advantage. He would cleat runners and would throw at runners when he could not record an out. He would cut third base short. He was notorious for spiking opponents with intent to injure.

Hughie Jennings

Jennings knocked down the Cincinnati Reds' Charlie Irwin at third base before he could catch Bid McPhee's pop-up. This resulted in a melee and in umpire Bob Emslie needing a police escort.

In 1899, Jennings was lost from the club due to an injured shoulder on his throwing arm. Upon his return, he was ejected by Emslie in the first inning for his continued "kickin'." We guess he had recuperated his tongue; anyway, it was not sure about the shoulder, since he didn't get to throw a ball at first base.

"That Baltimore gang is playing rough ball. They seem to be after my scalp. Jennings, McGraw and two others on that team did nothing but try to put me out of the business," said Tommy Tucker (Boston). *Baltimore American and Commercial Advertiser* (August 27, 1898) Jennings had red hair and a fiery temper.

In 1894, Jennings plowed into New York Giants shortstop Yale Murphy. Unbelievably, umpire Tom Lynch made Jennings go back to second base. Another time, Jennings stood in the base path, which resulted in the Phillies' Billy Hamilton running into Jennings and cutting his lip. Hamilton had been ready for Jennings' ploy and had pushed his hand out. Jennings was ready to fight. In the same game (fourth inning), Jennings spiked catcher Mike Grady at the plate. Jennings was a full-blooded, rowdy Oriole. In the season-ending Temple Cup series against the New York Giants, he blocked "Dirty Jack" Doyle and butted heads with George Van Haltren while trying to catch throws at second base. Jennings cut his eye and was removed from the game.

"Jennings ran between third base and home to block Philadelphia Jack Taylor. Taylor hit Hughie in the face. The Philadelphia press said Jennings bloody nose was a lesson well deserved." *Philadelphia Times* (April 19, 1895)

In 1896, Jennings tried to block the Chicago White Stockings' Bill Dahlen from reaching third base. However, Dahlen simply shoved him out of the way as the ball came sailing by, which gave Dahlen and the White Stockings the run. Jennings, a shortstop, would stand directly in the pathway between second and short, forcing runners to go around him.

Jennings ran over Cincinnati's third baseman, Charlie Irwin, who was blocking the base. This was considered a legal play.

"Boston's Fred Tenney blocked Jennings covering second on a pickoff attempt. When Umpire Tom Lynch did not call interference, a heated argument between he and Jennings was held." *Baltimore Sun* (May 3, 1897) Also, Jennings blocked Cincinnati's shortstop Claude Richey's throw to first base. Tim Hurst called Jennings out for interference. *Cincinnati Enquirer* (July 5, 1897) Jennings pushed Pittsburg shortstop "Bones" Ely off second base and then applied the tag without the umpire seeing the play. *Pittsburg Press* (July 23, 1897)

In 1898, "Jennings planted himself in the base path preventing Louisville's

Bill Magee from getting to third base safely. Umpire Jim McDonald called interference and awarded Magee the bag." *Baltimore Sun* (July 4, 1898)

"Jennings got in front of Louisville's catcher Mal Kittridge in order for Willie Keeler to steal second base." *Baltimore Herald* (September 21, 1898) John McGraw remarked, "Do you remember how Jennings so innocently can delay a catcher's throw to second or third until the steal is made? It has won a game many times." *Baltimore American and Commercial Advertiser* (April 6, 1899)

Tim Murnane, reporter, said, "Hughie Jennings is known to trip and play unfair ball every chance he gets." *Boston Globe* (May 17, 1897)

Jennings was transferred to Brooklyn during the 1899 season. He did not stop his dirty tricks. He had moved to first base, where he would now trip runners. He threw his bat in the direction of Chicago Colts catcher Tim Donahue.

Comments:

Teamwork:
Not one of us bothering [sic] about the other did. We simply stood on our own bottom, that was all [*Baltimore Sun* (Marsh 2, 1895)].

Umpire Kicking:
You can't imagine how hard it is on an enthusiastic ball player to see all his team chances of victory ruined by a rank decision. It is natural he should protest. Of course, I don't approve of any man making a nuisance of himself [*St. Louis Star* (January 9, 1899)].

Bill "Scrappy" Joyce (Washington)

Bill Joyce caused havoc whether batting or playing third base. The *New York Sun* (May 11, 1894) reported, "after a strike call, Joyce threw his bat on the ground with force, and squared his jaws at Umpire Tim Hurst. The umpire quickly picked up the bat and threw it to Joyce so hard that he stopped talking and resumed his position in the batter's box. On the next pitch, he struck out."

In 1898, while playing with New York, Joyce threw a ball at Cincinnati's Jake Beckley after Beckley elbowed him at first base. Joyce claimed that Beckley had insulted him, but he was ejected and fined $10 by umpire John Hunt.

Joyce blocked third base with his body "to prevent a runner reaching it, even if he does get a taste of the spikes," said New York captain Monte Ward.

Joyce got faked out of his uniform by Brooklyn second baseman Tom Daly. Joyce had stolen the base. Daly hit him in the back with his fist, causing Joyce to think he was out when Daly did not even catch the ball. The play prevented Joyce from running to third.

Joyce explained how he would stand in the pathway to the next base. "If a batter is trying for an extra base hit, all crack basemen walk in and stand on the direct line which the runner takes. They station themselves at the turn and make him run way out to get around them. This trick makes him run several yards more to the base." *St. Louis Republic* (February 26, 1900)

In 1892, Joyce ran directly into "Noisy Tommy" Tucker, who was blocking first base. Boston's King Kelly yelled to Tucker to fight Joyce, but he backed down.

In 1894, Washington's Joyce shoved Baltimore's Dan Brouthers off third base. Umpire Willard Hoagland called Brouthers out. The Orioles' Steve Broide threw Hoagland to the ground. After Hoagland landed, he threatened ejection to the whole team, and cool heads prevailed.

Cincinnati Times-Star (January 19, 1893) writer Ren Mulford said Joyce was "better known as 'Scrappy' because of his disposition to go around in a game with a chip on his shoulder and invitation on his lips to simply step on the tail of his shirt."

In 1896, Joyce was named captain of the New York Giants and requested to examine the ball thrown by Boston's Kid Nichols. Umpire Jack Sheridan gave Nichols five minutes or he would forfeit the game. "Joyce waited most of the five minutes before going back to the bench with a smile that could fry a doughnut." *Boston Globe* (August 15, 1896)

In 1897, Joyce told umpire Hank O'Day that the ball was torn and requested a new ball. O'Day refused the request. New York catcher Jack Warner picked at the seams when O'Day was not looking. Joyce went to O'Day after another pitch, demanding that he examine the ball. O'Day replied, "Go sit on the bench." Warner continued his picking of the ball while grinning. Warner gave the ball to O'Day, who did not look at the ball but threw it to the pitcher. The Giants got a new ball when Mike Tiernan hit a foul ball over the grandstand on purpose.

Bill Keister (Baltimore)

He had the perfect name because he was always landing on his keister. "Baltimore's Bill Keister grabbed Cincinnati's Tommy Corcoran before he attacked John McGraw. He threw Corcoran to the ground. Umpire Tom Lynch ejected both players." *Baltimore Sun* (July 19, 1899)

In a practice game, John McGraw told shortstop Keister to play deeper. On the first hit ball, Keister ran into McGraw as both went for the ball. Knocking him over, McGraw told Keister "not to come within his jurisdiction and to call out 'I'll take it.'"

"Bill Keister playing for St. Louis was blocked by the Chicago Orphans

Bill Everitt at first resulting in only a double. When a pickoff at second was attempted, Keister 'poked his fist' into the eye of shortstop Billy Clingman causing him to drop the ball and prevent the out." *Chicago Record* (April 26, 1900)

In a game against Detroit, Orioles Joe McGinnity and Bill Keister attacked umpire Tom Connolly. When the police escorted Connolly from the field, a clerk punched him. All three men went to court, with the clerk being fined $20 and Keister $1 for profanity in the courtroom. The other player, McGinnity, was released.

Malachi Kittridge (Chicago)

Kittridge was one player who stood up to Cap Anson. The *Chicago Post* (June 22, 1885) said, "Chicago catcher Malachi Kittridge attempted to catch a pop-up when a crank stuck his head out so the ball bounced off the top of his head and away from the catcher. The crank shouted 'There, blast you. I kept you from getting that.'"

He had many run-ins with Anson. He was fined $25 for getting dressed in street clothes before a game was over. When Kittridge got into Anson's face, he fined him another $50 and suspended him. A month later, another shouting match between them resulted in another suspension.

The *Cleveland Plain Dealer* (June 28, 1891) said, "Anson had roasted Kittridge for not taking charge of plays as catcher. Kittridge screamed to Anson, 'Why don't you stand there and not open your mouth?' Anson didn't say anything more."

The *Pittsburg Post* (July 22, 1891) reported that Anson yelled at Kittridge when he dropped a short pop-up, "Kit, now show that you're in it."

George "Candy" LaChance (Brooklyn)

LaChance was a tough player. When Denny Lyons attempted to block him, it resulted in LaChance doing a somersault and landing on his feet. Lyons was taken off the field and out of the game.

While playing shortstop, he put the tag on John McGraw, who got up and pushed LaChance. Umpire Jim McDonald did not see McGraw's action, or if he did he chose to ignore it.

By 1899, LaChance was playing with the Baltimore Orioles, resulting in an attitude change. He went to McGraw's defense against Patsy Tebeau and told Tebeau if he wanted to fight on the diamond, to fight him and not the smaller McGraw. Both agreed to fight after the game. They met under the grandstand and, after cursing from both opponents, blows followed. LaChance was beating up Tebeau, a well-known baseball pugilist, when the police arrived and restored order. The police arrested Tebeau and not LaChance, costing Tebeau $50 for "disorderly conduct." The bail was only $2.45, which Tebeau gave up as he happily left Baltimore.

Louisville's pitcher, Bert Cunningham, tossed the ball over the fence, resulting in a new ball. LaChance argued with umpire Sandy McDermott until he was tossed and fined $10.

Larry "Nap" Lajoie (HOF) (Philadelphia)

On May 31, 1900, Lajoie broke his hand in a fight with future Hall of Famer and teammate Elmer Flick. Lajoie was suspended without pay for five weeks.

In his first full season, Lajoie jumped out of the batter's box to be hit by a pitch. Umpire Jack Sheridan called the pitch a strike, saying Lajoie prevented the ball from crossing the plate as a strike. Lajoie refused to continue his at-bat. Sheridan ejected him, gave Lajoie five minutes to leave the field or cause a forfeit. Lajoie stood on home plate. Umpire Sheridan instructed Cincinnati's pitcher Frank Dwyer to pitch. The ball hit Lajoie and Sheridan called him out. Umpire Sheridan stated that Lajoie stepped out of the box for the purpose of being hit. At least the game continued." *Philadelphia Times* (May 20, 1897)

Lajoie hit a ball so hard that the center field fence had to be replaced. *Cincinnati Enquirer* (June 20, 1899)

"Nap" Lajoie showed up in Pittsburg drunk for the second time and was suspended," said the *Philadelphia Times* (August 28, 1897). Also in 1897, Lajoie was fined $50 by manager George Stallings for hitting a man standing by the team's carriage.

Walter Arlington "Arlie" "The Parrot" Latham (St. Louis)

Arlie Latham was the first "Clown Prince of Base Ball."

Latham was a third baseman who was more known for his antics as a coach than as a player. He was a crank favorite for heckling opponents to tears. Of course, his actions did result in more than a few fights.

"One of his famous crowd pleasers was to draw a line in the batter's box, he would then pull his 'Cap' over one eye, cross his legs, and lean on his bat and challenge the pitcher to stick three over." *New York Times* (March 7, 1915)

His comic routine while coaching first base would make any comedian proud. Cranks loved Latham wherever he went. Even his superstitions were weird. He would cross the street in order to keep from passing a Negro with a basket on his head, as he thought it would result in a team defeat.

In 1884, he signed a letter refusing to play against Negroes.

In 1885, when he coached first base before the coach's box was established, "he would stand next to the batter giving him instructions, which doubtless made a crowded plate." *Sporting Life* (August 19, 1885)

One of Latham's escapades was when he was a runner on third against Cincinnati. A ball was called that should have been a strike, and the whole Cincinnati team came in to argue. Nobody paid any attention to Latham. "Throw me your coat, Robinson," [third base coach] squealed Latham, and Robinson threw him the blazer. Latham put it on and coolly walked to home plate. The catcher thought it was Robinson coming in to make a kick until Latham walked over the plate with the winning run. *Sporting Life* (August 2, 1885)

In the "so-called World Series," "Latham lay down a bunt. Chicago's first baseman, Cap Anson, charged in to grab the ball and tag Latham out. Instead of running into Anson and being tagged out, Latham did a handspring and went right over Anson's head, safe at first. *Chicago Tribune* (October 27, 1885)

In early June 1886, Latham got into a fight with catcher "Doc" Bushong, saying he "needed a stepladder to catch his throws." Bushong responded, "You would drop them anyway." Latham resorted to a barrage of names, with Bushong retaliating with a fist to the neck. (Only Latham was fined.)

Latham got into it with "Yank" Robinson. Latham wanted the black team mascot to ride in their carriage. Robinson objected, and Latham tried to punch him. Robinson grabbed him and hung him over the side of the carriage. *Sporting News* (August 2, 1886)

The *Chicago Times* (October 19, 1886) had a different view of Latham, calling him "an antiquated idiot," "a hoodlum," and "the worst nuisance ever."

His pranks would often irritate teammates. While they were eating, he came in and told everyone the train was leaving. *Sporting Life* (August 5, 1886) reported, "Arlie yelled 'All Aboard' and everyone ran for the train leaving behind the food, drinks and $19 unpaid bills." (The train was not leaving.)

Latham was "fined for singing while on base." *Sporting News* (July 9, 1887) Latham hurt his arm in a long ball throwing contest against Bushong (catcher) for $100; Latham had failed to warm up before the throw.

Latham's antics at this time were very funny indeed. He stood on his head, on his hands, and threw about a half dozen flip flops. The party in the grand stand who had wagered two cigars with Latham that the Browns would not score two runs in the inning (they did) threw the smokers out on the grass in front of the grand stand. The crowd immediately took up the idea and everybody was throwing out smokers of all sizes and colors. Latham gathered up a hat full, gave all the boys half a dozen apiece and inserted six between his teeth and tried to coach. If Latham was ever cheered in his life, it was upon this occasion [*Sporting Life* (August 22, 1888)].

In 1889, an association with a gambler known as Mr. Lynch cost Latham an 11-game suspension. A collision at first base with Al McCauley (Phillies) injured Latham's arm and sent him to the bench for the rest of the 1890 season.

Latham was traded to Cincinnati for the 1891 season. He was blocking third base when "Jimmy McAleer slid into the base and gave Arlie an elbow to the ribs. McAleer was called out and kicked Latham in revenge. Latham came back with a right hand to McAleer's mouth bloodying it. McAleer grabbed a bat and threw it at Arlie." *Sporting Life* (August 22, 1891) When the incident produced a $25 fine from National League President Ban Johnson, Latham called "Johnson so rotund that it would take a dirigible to get him to his home in Circusville."

In 1893, while playing for the Cincinnati Reds, Latham was upset at umpire Tim Hurst's call. He threw his glove to the ground and kicked it toward Hurst, who kicked it back to him. The two continued the kicking exhibition until Hurst ejected him.

In 1894, a rule change affected Latham's play at third base. The infielders were no longer allowed to trap pop-ups to complete a double or triple play. The "Infield Fly Rule" eliminated the play. Arlie Latham showed his dissatisfaction by a play in April.

> Latham stood perfectly still in a game the other day, and to the amazement of spectators let a fly ball drop at his feet without putting his hand out to catch it. After it struck the ground, the irrepressible clown picked up the ball, tossed it to the pitcher and yelled "We don't have to catch them kind this year, Mr. Umpire." The Umpire McQuaid aroused himself and shouted "Batters out." There was a runner on first base, and Latham was simply showing up the asininity of the new rule which abolished trapped balls [*Sporting Life* (April 29, 1894)].

Latham was back in St. Louis for the 1896 season. His skills had diminished and he was booed often. He lashed out at umpire John Sheridan in his dressing room after a game. He cut a gash under the umpire's eye. Before June, his playing days were over.

Herman Long (Boston)

"Chicago's first baseman 'Cap' Anson threw the ball at Boston's Herman Long. His team ran to Anson, but he treated them as mosquitoes." *Boston Globe* (June 11, 1892)

"Herman Long is listed as one who fights honorably for his rights and does not threaten to slug umpires and apply vile epithets to them." *New York Sun* (August 2, 1897)

The *Chicago Record* (June 12, 1900) reported that "Boston's Herman Long changed his position in the batter's box on each pitch with the intent of drawing a walk. After two straight strikes, he grounded out."

"Boston's batter Herman Long stepped in front of Chicago's catcher Tim Donahue to prevent a good throw on a steal attempt by Billy Hamilton who was called safe. Umpire Tim Keefe denied an interference claim." *Chicago Tribune* (May 14, 1896)

In 1894, Long missed several games when ashes from his cigar got into his eye and irritated it. In 1896, Long spiked Brooklyn's Fielder Jones.

Bobby Lowe

Bobby "Link" Lowe (Boston)

The second baseman of the Boston Beaneaters was a jokester. The *Chicago Times* (October 4, 1899) reported that "Boston's Bobby Lowe had the Cleveland crowd roaring after being hit by a pitch he fell to the ground as laid out on a stage and then cried 'Is there a doctor in the house?'"

"Chicago's Bill Everitt was blocked by 'Noisy' Tommy Tucker from making a double. When he left the base to argue with Umpire Tim Keefe, the alert Bobby Lowe walked up and tagged Everitt out, who then exploded on Keefe." *Chicago Record* (May 14, 1896)

Boston's Bobby Lowe suffered a broken nose and fractured jaw when a foul tip hit him in the face. *Toledo News-Bee* (August 31, 1906)

Denny Lyons (Pittsburg)

Buck Ewing called Lyons "emotional with his mitts and his spikes." *Washington Post* (July 3, 1898) One trick was to get in front of catchers to cause inaccurate throws to second base. He would block runners while playing third base.

"Lyons tripped Cincinnati's Ollie Beard to keep him from scoring." *Cincinnati Enquirer* (July 7, 1889) Lyons tripped Columbus catcher Jack O'Connor preventing him from throwing to second base. Umpire Wes Curry called Lyons out at the plate costing his team a run." *Philadelphia Enquirer* (August 26, 1891)

In 1891, he used his craft to knock Columbus runner Jack O'Connor down. Umpire Jack Herins fined him $25. In 1893, he spiked Brooklyn Bridegroom David Foutz. In 1894, he sent an elbow to the chin of St. Louis' "Doggie" Miller, knocking him out. When he tried to knock the ball away from Cleveland's "Chief" Zimmer, Zimmer fought back by throwing sand in his face.

Brooklyn's catcher, Con Daily, turned the tables on Lyons by grabbing his bat, which prohibited his swing, and Lyons was out on a called third strike. Lyons shoved Daily into umpire Charles Snyder. On June 20, Lyons skipped second base to score the winning run.

In 1895, a collision between Lyons and Brooklyn's George LaChance caused LaChance to roll to the ground and be tagged out.

"Germany" Smith then hit him in the stomach. Smith got back later in the game and kicked Lyons in the back. Neither player's action was detected by umpire Bob Emslie.

Lyons, while playing for the St. Louis Browns, got Boston's pitcher Ted Lewis to throw him the ball while he was standing on third base. When Lewis tossed him the ball, he ducked and ran home, a legal play. His dirty tricks caught up to Lyons when Amos Rusie broke two of his fingers. He still managed to play with a splint.

During his early years, he was a troublemaker for managers. Billy Sharsig suspended him in 1889 for being AWOL. He was fined $100 for insubordination again by Sharsig.

James B. "Chippy" McGarr (Cleveland)

"Chippy" McGarr got his nickname for his quick temper, which did not take much to be released. He was small in stature, but there was not a tougher player. He was a skilled fighter with a poor bat. "Patsy" Tebeau used "Chippy" to challenge better players to get both kicked out of the game.

During one game, he picked up base stealer Billy Hamilton of the Boston Beaneaters and carried him to the stands. He then tossed Hamilton into the box seats. He was fined only $50 and was allowed to stay in the game.

In another game, he used so many curse words on umpire Tim Hurst that he was fined $200 and suspended for three games.

John "Muggsy" McGraw (Baltimore Orioles) (HOF)

"Muggsy" McGraw was a player of enormous ego whose mind was ever working on how to harm opposing players. He was the meanest, dirtiest, most contemptible player who ever put on a uniform. His motto was "win at all costs." One recognizes the name as the Hall of Fame Giants Manager for 30 years, but before that he was the star player of the Baltimore Orioles,

John J. McGraw

who won three pennants in the 1890s. He was detested by every opponent he ever played against. He described his play as "only fun when I am out in front and I don't give a damn for the rest of the game."

When a veteran player knocked him off the bench on his first day as an Oriole, McGraw picked himself up and proceeded to beat up the much larger player.

His nickname of "Muggsy" was given by his teammates from a tramp in the Sunday newspapers. He was a 5'5", 155-pound dynamite stick who chewed tobacco, smoked cigars, drank and gambled on anything. "He was a dirty demon," according to *The Sporting News* (June 30, 1894).

His first reported dirty tactic was when he deliberately spiked Arlie Latham on the hand. Latham's comment was, "McGraw eats gunpowder for breakfast and washes it down with warm blood." *Baltimore Sun* (July 12, 1893)

Patsy Tebeau felt McGraw's sting when McGraw hit him in the nose, leaving the field in a blood pool.

Even an exhibition game did not slow McGraw down. He spiked a Chattanooga shortstop sliding into third and slapped a runner in the face, which drew blood. The cranks in Tennessee stormed the field to attack McGraw. The police grabbed McGraw and took him to the police station for his protection.

On May 15, 1894, McGraw kicked the Beaneaters' Tommy Tucker in the head in the third inning. This resulted in a fight. Everyone was watching the fight and did not notice the fire in the right field stands which destroyed Boston's wooden structure.

In an exhibition game in Richmond, Virginia, McGraw shoved a runner to the ground. Umpire Tim Keefe was confronted by McGraw, who accused him of drinking. After the game, Keefe resigned, saying "I have taken enough abuse from McGraw." *New York Sun* (July 22, 1895)

McGraw was a heavy gambler. He bet on horse racing, but would also wager on pool shooting and prize fighting. He missed games by spending time at Pimlico track.

McGraw got into a heated argument with umpire "Lord" Byron, threatening to beat him up. When Byron remarked, "You were run out of Baltimore," McGraw swung and hit the umpire in the chin. The players broke up the fight, but McGraw sought revenge when he went to a notary claiming "Byron cursed me." McGraw was suspended five days for his rowdy play. Umpires refused to work Orioles games because of the players' harsh treatment.

McGraw was noted for his partying. In Marlin, Texas, he hired a "Negro band" to follow him around. He had a continual feud with the Cincinnati Reds' Henry Vaughn, who tried to round third when McGraw grabbed him with both arms. Vaughn got away from McGraw's grasp and scored the run. Later, after McGraw singled, he spiked Vaughn. After the third out, McGraw was walking to the dugout and Vaughn threw the ball, hitting McGraw in the back.

McGraw, after a close play at first in 1897, punched pitcher Frank Dwyer. Reds first baseman Jake Beckley knocked McGraw down. McGraw would again punch Dwyer in an August game. A year later, Reds catcher Heinie Reitz, after a dispute with McGraw, kicked him in the face and punched him in the eye. The police took both players to jail.

McGraw had a vile tongue. *The Sporting News* (August 9, 1899) said he was "so filthy that it is impossible to even hint at." McGraw was known for shouting insults at owners while playing third base.

McGraw hated "Dirty Jack" Doyle and said, he "wouldn't play on the same team with Doyle." "Hanlon said they were too much alike to share a bench. One altercation occurred when McGraw went after Doyle with a bat." *Morning Herald* (August 15, 1897)

NEWSPAPER ACCOUNTS OF MCGRAW'S DIRTY PLAYS

The *Baltimore American and Commercial Advertiser* (July 5, 1892) reported, "John McGraw called Umpire Bobby Mitchell an 'a' hole and Mitchell ejected him. Manager Ned Hanlon felt the UmpirUnmanageable Managerse should over look such a minor infraction. Mitchell, a rookie umpire, allowed McGraw to re-enter the game." This was one of McGraw's first misadventures into rowdy play.

During the 1890s, these episodes were reported:

- *Pittsburg Press* (July 6, 1893): "McGraw ran inside the base line so the pitcher's thzrow hit him in the back. Little Mac went wild with rage and called Umpire McLaughlin names. He was fined $35."
- *Cleveland Leader* (September 15, 1893): "McGraw is a light youngster so anxious to block men off bases. In the ninth he attempted to block big 'Buck' Ewing [Cleveland] who knocked him on his bottom."
- At spring training in New Orleans, the *Baltimore American and Commercial Advertiser* (April 8, 1894): "McGraw has developed some kicking qualities down here, which he invariably uses. A giant could not bluff him. Someone stole his bat and he was willing to fight a regiment. He had his bat returned to him."
- *Boston Globe* (June 19, 1894): "McGraw blocked runner Boston's 'Kid' Nichols at third base. Umpire Emslie called interference. Nichols was forced to slide."
- *Boston Globe* (June 20, 1894): "McGraw blocked Boston crank favorite Hugh Duffy at third base. Boston spectators hissed McGraw for several minutes and he was called every vile name in the book."
- *New York World* (July 27, 1894): "McGraw swung his bat around his head several times then smashed the plate when he was retired on a fly ball. He hurled his bat against the grandstand, splintering it. He gave a talking to with Umpire Charles Snyder who fined him $30 and ejected 'Muggsy.'"
- In the Temple Cup Series, the *New York World* (October 5, 1894) said, "McGraw ran full speed into New York second baseman 'Monte' Ward even though Ward had the ball when McGraw was five feet from the

bag. McGraw never stopped and threw himself into Ward which sent the latter reeling. McGraw knocked the ball from Ward and Umpire Emslie ruled McGraw safe."

- *Baltimore American and Commercial Advertiser* (April 27, 1895): "McGraw argued with Umpire Miah Murray when he accused 'Muggsy' of hitting a foul ball on purpose. McGraw threw his bat and 'Cap' in the air."
- *Baltimore American and Commercial Advertiser* (May 15, 1897): "McGraw attempted to block Philadelphia's Lave Cross at third but failed. There was no chance of the runner reaching home. However, Umpire 'Sandy' McDermott called interference and allowed Cross to score."
- *Pittsburg Commercial Gazette* (June 1, 1898): "McGraw tried in vain to hold Pittsburg's Fred Ely who still managed to score the winning run."
- *Brooklyn Eagle* (June 18, 1898): "When called out at second, McGraw pushed Brooklyn's shortstop George LaChance to prevent a double play. Umpire Jim McDonald did not notice anything."
- *Cincinnati Enquirer* (September 16, 1898): "In Baltimore, McGraw was tagged out in home. McGraw vented his anger by spiking Cincinnati's catcher 'Heinie' Reitz. Reitz then grabbed McGraw by the head and hit McGraw in the jaw. McGraw broke free and grabbed a bat when police stepped in."
- *Washington Post* (June 16, 1899): McGraw got in his rough house work by giving Washington's Cassidy an elbow loosening the ball. McGraw ran to third and Umpire Chippy McGarr had no response."
- *Baltimore Sun* (July 19, 1899): "McGraw holding on to second base told the Cincinnati shortstop, I'll make you jump hurdles. The two got into a fist fight. Umpire Tom Lynch ejected both players."
- *Baltimore Sun* (August 11, 1899): "St Louis Browns 'Patsy' Tebeau tried to block McGraw off first base with McGraw running full tilt at Patsy. Baltimore's Coach George LaChance came to McGraw's aid and challenged Tebeau to fight him. The players prevented LaChance and Tebeau from fighting under the stands after the game."

REPORTER COMMENTS

"McGraw used every low and contemptible method that a brain could conceive to win a play by a dirty trick." *Baltimore Sun* (August 3, 1895)

"He never let up and he had contempt for anyone." *Baltimore Sun* (June 11, 1892)

"His skin is full of baseball. He is fearless and would not get out of the way of anything or anyone." *Baltimore Morning Herald* (April 23, 1894)

McGRAW COMMENTS

"I made you what you are today." (regarding Ned Hanlon) *Baltimore Daily News* (August 3, 1897)

"We were a cocky, swashbuckling crew and we wanted everybody to know it. We won a lot of games before the first ball was pitched." *Baltimore Morning Herald* (September 8, 1903)

"A ballgame was something to fight for." *Baltimore Sun* (April 30, 1895)

Jimmy "Deacon" McGuire (Washington)

McGuire got the nickname "Deacon" because of his non-alcoholic lifestyle. His first catch caused him to injure his finger. His manager, George Wright, told him to play close to the plate. He had no mask or chest protector. Captain Arthur Irwin then told him to play 15 feet back from the plate, where he immediately had a passed ball. Manager Wright and captain Irwin stood on the field arguing about McGuire, continuing for 15 minutes. Chicago's captain, Cap Anson, said, "We withdraw our point. Put in your other catcher." Anson accused Irwin of dirty tactics, but poor McGuire was just a pain.

McGuire deliberately ran into Baltimore's Heinie Reitz to break up a double play, without repercussions. "Washington's Jimmy McGuire while running the bases intercepted a throw from Chicago Colts' second baseman Jimmy Callahan. McGuire threw the ball into the outfield and easily scored. Umpire Hank O'Day was not watching the ball and didn't see the play." *Washington Star* (July 6, 1897)

Ed McKean (Cleveland)

"When Boston's Tommy Tucker tried to cripple Cleveland's Ed McKean, the little shortstop stepped on Tucker's ankle with his spikes. Tucker threatened to punch McKean but he was not worried as the Spider cranks hissed." *Cleveland World* (October 30, 1892)

"Baltimore's Steve Brodie came into second base standing up to block a relay throw. Cleveland's Ed McKean wild with rage flung the ball at Brodie's head and then punched him with his fist. The ball glanced off Brodie's head like a rubber ball and Umpire Tom Lynch ejected both players." *Baltimore Sun* (September 25, 1894)

"Chicago's Cap Anson was running to third when Cleveland shortstop Ed McKean got in his way. The old man made a great kick and maintained that Umpire Wes Curry awarded him third base. The whole Cleveland infield got into Curry's face. But Anson just puffed his way to the unguarded home plate." *Chicago Tribune* (August 13, 1889)

McKean was fined $10 by Cleveland manager Tom Loftus for a poor job collecting tickets before a game in 1889.

Cal McVey (Baltimore)

McVey was considered an undisciplined player in Baltimore. His temper tantrums were blamed for poor team play. When released to Boston in 1874, pitcher Al Spalding directed him in the outfield. McVey fired back to Spalding,

Ed McKean

"Go to Hell. I know how to play the position." Manager Harry Wright responded, "I feel confident that McVey's action was the cause of our losing. It upset Spalding so that he lost judgment in pitching." An unidentified Boston player remarked, "It is some of your cricket notions. You never see it done by other clubs."

McVey was characterized by the *Boston Herald* (October 23, 1875), which said "his vulgar and profane language threaten violence by his persecutors." In spite of his troubles, he captained the Cincinnati Reds in 1879. He gave a release letter to shortstop Mike Burke. Burke criticized McVey for not telling him directly. Burke went onto the field, grabbed McVey by his uniform, and tore the jersey. McVey used good judgment by pushing Burke away and ordering the police to remove him. McVey's method of instructing his players included getting right up in their faces and staring at them without a word. Lip Pike was a player of like record, when it came to vile language in front of the cranks.

In 1879, with rain pending, McVey went to the bat rack several times as a stalling tactic. Yet when he hit a double that was momentarily lost, he yelled to Chicago's Cap Anson, "We're waiting." A minute wait was required before a new ball could be inserted into the game. Another double brought the same results. The Chicago cranks yelled, "They're waiting. They're waiting."

Cal McVey used abusive language toward umpire Dan Devinney and was considered the vilest player on the Chicago Nine.

George "Calliope," "Foghorn" or "Doggie" Miller (Pittsburg)

Miller was from the mold of King Kelly when it came to trickery. Pete Browning, the Louisville Colonels outfielder, would touch third base when coming in from his position. "Doggie" Miller literally stole third base, so when Browning got there, he was dumbfounded to find the base missing. The cranks were roaring with laughter. Browning saw Miller in the dugout and began to chase Miller, who had the bag, all over the park until Browning finally gave up. At this point, Miller replaced the bag.

Another time, Miller did not leave the field after being ejected within the one-minute limit, even after being warned a second time. Umpire Jack McQuaid forfeited the game to Chicago. Pittsburg's manager, Billy McGunnigle, protested to Chicago's manager, Cap Anson. In the next game, Miller hit a pop-up to first baseman Anson. Miller pulled his glove from his back pocket and threw it at Anson. Miller was ejected for the second day in a row.

GEO·F·MILLER,
CATCHER–PITTSBURG–

George Miller

Then there was the time Miller thought he had been awarded ball four and headed for first base. Umpire Jimmy Macullar called it a strike. Miller began kicking with the umpire while standing on home plate. Cleveland's captain, Patsy Tebeau, told pitcher Nig Cuppy to throw the pitch. Cuppy refused because Miller was still standing on the plate. Miller turned and smiled at Tebeau, daring him to have his pitcher throw at him. Cuppy pitched and just missed Miller. Umpire Macullar called, "that will be ball four." Miller smiled and walked to first base.

In 1891, Miller was fined $100 for drinking and being late for games by manager Ned Hanlon. He was fined $25 later in the same year for drinking.

"Doggie" Miller got his nickname from his love of pets. He would hit the saloons at night. Sportswriters were amazed he had such a long career for one who indulged in alcohol as he did. Chris Von der Ahe hired to manage the St. Louis Browns in 1894. In the first series with his old team, the Pirates, former teammates attempted to spike him while running the bases.

Miller made several errors in a game against Philadelphia due to his drinking the previous night. Von der Ahe was so perturbed that he told his scorekeeper, Harry Martin, to go manage the team and "tell 'Doggie' to go to hell." Miller was glad to give him the job. The next day, both men were back in their regular spots.

Miller played a cowboy in a Wild West show that Von der Ahe had at the stadium during the off-season. This was Miller's way of paying off borrowed money. In 1895, Miller lost his manager's job to Al Buckenberger.

John Morrill (Boston)

"He's the worst kicker in the business," said King Kelly.

In a game against Chicago on September 29, 1888, "Morrill needed a pinch runner for himself and still stay in the game. Billy Nash ran for him by standing behind him in the batter's box." *Boston Globe* (September 30, 1888).

The Boston player-manager stated that Kelly has always been the most successful player in breaking the rules and escaping the consequences.

"Pitcher Jim McCormick threw four pitches directly at Morrill. Umpire Wes Curry awarded Morrill a walk even though the rules of the day required six balls." *Chicago Times* (September 16, 1885)

"John Morrill was in charge of the players but he was subordinate to 'King' Kelly. If he fined Kelly, he could get even by disciplining the manager during the game." *Boston Herald* (February 26, 1888)

Morrill had fined Kelly $25 for drinking during the 1887 season.

Morgan "Morg" Murphy (Philadelphia)

Murphy was known for his sign-stealing methods. In 1899, he was a substitute catcher. He would get behind a whiskey ad on the outfield fence and would use powerful field glasses to see the catcher's signals. He would alert the batter by using a white handkerchief. He also used letters on the advertisement to denote the pitch to be delivered. His manager, Bill Shettsline, said, "Murphy is playing a deep thinking game, and playing it well." *Philadelphia Inquirer* (July 16, 1899)

Another method was having signals sent from inside an observatory in back of the outfield by moving the curtain to the right or left. When the Phillies went on the road, they would still work a signal service but not as conveniently. Morg Murphy would get on the roof of an adjacent building and signal by handkerchiefs. *Louisville Courier-Journal* (September 17, 1899)

Eventually teams caught on to the spying and started reversing signals. Murphy was relegated back to the bench. The 1899 season saw Murphy not play a single game, yet no one knew how many wins he helped secure. The Phillies finished in third place, with Ed Delahanty leading the league in hitting.

Billy Nash (Boston)

In 1894, Boston was leading Philadelphia, 2–1. Philadelphia rallied in the top of the eighth inning to take an 8–2 advantage. With rain beginning, Boston's captain, Billy Nash, attempted to get the victory by delaying the game so the score would revert to the previous inning. The umpire forfeited the game to Philadelphia instead.

When a Boston game was delayed by a snowstorm, captain Nash gave manager Frank Selee a note saying that the weather had cleared. Selee ordered their players to hurry and pack for the 1:00 p.m. train. Selee had already paid the hotel bill when Nash whispered: "Send the gang back upstairs. There is no game." Tommy McCarthy and Nash got into a fight when Nash refused to argue a call. Nash battled with Selee over team power.

Vincent I. "Sandy" Nava (Providence)

"Sandy" Nava was a Mexican-American. On July 27, 1884, he was fined $100 for intoxication. This was ten percent of his salary and indicative of how bad the drinking had been. He was fined another $10 during the season when he would not play in a game. Outside the park, he was a non-stop smoker.

Nava's heavy drinking was being exposed by Providence club director Ned Allen. However, to blacklist him this late in the season would leave only one catcher, and that could be disastrous. Nava was released with two weeks remaining in the season.

The Sporting News (February 20, 1897) reported that "Nava had dropped out of sight. Drink got the better of him."

John Joseph "Peach Pie" or "Rowdy Jack" O'Connor (Cleveland)

"Rowdy Jack" O'Connor was a tough player who was ready to fight any opponent. He was the catcher for the pennant-winning Spiders of the 1890s. He weighed only 170 pounds. He served as Patsy Tebeau's team enforcer for violations. Tebeau described him as "no hitter, no fielder, but a great tough guy." When Tebeau was ejected or too drunk to manage, O'Connor was put in control.

His job was kicking with the umpire and agitating opponents. As a catcher, he wasn't the smartest player on the field. He was guilty of calling the wrong fielder on infield pop-ups. When questioned, he said he forgot the player's name. Also, he put on two chest protectors with no mask.

O'Connor faked an injury while catching to give Spiders pitcher Nig Cuppy a rest. O'Connor was known for his vile language. He got into a shoving match with Cap Anson when he was blocked from making a double.

Another trick play O'Connor used as a catcher was to overthrow second base with a runner stationed there. The center fielder would close in and handle the ball to nab the runner at third.

O'Connor would throw his mask in the base path, hoping for a tripped runner. In New York, he threw the game ball over the stands to get a new one. The umpire did not see his play. He threw another ball over the fence at the game in Philadelphia. The amount of $1.25 was taken from Cleveland's share of income from the game. He would regularly bend over to get hit by a pitch. He truly believed in taking one for the team. His actions would not be allowed today.

Fred "Dandelion" Pfeffer (Chicago)

In 1881, Pfeffer refused to play an exhibition game against a Cleveland semi-pro team with a black player, Moses Walker. Pfeffer made an error on purpose to demonstrate his displeasure with playing the black players. Spalding, who was not allowed to leave the stands, came down on the field to chastise Pfeffer. Umpire Powers ejected Spalding for his action.

The *Chicago Daily News* (August 23, 1887) reported that "Fred Pfeffer found a rock in Pittsburg, and declared that he wrapped it in tissue paper. There are three broken nails in it. When I found it I knew it was good luck and the three nails mean three victories. The players were excited about the announcement."

In 1887 at Philadelphia, Pfeffer coerced a 14-year-old black, Clarence Duval, to become the team's mascot. The boy was in a play called "Starlight."

Joe Quinn (Baltimore)

Quinn was one of the Baltimore rowdies, but he was not as good at it as his teammates. When he attempted to block Dusty Miller at second, he kneed him, causing pain. St. Louis Browns outfielder Tommy Dowd had an extra ball in the grass, and Joe Quinn ran to third, where he was tagged out. John McGraw jumped on him for falling for their tricks.

When Quinn played with the St. Louis Browns, the *St. Louis Globe-Democrat* (August 24, 1893) reported, "in a dark ninth inning Joe Kelley [Baltimore] hit what appeared to be a home run, when out of Quinn's shirt a ball appeared. Neither Kelley nor third base coach Wilbert Robinson had seen the play. Quinn had made a great catch or had he."

Henry "Heinie" Reitz (Cincinnati)

Heinie Reitz and fellow German-American pitcher Ted Breitenstein were often seen drinking beer and eating pretzels at local saloons. The Chicago cranks called the two "the Pretzel Battery." Reitz was a rough and ready catcher who used his size to block home plate. He could inflict pain on runners who attempted to run over him. He worked as a bouncer in a pub during the off-season.

The *Chicago Dispatch* (July 9, 1893) reported that "Reitz' sarcastic tongue resulted in Bill Dahlen throwing a bat at him. Umpire Tim Hurst prevented the conflict from growing." He was referred to as "having the fastest tongue on the team." *Pittsburgh Press* (March 4, 1907)

William H. "Yank" Robinson (St. Louis)

"Yank" Robinson was a cocky player. He wanted to be liked by his teammates and would drink with them. He could not hold his liquor, which resulted in trouble with management. He got in a heated argument with team owner Chris Von de Ahe, who levied a heavy fine. Robinson's reply was, "he fined me enough in aggregate to build a stone front house." *St. Louis Dispatch* (May 2, 1889)

He continued to be fined for coming to the park intoxicated.

Jack Rowe (Buffalo)

Rowe was one of the "Big Four" for the Buffalo Bisons in the National League. "Rowe was forced out at second base, but in leaving the field, he ran swiftly touching third base and heading home. Chicago White Stockings Ed

Williamson didn't realize the out and thinking Rowe was going to score threw to home allowing 'Deacon' White to move to third. The Buffalo cranks laughed loudly." *Buffalo Times* (May 28, 1884)

"Detroit's Lon Knight in going home cut third base short. Buffalo third baseman [Rowe] complained loudly to rookie umpire W. W. Jeffers. Jeffers did not see the miss, but aware that Rowe rarely argued called Knight out." *Buffalo Express* (May 9, 1881)

On a trip to Boston, Rowe and Dan Brouthers were asleep in the shade and the train was delayed until the two players could be located. When they did get on the train, it was traveling 60 miles an hour to make up time. Rowe got motion sickness and spent the trip at the rail.

George "Germany" Smith (Cincinnati)

W. H. ROBINSON, S. S.
St. Louis Browns

OLD JUDGE
CIGARETTES.
COODWIN & CO., New York.

Yank Robinson

Smith was the nemesis of dirty Denny Lyons of Pittsburgh. "After Lyons tripped 'Germany' then blocked him, 'Germany' gave up the opportunity to score a run. Instead he stopped and kicked Lyons in the back without Umpire Bob Emslie seeing any of the plays." *Cincinnati Times-Star* (April 17, 1896)

In 1886, while Smith was playing for Brooklyn, he missed the train. He was fined $200, which was an extraordinary amount, for this violation by owner Charles Byrne.

He is most remembered for making seven errors intentionally to show pitcher "Phenomenal" Smith he could win by himself. He was fined $500 for his part in the 18–5 loss.

John A. "Cub" Stricker (Washington)

"Cub" Stricker was a 5'3", rowdy fighter. At a St. Louis game, he jumped into the stands to fight a crank. This resulted in his release from the team.

Stricker was playing for the Senators. After being booed, he faked throwing the ball at the cranks. The ball slipped out of his hand and hit a child in the face. It broke the boy's nose. Stricker was arrested, paid a fine and apologized, saying "I meant to hit the fence." *Washington Post* (August 5, 1893)

Ezra Sutton (Boston)

Ezra Sutton knew how to rattle opponents. New York's captain, John Ward, screamed, "Got it! Got it!" Boston's third baseman, Ezra Sutton, followed his direction and let the ball drop. (1886)

In 1888, Chicago Colt Tom Burns threw Sutton to the ground when he was attempting to catch a ball thrown by first baseman John Morrill. Umpire Tom Lynch ruled interference. Chicago's Cap Anson argued for ten minutes.

Also in 1888, Sutton was on first when he attempted to rattle Giants pitcher Mickey Welch. After calling him several vile names, Welch simply picked Sutton off first base.

Sutton was a skillful bunter. When he bunted, the ball started fair and then rolled across the foul line, which was still considered legal in 1876. He was the master of trapping the ball which appeared to be a catch.

Fred Tenney (Boston)

Tenney pushed aside Baltimore first baseman George LaChance without any call. Another episode occurred when Tenney wrestled with Hughie Jennings. The match was so fierce that Tenney's uniform was ripped to pieces.

"When Brooklyn's 'Bad' Bill Dahlen attempted to block Boston's Fred Tenney, Tenney knocked him to the ground. Dahlen got up seeking revenge and kicked Tenney." *Boston Journal* (June 18, 1897)

"Boston's Fred Tenney thought he had an inside the park home run. As he touched third, he saw Chicago White Stockings' catcher Tim Donahue standing at home plate. So Tenney slowed to a trot not knowing the throw was coming. Tenney was out by ten feet." *Chicago Tribune* (June 23, 1899)

"Boston's Tenney was not a fast runner and he took a six step lead on a sacrifice fly tag up. He was safe on a call by Umpire Tim Hurst. Brooklyn's Manager Ned Hanlon argued intently without recourse." *Brooklyn Eagle* (October 2, 1900)

Thomas J. "Noisy Tommy" Tucker (Boston)

Tommy Tucker was the most irritating player of every season he played. He was more than "Noisy," he was just plain dirty. He was guilty of tripping, blocking, hipping, grabbing, pushing, running into, punching, and kicking. He would claim that those plays were unintentional, yet he stated, "Did you see me 'do' him?" *Baltimore Sun* (June 17, 1887) Tucker even kept a book on his dirty plays with date, name and team. *St. Louis Republican* (July 4, 1887)

The *Baltimore American and Commercial Advertiser* (June 19, 1887) said, "Tucker had the St. Louis ball players badly frightened while here, and only a few of them cared to get near him. Whenever they would get on first base, he would keep up conversation that if they ran into him he would knock them out, and other remarks that frightened the men."

In 1888, "Tucker blocked Brooklyn's George Pinkney from catching a pop-up. Umpire John Gaffney missed the play. *Brooklyn Eagle* (June 23, 1888)

Tucker purposely tripped Monk Cline of the Kansas City Cowboys, who crawled on his knees to second base. *Kansas City Times* (July 18, 1888)

The 1889 season brought more pushing, blocking and shoving. He grabbed Louisville's Harry Vaughn at first by the back of his pants. Tucker pushed St. Louis first baseman Charlie Comiskey on a pickoff attempt. Tucker scored from first base as the ball rolled around the outfield.

During a game with the St. Louis Browns, "Tucker brought out an umbrella to urge John Gaffney [Umpire] to call the game. St. Louis 'Yank' Robinson broke the umbrella which caused a fight between Robinson and Tucker. The police arrived to break up the action." *Baltimore Sun* (September 7, 1889)

The 1890 season began with "Tommy Tucker throwing a bat at Cincinnati's catcher Jim Keenan who was chasing a pop fly. Keenan made the catch. Umpire 'Sandy' McDermott fined Tucker $25." *Boston Globe* (May 25, 1890)

In 1891, "Brooklyn's John Ward was blocked from first base by Tommy Tucker on a pickoff play. Umpire Jack McQuaid did not see the block and ruled Ward out." *New York Press* (July 1, 1891)

Tucker sat down on Chicago White Stockings' Jimmy Cooney, which resulted in Cooney suffering an injured knee.

"Tommy Tucker pushed New York's pitcher Amos Rusie out of the way as he ran to first base. Rusie still made the catch to record the out." *New York Herald* (August 18, 1891)

More dirty plays occurred in 1892. He blocked Cincinnati's big Pete Browning and tagged him out, only to have the play overturned by umpire John Gaffney. He ran into Jake Virtue in an attempt to jar the ball loose, but failed.

The *Cleveland Leader* (August 16, 1892) said, "It seems justifiable to crack Tucker a good one across the shins, for there is no man so persistent in trying to injure other players. He is a nuisance to himself and everybody else."

He attempted to spike Ed McKean but missed. McKean gave him his own medicine by spiking him. He challenged McKean to a fight, without results.

The dirty play Tucker is most noted for occurred in 1893. "On a block, Tucker broke the collarbone of Cleveland's catcher 'Chief' Zimmer. He was reprimanded, but claimed he did not do it intentionally." *Boston Globe* (July 13, 1893)

He did not change his methods, as indicated two weeks later when "Runner Tom Tucker stuck out his paw and swept Brooklyn pitcher George Haddock from the baseline. Haddock still made the putout." *Boston Globe* (August 4, 1893) While coaching first base, Tucker intentionally ran into Cleveland's Patsy Tebeau, who still made the play. "Tommy grabbed Cleveland's pitcher Chauncey Fisher's arm to prevent a throw to home. Umpire Bob Emslie missed the play and Hugh Duffy scored." *Boston Globe* (September 21, 1893)

He was fined $50 for drinking by manager Frank Selee. In 1893, he reported to the game and began missing every ball thrown his way. He could not throw the ball either. Tommy Tucker was drunk. Boston manager Frank Selee realized the situation and benched Tucker. Tucker took the benching as one might imagine by abusively swearing at his manager, saying "I'll show you up as the figurehead you are in Boston."

In 1894, "Foghorn" Tucker left his glove on the field in the ninth inning, which was by rule allowable. When he went to get his glove, the Philadelphia cranks came out of the stands and accosted him. Tucker cursed them, and a crank shoved Tucker. Then another one punched him on the cheek. The police arrived and broke up the incident. Tucker was not hurt, but cursed the police, was arrested and paid a $25 fine.

Also in 1894, "'Foghorn' attempted to trip John McGraw twice. However, McGraw cleated Tucker in the face drawing blood. *Boston Globe* (May 16, 1894) The injury did not prevent Tucker from hip-checking McGraw, without incident. In Washington, Tucker used his hand to knock the ball free of catcher Deacon McGuire's glove to be called safe at the plate. Tucker had an extra ball in his uniform pocket. Umpire Jack McQuaid said he "saw the ball sticking out like a small pumpkin." He quickly ejected Tucker.

In a spring training game in Norfolk, Virginia, "Boston Beaneaters' Tommy Tucker punched [the] Norfolk Clams first baseman in the stomach, slapped the ball out the second baseman's glove, and he tripped a runner in the ninth inning." *Norfolk Virginia* April 10, 1895)

"Tucker kicked the ball away from Baltimore's second baseman 'Kid' Gleason while trying to break up a double play. However, Umpire John Hunt ruled the runner going to first was out because of Tucker's interference." *Boston Globe* (August 16, 1895)

In 1896, "Tommy Tucker blocked Chicago's Bill Everitt from getting to third base on a hit. Everitt argued with Umpire Tim Keefe. Boston's Bobby Lowe tagged Everitt during the argument and Keefe called him out because time hadn't been called." *Chicago Record* (May 14, 1896) "Tommy Tucker grabbed Chicago 'Cap' Anson's arm on a throw to third. The Umpire Tom Lynch just made the runner, Jimmy Bannon, return to second as if nothing had happened." *Boston Globe* (June 6, 1896) When Cleveland's captain, Patsy Tebeau, attempted to catch a pop fly, Tucker bumped him, preventing the catch. Umpire Hurst ruled the batter, Tommy McCarthy, out. Tucker knocked the ball out of Chicago shortstop Bill Dahlen's glove with his fist. Umpire Tim Hurst ruled him safe. Later in the same game, Dahlen used the same trick on Tucker, only to be ruled out for interference.

Tommy Tucker bickered with his Boston teammates and manager Frank Selee.

Playing with Washington didn't change Tommy Tucker's rowdy play. He interfered with Pittsburg Pirates catcher Joe Sugden on a passed ball. Umpire Jack Sheridan returned Gene DeMontreville to second base, and no out was called. The *Washington Post* (June 27, 1897) reported that "New York Giant 'Kid' Gleason fell to Tommy Tucker's hid ball trick and was called out."

In 1898, Tucker used the hidden ball trick to nab Chicago Colts rookie Frank Isbell. Playing the Baltimore Orioles, Tucker simply sat down on Hughie Jennings to prevent him from advancing. Tucker even attempted to block his best friend in Boston, Hugh Duffy. They were drinking buddies. Duffy was the stronger player and pushed Tucker away. Cincinnati's Henry Vaughn was grabbed by Tucker. Umpire Jim McDonald did not see Tucker's action so he was literally held at first.

Tommy Tucker, while playing with the Cleveland Spiders, attempted to block Louisville's Honus Wagner. The rookie and "Noisy Tommy" had a shoving match at first base before it was broken up. *Cleveland Plain Dealer* (May 2, 1899)

"Tucker got away with blocking Brooklyn's 'Doc' Casey off the bag by sitting on his legs. Tucker and first base coach Joe Kelley squared off before Umpire Tom Lynch threatened to eject both players." *New York Sun* (June 3, 1899)

Opposing teams would get revenge for Tommy Tucker's behavior by hitting him with pitches. Tucker led the League in hit by pitch in five seasons.

The *Cleveland Leader* (July 21, 1892) described Tucker "as one of the trickiest and meanest players in causing injury to others on the diamond."

Why did Tommy Tucker play the way he did? His methods were to get outs, score runs and win games.

Comments made by Tucker:

Opposing player "Oyster" Burns threw dirt at Tucker on a pickoff attempt.
TOMMY: It was a dirty trick.
CRANK: Oh, I dunno. How about yourself?
TOMMY: Who me? Why I never did anything like that in all my 12 years of playing. I might kick and yell, but I never threw dirt in a man's eyes. That's a dirty trick.
[*Boston Globe* (August 26, 1894)].

"John McGraw should leave Boston a cripple" [*Baltimore Sun* (May 17, 1894)].

"That Baltimore gang is playing tough ball. They seem to be after my scalp. McGraw, Jennings and one or two others on that team did nothing but try to put me out of business. They jumped at me with their spikes, trying to send me to the hospital. They had their spikes after me all the time" [*Baltimore American and Commercial Adventurer* (August 27, 1898)].

Henry "Farmer" Vaughn (Cincinnati)

Henry was good at one thing: throwing the game ball out of the stadium. He collided with St. Louis' Steve Brodie at home plate. Vaughn threw his bat at Brodie, playing third base, hitting him on the shoulder. Vaughn was ejected by umpire Jack McQuaid and arrested by St. Louis police. He paid the umpire's fine of $25 and court costs of another $25.

In 1897, when John McGraw spiked Vaughn, Vaughn fired the ball from five feet away and hit McGraw in the back. McGraw continued to walk off the field. The *Baltimore Herald* (May 22, 1897) claimed, "Vaughn deserves to be blacklisted." McGraw said he would spike Vaughn again if given the chance. Vaughn's comment was, "every time McGraw came to first, he tried to cut me down."

In 1893, Vaughn tossed the ball over the fence with the hope of getting a new one. Umpire Bob Emslie warned him but did not fine him. There were no more balls, so Emslie sent Vaughn after the original ball. Vaughn used this trick on several other occasions. Playing against Chicago, he threw the game ball to a club house boy. The umpire put a new one into play. In the ninth inning, Vaughn threw the ball into the press section. He was caught, and the original ball was put back into the game. He was fined $10 by umpire Horace McFarland for dirtying the ball while he was catching.

In 1898, Cincinnati owner John Brush fined Vaughn $25 for striking umpire Ed Swartwood.

Honus Wagner (HOF) (Louisville)

Honus Wagner is remembered as one of the greatest players in baseball history. The outstanding shortstop of the Pittsburg Pirates played the same rowdy baseball of the era as most players because that was how you won.

One maneuver that Wagner used to disturb the pitcher was to jump over the home plate to the other batter's box when the pitcher was in his windup. This action was prohibited in the 20th century. The *Chicago Times Herald* (October 4, 1899) said, "Louisville's Honus Wagner slid into third base spiking Umpire Tom Connolly.... Connolly's shoe was completely ripped off." When

Cleveland's Tommy Tucker attempted to block first base, Wagner easily pushed him aside.

The *Louisville Times* (April 26, 1897) said, "Honus hit what should have been a triple, but when he made the turn at first 'Dirty Jack' Doyle, the Baltimore first baseman gave him a hip." At second base, was future Hall of Fame shortstop Hughie Jennings forcing him wide, and he did not touch second. At third base waited none other than future Hall of Famer McGraw, who blocked him off the bag and then knocked the wind out of him by tagging him in the stomach. He had run the obstacle course called "scientific base ball Oriole style."

In 1897, he would go up against the Orioles again with different results. The *Baltimore American and Commercial Advertiser* (September 9, 1897) quoted Wagner: "I hit another to deep center for extra bases. I dumped Doyle on his behind at first, left Jennings in the dirt at second and trampled over McGraw's feet coming to third." Honus Wagner learned quickly to play "rowdy ball."

Also in 1897, when Jennings was attempting to tag him, Wagner hip-checked him, causing the ball to fly out of his hand and a safe call.

Chicago runner Matt Kilroy grabbed Louisville's first baseman, Honus Wagner, by the belt, preventing him from catching a ball. The umpire, John Heydler, missed the play. Later in the same game, Wagner held Button Biggs, preventing a double by forcing Biggs to remain at first base.

In another game against Baltimore, Wagner picked up the ball and threw it away so he could score. The rookie did not get away with this one. Umpire Ed Swartwood saw the play and sent him back to third.

Wagner shoved Pittsburg's catcher, Frank Bowerman. Wagner claimed he accidentally stepped on Hughie Jennings' toes. One other trick Wagner was caught doing by umpire Bill Betts was rubbing the ball in the dirt.

In a throwing contest, Honus Wagner threw a ball 404 feet for a new record.

Perry Werden (St. Louis)

Werden described his play in the *Cincinnati Enquirer* (May 22, 1893) by saying, "Give a player credit when he turns a trick and can get away, but there is nothing in blood-raw strong arm work when there is nothing to be gained."

Werden was notorious for tripping and kneeing runners at first base. Some of the players would require assistance to leave the field. In 1891, Werden was called out for running directly from first base to third base by umpire Phil Powers.

The *Louisville Times* (August 12, 1897) reported that "Louisville's first base man Werden dodged a bat thrown by Chicago Malachi Kittridge to catch a pop fly."

Edward "Ned"/"Ed" Williamson (Chicago)

Ned Williamson was an enthusiastic partier and carouser. He spent his time away from the park in beer gardens and taverns. He was spunky and got into a fist fight with his manager, Cap Anson. During the game, Williamson had fired a bunt as hard as possible to the barehanded Anson, who played first base.

He accused Anson of being abusive to his players. "He is not too bad with the old blood as the new, but he raves at both on the slightest provocation." Anson called for a first base coach, and Williamson's reply was, "Get on, old man" as he walked to the coaches' box. The same month, while getting on a streetcar, he dropped a cigar in a man's umbrella, which started a ruckus on the car as everybody bolted off. It was reported that "Big Ned" threw a baseball in a contest 400 feet (longest of the era), winning $280.

He was a fancy dresser and had an affair with John Clarkson's wife, Ella. Williamson and Clarkson got into a fist fight after a game. The fight did not last long and resulted in a bloody nose for Clarkson.

Williamson's biggest problem was his continual weight gain; he reached 257 pounds. He told questioners that he was going to lose weight by avoiding butter, sugar, milk and potatoes.

ANSON: I want to know if you fellows are coming out here?

WILLIAMSON: What did you say?

ANSON: If I bring you out, I'll get in there after you. (What?)

All the players and cranks laughed. Anson fined Williamson $10 for calling him a "fool."

WILLIAMSON, S. S. Chicago's
COPYRIGHTED BY GOODWIN & CO. 1887.
GOODWIN & CO. New York.

Ned Williamson

He continually borrowed money from the club and was usually broke. Yet he still kept candy and pennies to give to all kids who saw the big man. The White Stockings never lost a game due to poor play, according to Williamson, who would say, "We had won but the umpire was with them."

In 1888, Williamson had a conversation in spring training with "Cap" Anson.

ANSON: What's the matter with you? Don't you need any practice?
WILLIAMSON: The weather is too rough for me.
ANSON: Boys, a fine example for the younger players.

In 1891, Williamson opened a bar called "Base Ball Wigwam."

He was one White Stocking who was not afraid of Anson. He would take enough then tell Anson to "shut up." On one occasion, he yelled in front of the Chicago cranks, "Oh shut up, 'Cap,' for Christmas sake, shut up!" while taking batting practice. Williamson received a $100 bonus "for having abstained from intoxicating drinks and orgies." *Washington Post* (October 7, 1885)

However, during the 1886 World Series against the St. Louis Browns, he was accused of playing while intoxicated, and released.

"Fighting" Harry Wolverton (Chicago)

He was described by the *Chicago Tribune* (April 16, 1898) as "a quiet player, not given to talk." Were they wrong! On June 12 against St. Louis, Wolverton and catcher Albert Nichol collided while chasing a pop-up in foul territory. Both players began fighting and blaming the other for the mishap. Wolverton did not get along with his teammates and was sold to the Philadelphia Phillies. He promptly started two fights in St. Louis. On August 14, 1900, he spiked St. Louis first baseman Dan McGann. The two let fists fly until police broke it up. While returning home, he stuck his head out the window of the train, only to hit a pole, fracturing his skull. When he left baseball, he became a policeman.

Wolverton got a "welcome to the big league." John McGraw hit him in the eye at third base with both fists when he was out by 15 feet. McGraw was ejected from the game. The same day, Wolverton was determined to get even with a St. Louis player. He spiked first baseman Dan McGann. McGann fired the ball at Wolverton, hitting him in the head. Amazingly, umpire Bob Emslie did not eject either player. Wolverton was woozy but charged McGann. The result was a fight to be remembered.

The fight only lasted a minute but featured jabs, uppercuts and wild swings. Wolverton claimed "the spiking was an accident," and McGann said "he would have thrown a bat or bench but only had a ball."

Philadelphia third baseman Harry Wolverton held Pittsburg Frank Bowerman without being detected. Wolverton ran inside the first base line and stepped on Chicago's John Ganzel, who missed the thrown ball at first base.

Charles "Chief" Zimmer (Cleveland)

He was not an Indian, but got the nickname when he played for a minor league team in Poughkeepsie. He sold cigars to teammates and opponents to increase his income.

Zimmer threw sand in Pittsburg's Denny Lyons' eyes when he was playing third base, to prevent him from seeing a ball coming down to third. Another trick was when two Louisville players were called off balls when Zimmer yelled "Me! Me!" Tommy Tucker broke Zimmer's collarbone with a block at home plate. A reprimand was given by the National League to Tucker. After Zimmer had just become well enough to play, John McGraw applied a fist tag to his jaw.

Zimmer was one of the first catchers to attempt to deceive the umpire by pulling a pitch into the strike zone. Zimmer was likewise adept at losing the only ball, requiring the umpire to go to a new one.

5

DISORDERLY OUTFIELDERS

Bob Addy (Chicago)

Cap Anson described Bob Addy as "an odd sort of genius." The key word being "sort." Addy played only two years as an outfielder. He thought any ball hit in the outfield was his to catch. He caught a ball in short left field, although he was playing right field at the time. He would constantly talk to anyone on base in an attempt to distract them.

In one game, Addy had four teeth knocked out. He left the game to go to the dentist. He returned and reentered the game in the ninth inning. The cranks went wild at his entrance. He was a crank favorite because of his love for the game and his happy attitude.

When an exhibition game to raise money for an orphanage was rained out, a reporter for the *Chicago Tribune* (July 20, 1876) reported Addy as saying, "It was expected that they would be unlucky, for if they hadn't been unlucky they wouldn't be orphans."

George Bechtel (Louisville)

In a game against the New York Mutuals, Bechtel made three errors in a key situation. The *Louisville Courier* (May 20, 1876) reported, "Bechtel was a much suspected man." The Grays' management suspended Bechtel.

Bechtel wired first baseman Jim Devlin a message stating, "We can make $500 if you lose the game today. Tell Jack Chapman to let me know at once. Bechtel." Devlin gave the telegram to the Louisville owner. Bechtel was suspended from the National League before the 1877 season. Devlin would later be banned for being paid to lose games.

Steve Brodie (Baltimore)

Steve Brodie was reckless, and his flamboyant play in the field made him a crank favorite. He continually talked to himself in the outfield. He would scream "Brodie" whenever he made an error. He actually caught a ball behind his back with a 12–0 lead.

When Brodie struck out, he would hit the side of his head with his fist. His continual chatter often gave his managers a headache. Brodie often recited Shakespeare in center field.

"Wee Willie" Keeler told Hanlon, "Brodie's got it in for me." Hanlon asked, "What's Brodie got it in for you for?" Keeler responded, "I don't know, but he keeps yelling 'I'll get you, you dirty dog. I'll get you, you dirty dog'" (referring to the ball). The other players laughed and remarked, "Brodie screams that at every ball that comes his way." Once Brodie and Keeler chased the same ball in right-center. Brodie threw the ball to catcher Wilbert Robinson just as Keeler tossed in a planted ball. The umpire screamed at both players, but both stood and grinned.

Hanlon's job was to keep Brodie's high-strung attitude aimed at the opponents, and not at his teammates. Brodie once pulled off the umpire's mask after a third strike call. In a spring exhibition game in Petersburg, a fearless Brodie took on the biggest crank and shoved him into the wall. Brodie used him for a punching bag.

ATTACKS ON UMPIRES

Baltimore American and Commercial Advertiser (August 2, 1894): "Brodie caught the jacket label of Umpire Will Hoagland with both hands and gave an imitation of how to wake a man when he is in a trance. Fine $25."

Baltimore American and Commercial Advertiser (August 16, 1895): "Brodie deliberately kicked John Hunt who fined him $50. The next day he grabbed Miah Murray's mask and flung it to the ground for a $25 fine."

Baltimore American and Commercial Advertiser (July 22, 1896): "Brodie was called out on strikes by Bill Betts. He grabbed Betts by the arm and gave him a shake. Fined $25 and ejected."

Baltimore Sun (June 22, 1895): "Brodie gave Umpire Miah Murray a 'little sarcastic criticism' costing him $25."

Baltimore American and Commercial Advertiser (June 30, 1899): "Brodie argued the call with Umpire Al Manassau so strongly, he was fined $25 and ejected."

Chicago Tribune (September 7, 1899): "Brodie blocked catcher Tim Donahue's throw to second to catch stealing Willie Keeler. Umpire Al Manassau did not rule interference. However, Donahue threw sand in Brodie's face."

Tom Brown (Boston)

Boston Beaneaters outfielder Tom Brown attempted to steal second base. Chicago's second baseman, Fred Pfeffer, made a hard tag which Brown reacted to by hitting Pfeffer in the face. When Pfeffer got up, Brown blasted him with "You are a dirty coward and loafer." Pfeffer retaliated by putting his fist beside Brown's nose and saying, "Brown, I'll meet you later."

In 1892, Brown was playing for Louisville when "after getting a walk, he threw his bat hitting Umpire Sheridan on the mask," reported the *Louisville Courier-Journal* (May 9, 1892).

In 1896, "Washington's Tom Brown was fined $10 for yelling at Baltimore fielder Steve Brodie who was trying to catch a fly ball." *Baltimore Herald* (August 11, 1896)

Tom Brown blamed his poor hitting in Brooklyn on the "musty" balls because of the park's nearness to Jamaica Bay. He claimed the air "takes all the life and elasticity out of the ball." *Washington Post* (August 8, 1897)

In 1886, Brown was "upset that a new ball was taken out when an old one was returned to the field. Umpire John Kelly stated that a new ball cannot be brought into use until the original has been lost for five minutes. After continued arguing, in which Brown was superior, the new ball was used. While arguing, Cincinnati's Bill Kuehne was rubbing the new ball in the dirt." *Pittsburg Post* (May 12, 1886)

Eddie Burke (New York)

In 1893, when called out on strikes, Eddie Burke threw his bat 30 feet. The *Baltimore Sun* (July 17, 1895) reported that "during pregame warmups New York's outfielder hot-tempered Eddie Burke was being roasted by the cranks. After making some vile comments about them, several jumped on the field. Burke hit the first man who got to him. His teammates broke up the muse."

"Wilbert Robinson left his mask in the base path of a home run by Billy Hamilton. Teammate Eddie Burke took the mask and beat it till it was not recognizable." *New York Star* (April 14, 1890)

The Cincinnati Reds' Eddie Burke was caught drinking and claimed he just had Bass Ale. "I have been in the team's hotel during the time in question. I played pinochle with Billy Schriever and Jack Shoup until bedtime. I would like to get in a few punches on a busybody who has nothing to do but write lying notes about me." *Cincinnati Enquirer* (May 18, 1897)

Jesse "The Crab" Burkett (HOF) (Cleveland)

Jesse Burkett's teammates dubbed him "The Crab" because he woke up cranky and stayed that way.

The *Cleveland Press* (June 26, 1896) reported that in a game against the Louisville Colonels, "Burkett took Umpire Weidman by the shoulders and gave him a good shaking for what 'The Crab' considered a bad decision."

"Jesse was thrown out in the ninth inning of a double header. When he continued to argue, he was ejected for the second game. The police finally escorted him away and he was fined $200 for 'Disorderly Conduct.'" *Morning Herald* (August 4, 1897) Manager Patsy Tebeau benched Burkett for throwing a ball into the stands which hit a crank.

The *Cleveland Herald* (July 5, 1894) reported, "Jesse Burkett called down the wrath of the crowd. With two strikes called on him, Jesse dropped the bat and began to argue with the umpire. Another nice one came over the plate and Umpire Hurst very properly called an out for Burkett." While "chaffing" (arguing with umpire) was a big part of the entertainment of the game, Burkett had numerous run-ins with umpires. In one tirade with an umpire, he was quoted as having used 13 curse words, ending with "put you in a 'damn' museum."

On one occasion, "The Crab" jumped into the Negro section to clobber a fan. Two teammates pulled him out of the stands.

"The Crab's" opinion on Native American Louis Sockalexis: "don't tell me about that 'bead peddler.'" "He's a Jonah. I haven't batted over 100 since he joined the team! Wait till I strike my gait and I will make him go back to the woods and look for scalps," reported the *Cleveland Plain Dealer* (June 18, 1897).

On September 9, 1899, while Burkett was playing for St. Louis, Cincinnati's Bill Phillips quick-pitched him when he stepped out of the batter's box, for a third strike. Burkett exploded and was ejected by umpire Bob Emslie.

Cliff Carroll (Providence)

Carroll chewed what he called "fruit cakes" but was actually chewing tobacco. The nicotine would help relieve pain. Carroll soaked rookie tryout Jimmy Murphy with a garden hose, causing Murphy to leave the mound without throwing a pitch. Murphy came back with a pistol and shot at Carroll. Murphy was sentenced to jail time, but when leaving the court yelled, "Carroll, I'll get even with you, yet! I'll break your head if I ever get out again." Carroll was constantly in trouble. He once invited all the waiters from the Narragansett Hotel to the game and then attempted to smuggle the black waiters into an all-white crowd of cranks. Manager Harry Wright thought it was funny, and Carroll's trick for free food had worked.

Cleveland pitcher Jim McCormick hit Carroll in the face with a fastball, yet Carroll never left the lineup. The *Fall River Daily News* criticized Carroll for bunting for hits, saying they were "baby acts" or "punts."

On August 17, 1892, outfielder Carroll kept misjudging fly balls and grounders. A grounder even landed in his pocket without his knowledge as he turned in circles, oblivious to the location of the ball. The cranks were laughing hysterically, but owner Chris von der Ahe fined Carroll $25 for "indifference and rotten play."

Carroll was continually up to monkey business. In August 1886, he got into a fight with Otto Schomberg after Carroll called him a ... head. Carroll was suspended seven days but was back after the Pittsburg directors lifted the suspension and made him pay a $50 fine. *The Sporting News* (August 23, 1886)

Like King Kelly, Carroll had a pet monkey that he brought to the games. The monkey soon became the team mascot. When the monkey died, Carroll buried him under home plate. *The Sporting News* (July 12, 1887)

In Spalding's "Baseball Trip Around the World," the team played a game in Australia. Cap Anson had arranged a boat race, with each player putting up $25. There were seven contestants. Each boat had two oars. The race was between Anson and John "Egyptian" Healy. Suddenly, Healy grabbed Anson's oar. The boats rammed together and spilled Healy and Anson into the water. Billy Earle was about to take the lead when Anson grabbed his boat and tried to climb in. Cliff Carroll smashed Healy on the hand with his oar and raced past the two. Carroll received the winner's prize of $175. Carroll purchased a roulette wheel, which he used to pocket additional money on the trip home.

Carroll spent his non-playing hours chasing women and drinking. With a threat of returning to the minor leagues, he gave up the rowdy night life style. Carroll got into a fight with King Kelly and hit him so hard that, if the August 13, 1897, *Baltimore Herald* is to be believed, Kelly turned a backflip.

Pearce "Nuget" Chiles (Philadelphia)

He ran the bases with the idea of injuring the fielders. If a player hit a pop-up to him, he would yell, "What's the use." Chiles developed a method to steal the pitcher's signals. When coaching third base, Chiles got Morgan Murphy to sit behind the center field fence with binoculars. Murphy would then buzz Chiles with a buzzer which Chiles had hidden under the third base. The ground would vibrate to denote the type of pitch. "Nuget" was caught but not ejected, since stealing signals was not illegal.

The next day, Chiles was coaching first base and twitching his leg. The Cincinnati Reds stopped the game, but it was just a ploy to throw them off their game. Chiles stole $100 from a soldier on a train. He was sentenced to prison for two years. After his release, he assaulted a young woman, which prevented him from returning to the major leagues.

Fred Clarke (HOF) (Louisville)

Clarke warned players to "look out for my jump." He would sharpen his spikes on the bench so opponents would be terrorized by his furious slides into the bases, including first base.

In 1897, it started to rain while Clarke was a runner on second base. He loosened the bag tie and showed the base to umpire Hank O'Day, saying, he "was safe as long as his hands were on the base." The Louisville cranks roared with laughter. O'Day called him out and then called the game due to rain. In New York, Clarke's take-out slide at third base resulted in George Davis hitting Clarke's jaw with his fist. Umpire Tom Lynch ejected both players.

In 1898, Clarke yelled to Chicago Orphans third baseman Barry McCormick to "keep out of the way." He made a feet-first jump at Chicago shortstop Bill Dahlen on a steal attempt. Jimmy Ryan described Fred Clarke in the *Cincinnati Enquirer* (April 25, 1898):

> Watch out I don't get these into you, pointing to his spikes. Then he came feet first and he didn't miss me by a great deal. He cut my glove twice with his reckless slides to home. Showing 'em [cleats] to you is going too far. Clarke strikes me as looking for somebody's scalp. He would not be so gallant if he played on the infield. He is in the outfield where he thinks no one will get a chance to get back at him. I don't think of a meaner trick than injuring a player. He is trying to scare players into giving him a clear path by showing his spikes.

Clarke described himself to the *Cincinnati Enquirer* (May 9, 1898): "I had my spikes sharpened and shined and I came down to home plate yelling "Tim, look out. And I going to use 'em on you. Then I held up one of my feet and showed him the spikes and I had Tim badly rattled. I'll do it every time to help another player out."

Clarke spiked Washington's "Dirty Jack" Doyle by stepping on his foot. Clarke blocked "Bad Bill" Dahlen from completing a double play. Clarke would warn infielders when he got on base. Also, he blocked Chicago's

"Cupid" Childs on a double play attempt. Childs vowed to get even. That evening on a train platform, the two got into a fight. Childs cursed Clarke and hit him with his right hand. Clarke fought back. Clarke's teammate watched the five-minute tussle without stopping the fight. A policeman arrived and broke up the battle.

Duff Cooley (Philadelphia)

Duff Cooley was fined by St. Louis owner Chris Von der Ahe for being hurt and missing games. He was docked a second time for having malaria, which cost him $25.

In 1894, Cooley missed a game after drinking and was suspended. In 1896, Von der Ahe fined him $25 for what he deemed indifferent play.

Cooley celebrated a pitching victory with teammate Al Orth by drinking all night. Cooley was the team captain, so when he returned to the hotel, manager George Stallings blasted his actions. He was fined $25.

Cooley was continually criticized by the cranks. Cooley's night-life activities were met with disgust by Philadelphia owner John Rogers, who suspended him. This resulted in Cooley being eliminated as captain. The players wanted Cooley to return to the team, but Rogers stopped that decision. *Sporting Life* (April 8, 1900) said, "Cooley was being handled as a Russian laborer. He landed with Pittsburg Pirates where he promptly gave the new team the Philadelphia signals."

Abner Dalrymple (Chicago)

Ezra Sutton hit what appeared to be a grand slam home run. The field was hazy. As the ball soared over the fence, Abner Dalrymple pulled a ball out of his shirt, stretched out his hand and came down with the ball in his hand. The umpire ruled an out, and Boston was denied four runs.

Dalrymple was short on money in 1883 in Cincinnati. He knew Cap Anson would wager on anything. So Dalrymple wagered $50 that his man could outrace outfielder Billy Sunday. Anson knew Sunday was the fastest man in the league. When the team went out of the ball park, Dalrymple marked off 100 yards. A pistol started the race, and Mike Kittleman defeated Sunday by a yard. Abner told Anson that Kittleman was the U.S. 100 yard champion—after he collected his $50.

Dalrymple gave Anson a chance to get even. He made another $50 bet on Fred Pfeffer versus Billy Sunday. Sunday had beaten Pfeffer before, so Anson thought he had a sure thing. Dalrymple arranged for Sunday to fall down during the race. The race appeared to be going well until Sunday "stumbled" in the last ten yards. Dalrymple and the two other players split the winnings.

Edward "Big Ed" Delahanty (Philadelphia) (HOF)

When Ed Delahanty debuted in the National League in 1888, he was considered too fat to play for the Phillies. One night after a few beers, the local press heard him talking with teammate John Clements about quitting. He even packed his trunk but was talked out of it by Coach Harry Wright.

In 1891, Philadelphia's losing season took its toll on young Delahanty. Philadelphia's owner, "Colonel" Rogers, made matters worse by pestering Delahanty for a small loan. The fans did give him a horseshoe of flowers, which is every player's dream. Harry Wright over-managed the team to the point of objecting to Delahanty's female companion. So Delahanty left the game and put on his street clothes. Wright fined him $100 and suspended him indefinitely. Delahanty apologized, the fine was reduced to $25, and he was allowed to return to the team.

He was fined another $50 for bringing a boy to the field. Later in the same season, after failing to run to first base and talking back to his manager, Delahanty was fined another $25.

In 1892, he was hit by a pitch in the groin that sidelined him for nine weeks. In 1893, he was given a $300 pay cut. Delahanty complained to O. P. Caylor of *The Sporting News* about the hard practices, wind sprints, and two practices a day. He believed in "hoodoo." He frequented the races and blew his money entertaining friends at his hotel. He was one of the big spenders. He founded his own social club, the Ancient Order of Jabawauks.

In 1895, he hit 450 home runs and was met at home plate by pitcher "Adonis" Terry. This sight you would not see in modern baseball. Delahanty was constantly chastised for fouling off so many pitches. None of the other players understood his attitude, saying he was delaying the game. But Delahanty would sulk even though he was right. He bet $200 on his friend James Corbett in a prize fight. His teammates collected when Jim Fitsimmons knocked out Corbett in the 14th round. Delahanty was very superstitious, and when the Phillies team got on the 1:13 p.m., #13 train on track 13, on March 13, he said the train was cursed and did not get on board.

Delahanty had signed a document pledging to stop drinking whiskey. The front page of the *Detroit Times* showed the following headline: "Del Mighty Hitter, Signs Pledge." The article made him look like a teenager taking advice from his mother. He had hoped to be traded from Washington to the

New York Giants, a deal which had failed to be completed.

In a letter to his wife, Norine, he alluded to a lapsed insurance policy and said that he had bought a ticket to New York. In the letter, he mentioned that he hoped the train would jump the tracks. He did not speak to his family and left for the train. He got on the train, went to the Pullman car and ordered whiskey. He was seen smoking consistently, which was prohibited in that car. The train's service bell was continually ringing, which angered conductor John Cole. After Cole's talk, Delahanty stopped smoking. The porter refused to serve him any more whiskey. Conductor Cole again went to talk to a distraught Dela-

Ed Delahanty

hanty, who had broken his glass and created a minor mess. Now Cole required Delahanty to pay $3 for the glass. The conductor warned Delahanty that the train was in Canada and under Canadian laws. Delahanty's reply was that he "didn't care if [he was] in Canada or Hell." Cole ordered a whiskey for him. Later, Cole saw Delahanty stumbling in the walkway when the train stopped in Bridgeberg. While stopped, Delahanty went to the wrong berth, startling a woman. The disturbance brought conductor Cole back to the situation. Cole ordered Dalahanty off the train.

Delahanty started following the train track, and in spite of a sign warning "Keep Off the Bridge," forged ahead, only to be met by another train. He stood on the chord as the train passed. The bridge watchman came out to see the lone man on the bridge. The watchman, Samuel Kingston, claimed Delahanty threatened him with a rock. Kingston attempted to grab Delahanty, catching him by the collar. Both men tumbled to the tracks. Kingston got up and heard Delahanty splash into the river. Delahanty hollered for help, to no avail. A nearby tug searched for Delahanty, but was only able to find a derby hat. Eventually, his naked body was found in the Canadian side of Niagara Falls.

Foul play, suicide, or just the plain accident of a drunk at night on a railroad track, that was the final inning for Delahanty.

Charlie Dexter (Louisville)

Dexter was a baseline bruiser. He stood on third base as Cincinnati's Tommy Corcoran headed for the base. Corcoran bent over like a "bull." At the last second, Dexter jumped away and laughed when Corcoran ran past third and was tagged out. Baltimore's John McGraw rounded third base, only to have Dexter spike him.

In 1898, Baltimore first baseman Dan McGann went after a bunted ball, only to be run over by batter Charlie Dexter. McGann was knocked to the ground. Umpire Jim McDonald ruled Dexter safe. Umpires let a lot of illegal tactics go rather than suffer abuse.

The *Baltimore Herald* reported, "Louisville Colonels third baseman Dexter skipped running to third base by five feet and was called out by Umpire Charlie Snyder."

Even as a base coach, Dexter brought trouble to the field. New York Giants first baseman "Dirty Jack" Doyle was going after a ball thrown into the grandstands by catcher John Warner. Coach Dexter yelled, "Throw me the ball!" Doyle, without looking, threw the ball to Dexter, allowing the errant throw to score Honus Wagner. *Chicago Times-Herald* (May 14, 1899)

"Turkey Mike" Donlin (St. Louis)

Donlin was a player who got his call-up to the major leagues while in jail due to drunkenness. He had a volatile personality and was an instant crowd pleaser. He painted his bat in red, white and blue to symbolize America's victory in the Spanish American War. As an orphan, Donlin had to learn to fight for himself.

However, his love for partying and alcohol had a higher priority than baseball. He got the nickname "Turkey Mike" because of his love for booze. He would be there during bed check, then climb out a window and shimmy down a drainpipe for a night on the town. "Turkey Mike" was sentenced to six months in jail for a drinking binge.

Donlin left baseball for a Hollywood career and appeared in many movies.

Sam Dungan (Chicago)

During 1892 in Pittsburg, Cap Anson walked to first base, but it was only two balls. Anson angrily yelled, "Dungan, pick up my bat and hand it to me." Red-faced, Dungan picked up the lumber and handed it to Anson. Dungan was offended by Anson, but simply took the belligerence as the cranks hissed Anson.

Dungan purchased a new bat. When he got back to the hotel, the other players showed interest in his new bat. Dungan's plan was to sell half-shares in a 75-cent bat. He got four players to purchase halves, so he made $1.50 profit. Then, Dungan obtained a gross of bats and became a bat salesman.

Dungan was not the smartest player, and when taken on a train trip to St. Louis, he got into a card game. Dungan's first hand had four kings. He bet $50 and a diamond ring worth $4,000. He lost and realized he had been cheated! When Dungan told Anson, he fined him $25 for being taken. Dungan told a policeman at the next stop, and he did get his ring back.

In 1893, after an outstanding catch, Dungan leaped around with such excitement that Anson chided him for not getting the ball back into the infield. After Dungan was traded to Louisville, Anson still rode him by calling him a "rat hole" and chastised him to "git in de game."

Jimmy Fogarty (Philadelphia)

Fogarty would have been just as happy on vaudeville.

A player whose life was cut short by tuberculosis at 27 years of age, Jimmy Fogarty was a prankster. In 1888 in an exhibition game against the Chicago White Stockings, Fogarty was coaching third, pretended he was the runner on third, and ran home. Cap Anson was catching and when the ball was thrown home, Fogarty reversed directions with Anson close behind. Anson chased Fogarty off the field. Finally, Fogarty dropped to the ground, laughing away. Anson accused him of a "schoolboy trick which ain't base ball a little bit." *Sporting Life* (November 14, 1888)

Fogarty would put ice down players' backs when they were asleep on the train. On a post-season trip to Hawaii, he serenaded a seasick Ed Crane with a ditty:

> There is a boarding house not far away
> Where they have ham and eggs three times a day.
> O how those boarders yell
> When they hear the dinner bell.
> O how those eggs do smell.

Ed Crane was heard singing "Home Sweet Home" while barfing over a bucket.

In Australia, Fogarty was in a boat race with Anson which was bet on. Fogarty lost. He was supposed to warn his teammates of a cannon salute off Ceylon. He didn't. This caused players to grab bats, thinking they were being invaded by pirates. (Not Pittsburg.) Anson put on his wife's gown.

Other players were locked in a closet. The whole team wanted to throw Fogarty overboard. Fogarty threw a baseball that hit the right eye of the Sphinx in Egypt. This resulted in giving all the Americans a black eye.

Fogarty was fined $50 for drinking and $12 for missing the train.

George "Budweiser" Gore (Chicago)

George Gore was King Kelly's frequent saloon buddy. Gore began his playing days with the powerful Chicago White Stockings. He was fast and set a record with seven steals in one game. He loved beer and the nightlife.

Cap Anson believed in sobriety and continually berated drinking buddies Gore, Kelly, Silver Flint and Ned Williamson, who often frequented Mickey Finn's Lone Star Saloon in Chicago. Tom Burns, Gore, Kelly and Anson were riding in a carriage when Anson was hit in the face by a wad of chewing tobacco. Gore and Kelly jumped from the carriage and attacked the hooligans.

In a World Series game against the St. Louis Browns, Gore played under the influence of alcohol. Anson was so mad he suspended Gore for the balance of the series.

Anson released Gore with the comment, "Women and wine brought about his downfall." *Chicago Tribune* (October 9, 1886)

Anson chastised him for errors with vile language. Gore had the bad habit of laughing when he struck out, which made Anson angry. In Cleveland in 1884, he was so drunk that he climbed out of a sixth floor window and hung by his fingers until his teammates got him back into the hotel room. In 1885, he

OLD JUDGE CIGARETTES Goodwin & Co., New York.

George Gore

missed a game due to his drinking. Once traded to New York, he was caught drinking in the clubhouse. In 1888, he even dressed in the wrong uniform because he was so drunk. In 1890 in the Players' League, his drinking irritated his teammates so much that they wanted to beat him. When a dog got close to him, he felt the dog was a "hoodoo" and threw objects at it.

Paul Hines (Providence)

One of the real characters of the game was Paul Hines. He carried a horseshoe wherever he went. He was partially deaf and talked loudly. He said he was from an affluent Washington family, when he actually had lived in a poor shanty.

At a hotel, he discovered a sportswriter's scorecard. He used a pencil to change his singles into doubles. Boston caught Hines using an illegal bat.

Hines was fined for poor play and missing games. He had a hot temper. New York Giants pitcher Jack Lynch hit Hines with a pitch. Hines fired the bat at Lynch, only to have him duck. The bat landed at second base. The *Providence Star* (August 25, 1882) reported, "Lynch hit Hines in Washington, Baltimore, New York and elsewhere and deserved to be hit."

Hines was knocked down at second base by Jack Glasscock, but when he got to his feet he flew into Glasscock. Neither player was ejected. Hines was involved in the same game with a collision at first base with runner Kid Gleason.

In 1886, Hines was playing third base when King Kelly plowed into him. Hines fell on top of Kelly while at the same time grabbing his uniform. Umpire Red Connolly ruled that Hines had interfered and allowed Kelly to score. Hines was fined $250 for indifferent play and arguing with his captain.

Howard "Ducky" Holmes (Baltimore)

Holmes' attitude made it hard for him to get along with teammates. While playing at the Polo Grounds, he struck out. The Giants cranks, where he had played in 1897, were yelling, "Oh! 'Ducky,' you're a lobster." Upon spying his former owner, Andrew Freedman, Holmes shouted, "Well, I'm glad I don't have to work for no sheeny anymore." ("Sheeny" was a derogatory term for Jewish people.) *Baltimore Morning Herald* (July 26, 1898)

This comment by Holmes enraged Freedman, who went onto the field to ask the umpire to eject Holmes. Umpire Tom Lynch acknowledged that he had not heard the comment. Freedman, in frustration, fetched two policemen. Lynch ran the policemen off his diamond. Freedman did not allow his players to continue playing the game. Lynch declared a forfeit for the Orioles.

The cranks demanded their money back. Freedman was barred from the park, and the league office suspended Holmes for the rest of the season.

Holmes became a crank favorite for taking on the league, and the directors backed down and lifted the suspension.

Michael Joseph "Ubbo Ubbo" Hornung (Boston)

Joe Hornung was an excellent fielder who upon making a good catch would yell "Ubbo Ubbo." Hornung also made the same "Ubbo Ubbo" yell upon getting a hit. "Ubbo" is a Nordic or German word meaning "boy."

He was an aggressive player who slid hard, using his cleats. He spiked Pittsburg's third baseman Art Whitney so badly that his shoe was in pieces. Amazingly, Whitney's foot was not damaged.

The *Washington Post* (June 7, 1887) stated, "Boston left fielder caught the ball but dropped it when he turned his back. The boy who marked the scores on the scoreboard was questioned by Umpire Phil Powers about the play. The boy said he made the catch. After the game, the boy said Hornung offered him a dollar to say the ball was caught."

In 1886, Hornung scored without coming near third base. Umpire Joe Ellick was not looking and did not accept Kansas City's kicking.

Richard "Dick" Johnston (Boston)

Johnston was quoted in the *Boston Globe* (October 16, 1887) as saying, "When we have two men on and we're one run behind with two outs: That is the time for scheming."

In Philadelphia, a single brought in Boston's winning run. But batter Dickie Johnson, in the team's celebration, did not run all the way to first base. This play occurred in 1889, however, the rule about touching the next base on a game-winning hit was not enforced by the lone umpire. Johnston was fined twice for drinking in 1887.

The *Boston Globe* (July 18, 1888) reported this trickery: "With the score tied and Dickie Johnson on second base, Boston's John Morrill grounded out to first. Johnson cut third base short 20 feet and crossed the plate. Umpire John Kelly did not see the trick. Detroit's Captain 'Deacon' White yelled Johnson was out. Umpire Kelly replied 'No, he's not. I didn't see him do it; but next time I'll fine you $25.'"

Joe "Handsome" Kelley (HOF) (Baltimore)

The Baltimore press added an "e" to Kelly's name (making it Kelley) as a status symbol. Kelley was handsome and drew many female cranks. He would scream at the top of his lungs at the umpire on a close call. Kelley would insult the cranks just to get them riled. He got in several fights and actually went into the stands after cranks. Kelley was notorious for making snide comments in the newspaper about the intelligence of Willie Keller and Jack Doyle. He also sometimes hid balls in the outfield.

When accused of playing dirty, Kelley replied, "We bathe as much as the next and the talk is nonsense. We Baltimore boys only defend ourselves when playing against teams that treat us mean, especially Cincinnati." *Baltimore Morning Herald* (September 1, 1898)

During one game when Kelley was ejected, the umpire pulled out his pocket watch and gave Kelley one minute to leave. Kelley knocked the watch out of the umpire's hand and stomped on it. The umpire replied, "it was your watch." (The umpire had borrowed the watch from the clubhouse before the game.)

Kelley was a perfectionist and ribbed his teammates when they made errors. He carried a mirror in his back pocket to check his looks.

Mike "King" Kelly (HOF) (Boston)

Mike Kelly was the greatest trickster of the era on any diamond. He was a notorious night life player who loved to party with the cranks to the wee hours of the morning. He seemed to do well until he switched from beer to whiskey. He was noted for kicking (arguing) with the cranks.

Kelly normally got along with reporters because he always had quotable comments after the game. His notoriety came from his circumventing the rules. He would tick the bat with his fingernail while catching, resulting in a foul tip call and ensuing riot. He would stick a ball in his trousers when playing the outfield to save for the late innings, using it to pretend to make a catch, when it was actually hit over the fence.

Kelly took a horsewhip after a reporter who said Kelly quarreled with his teammates. With only one umpire, Kelly would cut third base short when possible. On more than one occasion, he faked an injury at such length that the game was called for darkness.

In 1886, Kelly and Jim McCormick were so drunk before a game that Al Spalding fined them $250 each. Kelly led the league in hitting with a .388 average, but Spalding was put out at Kelly's antics and sold him to Boston for $10,000, the largest sum at that time.

For Kelly's first game in Boston, he showed up in a horse-drawn carriage. He was wearing a tuxedo and mink coat, and had his pet monkey at his side.

At one away game, Kelly was so drunk that he attempted to jump from the hotel's tenth floor until restrained by a teammate.

Another tactic employed by Kelly was to get in an argument with a base-man. When the umpire came to intervene, Kelly would take off for the next base.

A visit by the Chicago team to the White House resulted in President Grover Cleveland calling the team "Ball Niners." This infuriated Kelly to the point that he gripped Cleveland's hand like a vise. The other players did the same, causing baseball players to not be invited back to the White House until Nixon was President. Even the song written about Kelly referred to his antics.

Slide Kelly, Slide
Slide Kelly slide, Your running is a disgrace
Slide Kelly slide, Stay there and hold your base.
If your batting doesn't fail you
They'll take you to Australia.
Slide Kelly, slide.

When A. G. Spalding had a detective follow Kelly, Kelly rebuked the detective's report. "I have to offer only one amendment. In the place where the detective reported me taking a lemonade at 3 AM, he's off. I never drank a lemonade at that hour in my life! It was straight whiskey!" When asked by a crank if he drank during games, Kelly replied, "It depends on the length of the game." *Chicago News* (September 1, 1886)

One night, George Gore and Ned Williamson got Kelly so drunk that he completely passed out. When they told Anson that Kelly was sick, he refused to believe it and told them to go get Kelly. So Gore went to Kelly and suggested he play in disguise. Kelly agreed and shaved off all of his hair. Everyone in Boston still recognized him by his mustache. But they enjoyed the joke and cheered for him on that day.

"'King' Kelly showed up drunk and was taken by the police when he threatened Umpire Jack McQuade." *Boston Globe* (October 2, 1889)

Kelly claimed to have injured his hand in pre-game warm-ups and planned to sit the game out. However, the Cleveland cranks said Kelly was drunk. Kelly went to sit on the Cleveland bench next to the Cleveland manager, and shouted comments such as these at his own teammates: "You never win when I don't play," "Kelly is king," and "I am the king." *Cleveland Plains Dealer* (October 2, 1889)

After a call against the Beaneaters, he charged umpire Jack McQuaid and accused him of robbing Boston. Kelly told McQuaid that "he would give Boston a roasting." McQuaid called a police officer from the stands to remove Kelly. Kelly broke away from the police officer and ran straight for McQuaid. This brought more police "with drawn clubs, making a ridiculous display over one man." *Cleveland Plains Dealer* (October 3, 1889) As Kelly left the park,

King Kelly

he lit a cigarette and then attempted to reenter the grounds, but the gate was locked.

"'King' Kelly played the entire game dressed as an English dude." *Chicago Tribune* (July 11, 1892)

In a Temple Cup game against the Cleveland Spiders, Kelly used his bat to knock the ball out of catcher Chief Zimmer's hand on a steal of second by Tommy McCarthy. He was called out for interference.

In New York, Kelly attended a clambake and then went to the horse races at Morris Park. John Ward suspended him for seven days.

Kelly spent a lot of time at the race track betting on the horses. He even had a favorite horse named Salvatore. Kelly often watched the races at the Sheepshead Bay track. Betting on Salvatore could bring heartache. Although Salvatore was not always a winner, Kelly stuck with his horse. Kelly was given the privilege of starting races, which only required holding a string, but it allowed Kelly to watch from the track level. Kelly's presence at the race brought in the baseball fans.

Teammate Fred Pfeffer spoke of Kelly as the greatest ball player: "He played the umpire as intelligently as he did the opposing nine. He would make a friend of him, engaging his confidence, and in various ways, get the best of close decisions. I have seen him make plays that others never dreamed possible. He plays not by rules or instruction, but by instinct, and to him belonged the degree of perfection, that faculty known as base ball sense. I never knew Kel to hesitate in a close play."

"In 1886, Kelly ran home from the coaching box. St. Louis Browns shortstop Jack Glasscock threw home allowing Tom Burns to be safe at first base. Chicago reported 'it requires considerable nerve to attempt a play like this one.'" *Chicago Tribune* (August 14, 1886)

The Kansas City Cowboys' Pete Conway trotted to second base on a passed ball. However, when he got to second, he made the mistake of asking Kelly if it was a foul ball. Kelly, as usual, lied and said yes. Conway walked back to first, where he was tagged out. Kelly told Conway, "Oh, I thought you asked if it was a passed ball." Kansas City Cowboys captain Dave Rowe argued without result. The duped Conway headed to the bench with his head down.

"Dirty Jack" Doyle told this humorous story about Kelly blocking home plate. In extra innings, the go-ahead run was about to score. Kelly threw his mask to block the runner. He ran to the bench and gathered several bats. He was building a blockade that the runner had to slide into to bust it up. He was easily safe.

On owner Al Spalding's sale of Kelly in 1887 to Boston for $10,000, this letter by Kelly shed more light:

> I cannot understand why you think it necessary to speak of me in such a belittling style whenever you find an opportunity to do so. Certainly you can say that I will play with you next season if the saying gives you any pleasure, and words cost but little, especially to the management of the Chicago club. But I think it altogether unnecessary for you to take pains to lead the public to think I cannot survive without your well known generosity. Again, I fail to see why you think it necessary to always speak unkindly of me. I have always done a man's part for the success of your club. That you have paid me much or little, early or late, in parts or whole, I understand it. It is nobody's concern but our own. I have played ball for you for much less than I could have had anywhere else, but did shirk from knowledge of this fact. I have never taken one advantage of

you, while you have taken advantage of me. This fact could be shown in many ways. I have told you that I would not play ball with you, and I will not.

The wildest thing he did while sitting in the stands as a crank was when the Philadelphia Phillies were playing the Detroit Wolverines. Kelly whistled signals to the Philadelphia hitters. Kelly remarked, "Had I commenced on the start, I would have won the game for the Phillies." *Detroit Free Press* (September 15, 1888) The next day, after players, umpires and press had judged his action as deplorable, Kelly cursed "the official score keeper for exposing him." *Detroit Free Press*

In 1893, Kelly signed with the New York Giants, but he began drinking heavily. Captain "Monte" Ward sent Kelly to a Turkish bath every morning to get him sober. However, King skipped the bath, went to a clambake and bet on the horse races, which resulted in his suspension and eventually his dismissal.

Comment by Kelly:

> Many times I have been asked the question "To what do you ascribe the great popularity of base ball?" This seems to me, can be answered in two words. "The excitement." People go to see games because they love excitement and love to be worked up. That is one reason why I believe in "kicking" now and then on the diamond. It may be all right for newspapers to say that base ball will become more popular when played without kicking. I disagree entirely with those authorities on the subject. Look at the Chicago Base Ball Club. It has been the most successful in the country. Why? One good reason is because they are "chronic kickers" and people flock to see them to witness the sport. You won't find the ordinary man going out to a base ball field when it is 80 degrees in the shade to see two clubs play ball for a couple of hours without a word being said on either side. The people who go to ball games want good playing, with just enough kicking to make things interesting thrown in.

William A. "Big Bill" Lange (Chicago)

Bill Lange irritated his teammates with his constant practical jokes. He was a crank favorite, resulting in plenty of free drinks after home games. He partied hard and was a playboy with the women. Clark Griffith described Lange as "the toughest, roughest base runner who ever strode the bases." At 6'2" and 210 pounds, he would body-block the basemen.

Lange's humor in the clubhouse had grown old by 1895. The players had gone to management about his negative effect on the team. Cap Anson was being criticized for not reeling in Lange. Still, Lange was voted a favorite by cranks, according to the *Chicago Tribune*.

Lange was a hit in Chicago's saloons as well as boudoirs. Lange and Bill Dahlen would miss curfew, miss trains and even miss games. They called themselves the "Dawn Patrol." On May 23, 1897, Lange got into a fight with

Washington Nationals second baseman John O'Brien after he plowed into him.

Umpire Ed Swartwood called a game due to darkness when Lange was at bat. Lange attacked the umpire and pulled his ear. Lange was suspended for this altercation.

Unfortunately, Lange's practical jokes were primarily aimed at Cap Anson. His treatment of Anson had not gone unnoticed, and he was called out by the dirtiest player of the era, John McGraw.

Lange's foolery at a train station after a loss caused Anson to erupt, and Anson called him "a loafer and drunkard." An 11th-place finish resulted in the release of Anson.

Lange left the team to take care of personal business (a race track). This resulted in a suspension by club president James Hart. Hart said, "he shows a lack of regard for the welfare of the club that could not be forgiven." *Chicago Tribune* (November 28, 1898)

Lange retired from baseball in his prime to marry, and then divorced.

Fred Lewis (St. Louis)

Fred Lewis got into a fight with teammate Tony Mullane early in the season. However, on August 30, 1883, Lewis chased their manager, Ted Sullivan, and hit him in the head in a saloon. Lewis and Pat Deasley were totally drunk and were soon arrested by Columbus police officers for disorderly conduct.

The arrests were associated with an altercation with Columbus Buckeyes players (Lewis had been "released by Philadelphia previously for lushing"). After an intoxicated episode on September 15, 1883, Chris Von der Ahe released him. The *St. Louis Globe-Democrat* reported, "he has no one to blame but himself for his downfall."

Tommy McCarthy (Boston) (HOF)

Tommy McCarthy would trap fly balls and pretend it was a catch, with the umpire signaling an out. He pretended to misjudge a fly ball and used his speed for a catch. He would then double up the unsuspecting runner. While playing for the St. Louis Browns, when they failed to take the field in Brooklyn, the fans threw stones and bottles at the players, breaking McCarthy's jaw.

McCarthy and Hugh Duffy purchased a saloon together in Boston. This became a problem when McCarthy started drinking with the patrons. As his beer drinking increased, so did his weight, therefore reducing his speed. He was a constant winner at poker with his teammates.

McCarthy's temper dominated the dugout, with foul language being administered to anyone who made an error. He got into a fight with pitcher Jack Stivetts. *Boston Globe* (May 27, 1892)

His actions became intolerable when he started criticizing manager Frank Selee. McCarthy's contract was sold to Brooklyn in 1895. He would still become a Hall of Fame outfielder, nicknamed with Hugh Duffy as the "Heavenly Twins."

When a batter hit a ball to him, he would simply keep juggling the ball as long as he could while running to the infield. Since the putout did not occur until he took possession, the runners had to hold their bases. This maneuver kept the runner from tagging up on the fly.

McCarthy's inclination to solve every teammate's problems gave management the opinion that he was a malcontent. McCarthy was noted for

Tommy McCarthy

sitting out games due to minor bruises.

McCarthy's loafing on balls and not running on outs for the Brooklyn Bridegrooms, his new team, resulted in the following comment: "It is gradually dawning on the minds of base ball people in general that Brooklyn secured a gold brick with the purchase of Tommy McCarthy." *Brooklyn Eagle* (July 11, 1896)

Charles "Dusty" Miller (Cincinnati)

Louisville's Bill Donovan hit "Dusty" Miller with a pitch. His next at-bat, Miller warned Donovan, "If you hit me I'll make you jump over one of those fences." After the game, Donovan questioned Miller, "Which fence would you have had me jump over?" Miller just smiled. *Cincinnati Commercial Tribune* (June 26, 1898)

Boston's Tommy Tucker hit Miller with a shot to the nose at first base which bloodied Miller's nose. In the same year, Miller kneed Baltimore's Joe Quinn at second base, resulting in an out call.

During the 1895 season, while on base, Miller yelled the name of a Philadelphia outfielder when the fly ball was in the area of second baseman Billy Hallman. Hallman stopped running, and the ball dropped. Miller was criticized by the *Philadelphia Public Ledger* for his dirty play.

Miller inadvertently bumped into Chicago's Clark Griffith, causing him to lose his temper. Griffith threw the ball down and tried to slug Miller. Griffith threw three wicked blows to Miller's neck in a ruffian assault. Griffith's abuse allowed "Germany" Smith to score from first base, since time had not been called. Umpire Bob Emslie did not eject any players. *Cincinnati Enquirer* (April 30, 1895)

While playing for the St. Louis Browns in 1890, Miller was fined $25 for drinking. He had the same problem in 1896, when Buck Ewing fined him $25 for drinking.

Hugh Nicol (Cincinnati)

Nicol was a small player who would back down from dirtier players. Only in 19th century baseball would the following play occur. Cincinnati's "Frank Fennelly stroked a single and advanced on an error. The ball rolled into centerfield, however, Fennelly had lost track of the ball. St. Louis second baseman 'Yank' Robinson made false bluffs about going after the ball while Fennelly simply stood on the base. Cincinnati's third base coach Hugh Nicol ran to second base and told Fennelly the play. Fennelly with Hugh running beside him went to third base safely." *Cincinnati Times-Star* (June 23, 1887)

Boston's Tommy Tucker held Nicol off first base, resulting in his being picked off. He attempted to block Nicol in the ninth inning, but this time Nicol slid cleats-first and Tucker gave Nicol plenty of room. *Cincinnati Times-Star* (August 13, 1889)

While playing outfield for the St. Louis Browns, Nicol hid extra balls under the right field seats. When a fair ball came into that area, he would grab the nearest ball to make a play.

Hugh Nicol cut first base short by ten feet. He was not caught by Umpire Al Bauer.

Lipman "Lip" Pike (St. Louis)

"Lip" Pike ran himself right out of baseball. At Baltimore's Newington Park, Pike raced against a horse named "Clarence." Pike won in ten seconds flat. He played second base but was left-handed, which made it difficult to make the double-play pivot and moved to the outfield. Later in his career, Pike was called up on September 3, 1881, by the Worcester Ruby Legs. While playing center field, he made three errors in the ninth inning. He was accused of throwing the game and was suspended.

At the National League meeting in Saratoga Springs, New York, he was blacklisted from the National League by a unanimous vote of the club presidents. He was reinstated in 1883.

Jimmy Ryan (Chicago)

Jimmy Ryan was a high-spirited player who was often moody. When manager Cap Anson made negative comments about Irish players, Ryan called Anson a "big stiff," which resulted in a shoving match. In 1891, Ryan and others threw a keg of beer out a hotel room window that almost hit Anson. Ryan on several occasions assaulted reporters, which resulted in fines, not suspensions. In 1896, he knocked out a train conductor who was attempting to quiet him.

High class or no class!

Ryan had an expensive ring and pin costing $700 ($14,000 now). This resulted in him carrying a gun to keep from being robbed. He was a very rowdy player, punching *Louisville Courier Journal* reporter Dan Sullivan, *Boston Globe* reporter Charlie Ganziel, the *Cleveland Plains*

Jimmy Ryan

Dealer's Jack O'Connor, and the *Daily News'* George Bechtel, who was beat up harshly. Ryan was not arrested on any of these attacks.

Ryan was not popular with his teammates. He would continually voice his opinion, so when Anson told him to shut up and he failed to do so, Anson fined him $100, which caused Ryan to ask to be released.

He was fined another $10. The *Cincinnati Commercial Gazette* (April 30, 1893) recorded Ryan's comments on Anson: "Why you big fat duffer, what do you know about ball playing? You've got a man at second who can double discount you at playing first. Now, I tell you right now the fine doesn't go with me. If you insist on taking it out of my pay, I'll not go with you to Pittsburg, but will board the first train to Chicago. I'll run my little German saloon before you'll do me in this style. This spring I forced you to come to my terms, and now I can get along without a position on the Chicago Club."

When Ryan hit a single, he would walk to first base, resulting in boos from the cranks.

Ryan's drinking was another problem. On July 22, 1894, he played only one inning in St. Louis because he was drunk.

Anson fined Ryan for walking to first base on a ground out. Anson stated, "I repeatedly fined Ryan, but those fines did little good." Ryan's reply was, "It is lucky you think so well of your position. For if you lay your hands on me you big stiff, I will shoot you full of holes." Ryan was released to St. Louis, where he became Charlie Comiskey's problem.

Tip O'Neill, a star player for St. Louis, rebuked Ryan for not sliding. Ryan used every curse word in the book in responding to O'Neill. O'Neill did not say anything but stood in left field without moving. Ryan was chasing balls all over left field. Comiskey did not even chastise his left fielder.

Ryan criticized Comiskey's managerial style by saying "He is afraid of hurting your feelings." Ryan returned to Chicago, but said he "would not again under the same conditions."

Anson accused Ryan of "playing poorly in a bid to get him fired." Ryan was made the team captain to replace Anson, but he was unpopular with the other players. The players threatened a strike, and Ryan was released.

Jimmy Sheckard (Brooklyn)

Jimmy Sheckard was known for his horseplay. He once threw his glove in the stands after a teammate's error. He retrieved his glove. The pitcher yelled for him to take his position. Instead, Sheckard stayed at the left field foul line. The pitcher delivered the pitch, which was a line shot from Fred Clarke right at Sheckard. He caught the ball and claimed that play made him a better fielder from that day forward.

Sheckard got into a fight with teammate Heinie Zimmerman, who threw a bottle of ammonia, hitting Sheckard in the eye. This incident caused him to lose eyesight in his left eye.

Elmer Smith (Pittsburg)

On July 20, 1894, Pittsburg Pirate's left fielder Elmer "Mike" Smith chased Cincinnati's Germany Smith's ball that bounced into the stands. When Mike attempted to get the ball, he was confronted by a Reds crank who had a gun. Mike decided the ball could stay, and Germany scored the winning run.

Mike Smith spiked the rowdy Cincinnati third baseman, Arlie Latham. Smith told the *Cincinnati Post* (May 1, 1895) his side of the story: "Latham stood right in my path, but at that he would not have hurt had he not toppled over backward and struck his leg on my spikes."

The *Baltimore Herald* (June 4, 1896) reported that "Pittsburg's Elmer Smith threw the base ball over the grandstand without the umpire seeing him. A new one was put into play."

The *Cincinnati Enquirer* (January 29, 1898) said, "Pittsburg's Elmer Smith boiled meat bones and used the bones to scrape his bat. He thought it would make the bat harder."

Louis Sockalexis (Cleveland)

Louis Sockalexis was the first Native American Indian to burst on the scene with high potential as a hitter and a speedy base runner. He was so popular in 1897 that a three-foot-tall wooden Indian was placed at the entrance to the Cleveland Spiders' stadium.

However, by 1898, Sockalexis was drunk more days than he played. He was so drunk that he missed the team's train home. He wired club president Frank Robison for ticket money. When Sockalexis received the wired money, he spent it on alcohol.

On May 15, 1899, Sockalexis was fined in Cleveland for public intoxication, causing him to be released by the Spiders.

Billy Sunday (Chicago)

Sunday did not drink. The *Chicago Mail* (September 6, 1887) reported that "Sunday is the good boy both on and off the field. His only vice is smoking." He would get on umpires, but it was not considered wrong. He said about umpire Charley Fulmer, "We had to fight hard for the pennant. Fulmer's umpiring at Philadelphia was the worst I ever saw. He robbed us of two games and he gave us the worst of every decision." *Chicago Herald* (October 12, 1886)

In the 1885 World Series, "After a call by Umpire Bill McLean against Billy Sunday he went to McLean with his fist clenched in order to strike up. Only 'King' Kelly's interference prevented a melee." *St. Louis Republican* (October 18, 1885)

King Kelly said, "Sunday is all heels and no head." Kelly felt Sunday was the fastest player in the league but could not hit. Fred Pfeffer said he "could not catch anything and no more judgment on balls than an umpire." Cap Anson said, "Sunday's throws seemed to gain in weight as they sailed through the air and were heavy and soggy when they hit your hands."

In 1888, he was released by Anson and picked up by Pittsburg. "While coaching he shouted to hitter Bill Kuehne, 'if you strike out, Billy, run it out.' The cranks roared with laughter. Umpire Valentine cautioned him about 'coaching' the batter." What? *Pittsburg Chronicle Telegraph* (May 17, 1888)

Sunday felt Ed Williamson was a bad apple, saying "As for Williamson, I would not trust him out of my sight."

In 1887 "Billy Sunday was on third base with pitcher Ed Morris pitching. 'King' Kelly the third base coach broke for home. Morris threw to home and catcher Fred Carroll held the ball. John Clarkson was able to walk from first base to second." *Pittsburg Commercial Gazette* (September 25, 1886)

Mike Tiernan (New York)

Tiernan was a tough, no-nonsense player. When Pittsburg's third baseman, Billy Clingman, stood in his way, he bulldozed Clingman with such force that he broke his collarbone. *Pittsburg Press* (July 28, 1895)

In the ninth inning with the score tied, the New York Giants needed a run against the Boston Beaneaters. "Giants Mike Tiernan asked Jim O'Rourke to stand in the left handed batter box. Mike quickly stole second base and O'Rourke knocked a single to score Tiernan with the winning run." *Boston Herald* (July 25, 1888)

The *Cleveland Leader* (September 13, 1893) reported that "New York Giants Mike Tiernan cut first base short by ten feet to record a double. Umpire Bob Emslie was not looking. Tiernan would score the go-ahead run in a 5–4 win for the Giants over the Cleveland Spiders."

George "Rip" Van Haltren (New York)

Van Haltren began his career as a left-handed pitcher, but soon found his place in left field. He was always a disgruntled player and a problem for his manager. His tricks on the base paths made him a crank favorite.

However, his claim to fame was "Rip's Stealing Home as a Coach" on July 31, 1897, while coaching third for the Giants. The Brooklyn catcher turned his back to argue with the umpire without asking for time. Van Haltren dashed from the coaching box to home plate. The pitcher yelled and fired the ball, thinking Van Haltren was trying to steal. The catcher missed the ball, and the runner who had been on second ran all the way home to score. This was called the dirtiest play of the year.

Curt Welch (St. Louis)

When he started with the St. Louis Browns, Curt Welch already had a reputation as a hard drinker. He proved to be a speedy outfielder and was best known for stealing home with the 1886 World Series-winning run. (It was called the "$15,000 slide" because of the earnings for the Browns.)

Welch was known for keeping a case of cold beer behind the billboard in the outfield. Occasionally, he would sneak a drink between innings. Due to either his temper or the alcohol he had consumed, Welch attacked Philadelphia pitcher Gus Weyhing and spouted foul language as he blasted him. The Athletics' management sought an assault charge, resulting in a $400 fine. A drunken Welch hit umpire John Kelly at a train station and accused him of betting on the Giants. He was fined $200.

Welch almost caused a riot in Baltimore when he ran over second baseman Bill Greenwood in an attempt to steal. Welch was arrested after the game by the Baltimore police. It cost $200 to bail him out. Tip O'Neill, Comiskey's discipline enforcer, allowed a bat to slip and strike Welch, in the on-deck-circle, in the face.

Manager Comiskey suspended Welch for "boozing" in 1892.

Walt Wilmot (Chicago)

Wilmot's nickname should have been "Cutter." While playing for Chicago against Cleveland, he was arrested for playing baseball on Sunday. He represented the whole team, and each player was fined $3. Their lawyer appealed the case and won.

Wilmot was noted for his speed and used it to cut third base short. Umpire Bob Emslie missed his play as he scored the winning run. *The Chicago Times* reported the play on May 23, 1894. Wilmot was listed as one of the top five at this trick.

In 1895, he was caught in the club house with the game ball in his possession after the game. Umpire Fred Jevne made Wilmot give up the ball.

When discussing his injury with Cap Anson, the *Cincinnati Enquirer* (May 26, 1889) reported this conversation:

WALT: My knee is sore. I would like to lay off today.

ANSON: You go in, Walter.

WALT: My back is stiff.

ANSON: My leg is just as sore, it will be sore tomorrow as it is today. I am going to work the same. As Manager, I could excuse myself.

His words were met with silence.

In 1893, Wilmot was sulking as he took his place at third base. Anson commented, "You can hand in your resignation when you feel like it."

"In 1894, Walt hit a crow with a thrown ball. Anson told Wilmot to put the bird in the bat bag for a mascot." *Brooklyn Eagle* (August 16, 1894)

6

Unruly Umpires

General

From 1876 to 1898, there existed only one umpire for a game. Low pay and abuse from cranks resulted in a high turnover. The umpire needed full body armor to protect him from being assaulted with balls, bats, beer mugs, umbrellas and any other handy objects. Most of the umpires stood behind home plate to make calls they could barely see, as well as plays they did not see. The antics of the players were impossible to stop and often made the umpire a laughingstock. The man in the blue blazer was responsible for maintaining order. Without these men, we would not have baseball today.

Unfortunately, umpire abuse became a source of entertainment to the cranks. It was called "kicking," which meant browbeating and intimidating to gain an advantage in the game. No other era can compare to the physical tactics used, some of which would now be considered criminal.

The call most disliked by the cranks was calling games due to darkness, which in some instances resulted in tie games. The cranks felt they had been cheated when paying for a game called due to darkness.

Only 40 percent of the umpires lasted beyond one year. The high turnover prevented stability and promoted greater testing of a "rookie" umpire.

This interesting play demonstrates how wacky umpiring was in its early days. The lone umpire was John Egan. The Providence second baseman touched the runner, Cincinnati's "Buttercup" Dickerson. However, the umpire did not see the play, so he asked Providence Grays first baseman Tim Murnane, who made the out call.

Arlie Latham, in *Sporting Life* (September 6, 1899), said the following about Wilbert Robinson trying to influence an umpire. "When a poor inoffensive and well-meaning umpire appears in Baltimore, 'Robbie' meets him at the plate, shakes hands with him and remarks 'I'm glad you came over. They tell me you're doing a great work out west, glad you're here. These are pretty tough games, old man and that other fellow we had here was a little to the bad.... You want to watch this pitcher we're trying today. Great lad. Keep your eyes on the outside corner. We get lots of them on the edge and the other fellow missed a lot of them."

There was no coaching box, so the first base coach (a player) could wander where he chose. Along came Arlie Latham, a comic, acrobatic player, who would stand next to the batter and do cartwheels and flips down the first base line. He was constantly shouting at the pitcher in a blind rage. He became a crowd pleaser, even at road games.

Rule 7 in 1886 established a coaches' box which was 75' from home plate. Wandering outside the line resulted in a $5 fine. The *National Police Gazette* (June 26, 1886) attributed the rule change to Latham saying, "Latham has not been heard from since the American Association tied his tongue to his toes."

Latham still did his little dances in the box, along with his comic remarks that kept the cranks laughing. Some umpires resorted to fining coaches who spoke to anyone other than the batter.

Anonymous Umpires

No Leaving the Game: On August 5, 1884, Tom Lynch was pitching for the Chicago White Stockings. In the eighth inning, he experienced a cramp in his pitching arm. The umpire would not allow Lynch to leave the game, so Cap Anson came in to pitch. The White Stockings lost the game, and Lynch would not pitch in the major leagues again.

Home Run or Not: At an 1884 game between the Philadelphia Athletics and the St. Louis Browns, St. Louis captain Charlie Comiskey failed to go over the rules prior to the game on balls hit over the fence. Harry Stovey of the Athletics hit a ball over the right field fence. The St. Louis owner, Chris Von der Ahe, jumped on the field to intervene. Von der Ahe addressed the umpire as follows: "Look here, Mr. Umpire, vot's knocked in knocked. Vot's over de fence is over. Go ahead mit der game." The confused umpire ruled a double. The fence in right field was short, therefore it was only a double.

No Room: Chicago's West Side Grounds added 10,000 seats inside the outfield fence for their crucial game with the New York Giants on September 29, 1885. The umpire ruled before the game that any ball hit into the seats would be a triple.

Not Enough Players: On September 12, 1888, the New York Giants forfeited a game in the sixth inning when Buck Ewing was injured and no substitute was available.

Who's on What Base: On June 27, 1893, the Brooklyn Bridegrooms were playing the Chicago Colts. Brooklyn's Oyster Burns was on second base and Con Daily was on third base. Dan Brouthers hit the ball up the middle to Chicago shortstop Bill Dahlen. Dahlen threw the ball to catcher Malachi Kittridge. Daily, running home for an unknown reason, retreated and ran back to third, which was now occupied by Burns. So Daily continued to run to second base. Malachi could not catch Daily, so the confused umpire yelled "safe." When Cap Anson came to argue the play with his loud tone, the umpire reversed the call to out.

No Time Out: On May 8, 1896, Bill Nash of the Philadelphia Athletics argued with the umpire about a called strike two. While he remained in the batter's box, the Chicago Colts' quick-thinking pitcher, Clark Griffith, threw a pitch, striking Nash's bat. The ball rolled to Griffith, who started a double play. Nash exploded at the correct call and was ejected. In addition, he was fined $25.

Different Ball: The New York Giants were playing an exhibition game against the Washington Nationals of the American Association. *Sporting Life* (May 6, 1885) reported Jim O'Rourke of the Giants switched a dead ball into the game in the first inning. The next batter noted the change and alerted the umpire. After a half-hour of wrangling, the umpire threw the ball out. The Nationals cancelled the next game.

Cut Ball: "Blondie" Purcell was fined on April 24, 1885, for cutting the ball. The umpire did not issue the fine but New York Mutuals manager Jim Mutrie fined his pitcher $100, a very high fine.

Forgot to Touch First Base: On August 26, 1889, Boston's Dickie Johnston hit a game-winning single, scoring King Kelly. In the excitement, Johnston failed to touch first base. Philadelphia Phillies outfielder Ed Delahanty threw the ball in to the Boston bench. Phillies first baseman Sid Farrar noticed the miscue and headed for the Boston bench. But the ever-present Kelly grabbed the ball. Kelly and Farrar wrestled for the ball with the Philadelphia cranks yelling their lungs out. By now the two umpires had left the field. The Phillies protested the game to no avail.

George "Ed" Andrews

Andrews was attempting to umpire with veteran umpire Jim Gaffney on April 28, 1899. Baltimore Orioles captain John McGraw was protesting to have the game called due to darkness with Baltimore up, 12–11. The tactic worked as Brooklyn players surrounded Andrews. Then the Brooklyn cranks jumped on the field, and Andrews forfeited the game to Baltimore.

Al Barker

In 1881, King Kelly of the Chicago White Stockings ran from second base to home plate without going within 20 feet of third base. Umpire Al Barker was watching first base and "refused to call Kelly out."

William Betts

Betts was an umpire who was often attacked. Denny Lyons (Pittsburg Pirates) was a runner on third base when he asked Boston Beaneaters pitcher Ted Lewis to let him see the ball. Lewis tossed it, and Lyons stepped aside, then ran home and scored. Umpire William Betts upheld the play. *Boston Globe* (July 10, 1896)

The *Baltimore Sun* (July 11, 1896) reported that Betts was hit by John McGraw in a tender spot by a thrown ball. He fined McGraw $5.

The *Baltimore American and Commercial Advertiser* (July 22, 1896) reported "a dispute between Baltimore Orioles Steve Brodie over a third strike call. He walked away, then turned and grabbed Betts and shook him. Betts ejected and fined Brodie $25."

"Louisville was beating Baltimore 6–5. Louisville's Honus Wagner rubbed dirt all over the ball. Umpire Betts caught the play and put a new ball in the game. However, Louisville Colonels pitcher Bert Cunningham would have no part of the new ball and threw it to the bench. Cunningham stomped off the mound and refused to pitch. The umpire ejected Cunningham. 'Deacon' Phillippe finished the inning without giving up a run." *Baltimore Herald* (September 15, 1899)

One humorous story occurred (August 1894) when the Chicago Colts' Jimmy Ryan was batting. Betts had just called strike two when the first base coach, Willie Hutchinson, complained about the pitch. Ryan shouted to Hutchinson, "The ball was right over the plate." All the cranks roared with laughter that Ryan would agree with the umpire!

George "Foghorn" Bradley

Bradley was nicknamed "Foghorn" for his deep voice. On August 18, 1882, he was umpiring a game between the Detroit Wolverines and the Providence Grays. The game went into extra innings. In the 15th inning, George Wright hit a ball that went through an open gate in the outfield fence. Detroit's left fielder, George Wood, ran through the gate, retrieved the ball and fired it into the infield. The infielder threw to the catcher, who tagged Wright out.

(The correct call was a ground-rule triple.) The missed call did not affect the outcome as the Grays won, 1–0, in the 18th.

Bradley was umpiring in the American Association in 1886 when St. Louis captain Charles Comiskey complained that the Philadelphia field had too much sand. The umpire ordered the groundskeeper to use wheelbarrows to remove the excess sand. One wheelbarrow-full had been used on first base alone. The game was delayed for 15 minutes.

Later in 1886, Bradley was hit by a beer mug thrown by a crank in Cincinnati. He left the field and hid in the clubhouse. He eventually returned to complete the game.

George "Watch" Burnham

Burnham is most noted for one game he umpired in 1889. The umpire was required to have a watch. He didn't have one for a game in Baltimore. He asked to borrow one from the clubhouse attendant. Burnham put the watch in his pocket and proceeded to umpire the game. In the fifth inning, he called Joe Kelley out at second base. Kelley had a short temper and began to curse Burnham. Burnham replied, "Now for saying that, you're out of the game." Kelley continued his kicking to Burnham. Burnham reached into his pocket for the watch and said, "I am giving you one minute to get off the field." Kelley slapped the watch out of his hand and stepped on it. Burnham said, "Mr. Kelley, that will cost you $25 and the watch will cost you $100." Kelly replied, "I will pay the $25, but you're crazy if you think I'll pay no more than $3 for that watch of yours." Burnham exclaimed, "It's not my watch, it's yours." After the incident, Burnham was given the nickname "Watch."

Later in 1889, he was the first umpire to use spikes.

Burnham was umpiring at Boston in a game against his former team, the Chicago White Stockings. King Kelly scored a run but missed home plate, which Umpire Burnham noticed. The *Chicago Herald* (May 31, 1889) reported "that Kelly diverted attention from himself by complaining that White Stockings third baseman Tom Burns had attempted to stop him at third. Pitcher Gus Krock was standing on home plate with the ball in hand, but he looked to see what Burns had done. When he turned his eyes, Kelly strolled back to the plate and touched it with his foot saving the run. Umpire Burnham smiled and the cranks roared their approval."

Cap Anson caught Kid Gleason applying tobacco juice to the ball and alerted Burnham, who promptly put in a beat-up ball that prompted Anson to go "into a seizure."

The *Cincinnati Enquirer* (May 30, 1897) reported, "George 'Watch' Burnham stated that 'People in the stands have no idea of the bombardment of slurs and exasperating remarks that players make at the expense of the umpires.'"

John Burns

Burns was an umpire who wanted the game to come to him. He allowed a ball hit by Pittsburg's Jack McCarthy to go through a door in the outfield, and then a crank shut the door. He ruled a home run, but the National League ordered the game to be replayed. The game occurred in April 1884.

"Fatty" Briody, catcher of the Providence Grays, described Burns umpiring on May 2, 1884, by saying, "Well, he is a daisy. He dodged away from the ball and failed to see it squarely. It would make a stone statue weep. Burns complained to pitcher 'Hoss' Radbourn, 'If you wouldn't curve 'em so much, I'd give you more strikes.'"

The Grays were playing the Cleveland Blues on May 8, 1884, when it began to rain. Providence was ahead, 7–0, in the fourth inning. Cleveland's players wanted Burns to call the game. Blues manager Charlie Hackett had his players pack their bats. Burns motioned for the game to resume. The Cleveland club hurried back through the exit gates. The clouds opened up, and the rain came down. Burns finally called the game.

The *Sunday Morning Telegram* referred to Burns' umpiring by saying, "It isn't impossible that he had admirers outside of the deaf, dumb and blind." He was released in August.

Tom Burns

Tom Burns was known as the "hobo" umpire. In his debut in 1892, he wore a torn blue coat, checkered shirt, and striped pants. The *Louisville Commercial* (August 26, 1892) said, "Burns called the game in a very-lady fashion, his soft, mellow decisions not being heard 20 feet away." He umpired only in 1892.

L. W. Burtis

He was one of the original National League umpires in 1876. Warren Burtis was accused of brokering a fix of St. Louis Browns Stockings games. In 1877, Burtis had been seen dining with Chicago gambler Mike McDonald. It was believed that he was betting on games and then making calls to influence the outcome. Burtis, though not proven guilty, was released at the conclusion of the season.

Albert John "Doc" Bushong, D.D.S. (Sub Umpire)

Doc Bushong gave up being a dentist to be a catcher without a mask. Was this ironic? He was a substitute catcher for the Brooklyn Bridegrooms when he was called on to umpire after none of the three listed umpires were available. Brooklyn owner Charlie Byrne had provided a list. The three names on the list were all found in a local graveyard. Kansas City Cowboys manager Bill Watkins accepted Bushong to umpire. The game was played without disputes. The score was Brooklyn 14, Kansas City 4. This occurred in August 1889.

Billy Carpenter

He umpired a "Ladies Day Game" in Washington, D.C., in 1897. A large crowd of ladies had gathered to watch handsome Nationals pitcher "Win" Mercer. Mercer was pitching great until the fifth inning, when he walked a batter on what he considered strikes. His temper got the better of him and he exploded with curse words at the umpire. Carpenter quickly threw up his right hand to eject Mercer. Then the ladies stopped being ladies and jumped on the field to attack the umpire. Carpenter ran for the clubhouse. The ladies even tore the seats off. Carpenter resigned at the season's end.

Frank Caughey

Frank Caughey was a one-game blunder of an umpire. He was a rookie umpire who worked at a spring training game in Savannah, Georgia. Orioles John McGraw and Wilbert Robinson had his clothes trunk refused by the steamship agent when he attempted to leave. The next day, he was turned back again and returned to the hotel. Robinson spoke to the railroad agent, where he met the same fate. Fed up, Caughey picked a different destination and resigned as a National League umpire without ever umpiring an official game.

Tommy Connolly (HOF)

Umpire Tommy Connolly had a long and illustrious career. He began late in the 19th century. When Connolly called Jack Dunn out at first base, Joe McGinnity left the Orioles' coaches' box, stomped on Connolly's toes and spat tobacco juice in his face. Mike Donlin (Orioles) and Kid Elberfeld

(Detroit) got into a fight. The police attempted to arrest Elberfeld, who tried to get in the way. McGinnity was also arrested, so Connolly declared the game a forfeit to Detroit. Connolly received a mounted police escort from the field.

Years later, New York Highlanders manager Clark Griffith attempted a stalling tactic that was detected by Connolly, so he called a forfeit. The cranks responded with cries of "Kill the Ump."

Umpire Connolly kicked Jesse "Crab" Burkett out of a game when he attacked Tom Loftus on the Senators' bench. Both players were suspended for five games.

John "Red" Connelly

Connelly was one of the smarter umpires of the era. "Umpire John M. Connelly caught a stupid play by Chicago's third baseman Tom Burns. The game came to the ninth inning. Burns' single brought in the winning run. But, Burns thought the ball had been caught, so he did not run to first base. The game ended in a 7–7 tie due to darkness." *Chicago Tribune* (April 8, 1886)

"Umpire John Connelly caught a trick of Chicago's 'King' Kelly where he snapped a rubber band on his glove before the batter swung to throw them off. Connelly stopped Kelly from using the trick." *St. Louis Post Dispatch* (September 16, 1888)

Wes Curry

Umpire Wes Curry moved back and forth between both major leagues. The *Chicago Times* (September 16, 1885) reported that Chicago White Stockings pitcher Jim McCormick "became so angry at Umpire Curry changing the game ball, he vented his spleen in a most blackguardly fashion by trying to hit Boston's John Morrill, the batter. After McCormick threw four pitches directly at Morrill, Curry awarded Morrill a walk, even though the rule requires six balls were needed for one."

On July 9, 1887, Brooklyn took a 4–2 lead over Louisville. The Colonels loaded the bases. Reddy Mack scored on a single but remained at the plate. He saw that the second runner was going to be tagged out and jolted catcher Bob Clark, allowing the runner to score. Mack and Clark started wrestling on the ground. Curry declared the second runner, Deacon White, out and charged Mack with obstruction, even though there was no rule that covered the play. Curry's decision resulted in a new rule in 1888.

Sporting Life (June 19, 1889) reported that after a bad call by Curry, "Kelly stood on his hands waving his feet in air while in right field. He then got on all fours and brayed like a mule."

While playing third base, Cleveland manager Patsy Tebeau pushed Walt Wilmot off the base and tagged him. Curry called Wilmot out, saying he saw only the tag. The *New York Clipper* (August 3, 1889) said that "Curry noticed the interference but did not consider it."

In 1889, Curry sent King Kelly back from third to second base after he knocked Pittsburg's third baseman Bill Kuehne to the ground.

The *Baltimore Herald* (July 10, 1889), said, "Boston's 'Kid' Madden advanced to third on a balk. Cleveland third baseman 'Patsy' Tebeau with the ball motioned to Madden to come to the plate, implying that Umpire Wes Curry had ruled such. Madden declined the invitation. Tebeau had attempted to trick Madden so he could be tagged out."

Charley Cushman

He umpired two seasons 13 years apart but was noted for his incompetence. The *Philadelphia Times* (May 19, 1885) said that "Philadelphia second baseman Al Myer was held by Chicago White Stockings 'King' Kelly to prevent a double play. Further, Stockings third sacker Ned Williamson threw his arm around Jimmy Fogarty to keep Myer from scoring. Umpire Charley Cushman was oblivious to either play saying after the game, 'I saw nothing.'"

John Dailey

Dailey was an umpire who felt the dangers of the profession. On April 24, 1884, the Providence Grays (NL) came to play the Brooklyn Trolley Dodgers (AA). Dailey was noted as a hometown umpire. Providence manager Frank Bancroft stated, "I feared there would be unpleasantness if he is allowed to umpire."

Dailey started calling balks whenever Providence pitcher Charlie Sweeney brought his arms over his head, so Bancroft urged Sweeney to throw underhanded. However, this delivery resulted in Sweeney having shoulder problems. Bancroft sent Sweeney to right field and brought in Shorty Radford, who quickly gave up eight runs. Meanwhile Brooklyn pitcher Adonis Terry was clearly throwing overhand. (American Association rules still requiring an underhanded delivery.)

Bancroft went into the stands to seek out Brooklyn part-owner Joe Doyle about the umpire's unfairness. Instead, Doyle cursed Bancroft out. Providence captain Joe Start was pleading for another umpire for the last inning. A crank yelled, "Five minutes are up." Doyle ordered Dailey to award the game to Brooklyn. Daily cried, "Play!" The Grays did not go on the field, and the game was forfeited to Brooklyn. Brooklyn refused to pay the $100 guarantee to Providence, but Dailey received his $25.

He was an umpire in the National League in 1884 when a foul ball caught him in the face. The *Brooklyn Eagle* reported the "ball almost drove the side of his face in." His jaw was broken in two places. He was given a liquid diet for a month. The low pay was not worth the dangers of umpiring, he decided.

Charlie Daniels

Daniels had a 12-year career as a major league umpire. Early in the 1883 season, St. Louis owner Chris Von der Ahe was so upset that umpire John Kelly was playing poker with the Louisville team players that he refused to let Kelly umpire the next game. He wired that he wanted Charlie Daniels for the next game. The last train for St. Louis had already left, so he hired a "special train" for $300 to get Daniels to the next game.

The Philadelphia Athletics were leading the St. Louis Browns, 13–8, when the rain began to pour. Daniels called the game due to rain. However, Von der Ahe protested to Daniels and ordered the game resumed. The teams went back on the field, but the rain was so hard the umpire could not determine when the ball was being caught. Daniels simply called any fly an out. The final score was Philadelphia 13, St. Louis 11.

On May 3, 1883, Daniels was at the park but was too sick to umpire. The Pittsburg Alleghenys wanted to play the game to get their portion of the gate receipts. Both team captains had to agree that the game was a "championship contest." If not, it would be an exhibition game and all revenue would be retained by Philadelphia. Two cranks from the stands were selected, and Pittsburg won, 15–2.

Daniels was involved in a delay trick pulled off by the Cincinnati Reds on July 21, 1883. Third baseman Hick Carpenter had missed the train and was late for the game. The Reds had only nine players. The Reds' Chick Fulmer pretended he had cramps, and his head was damp when Daniels came to check on him. Even the Columbus players thought he had the "Egyptian plague." He was given ginger as a remedy. When Carpenter arrived wearing his uniform, Fulmer jumped up, declaring that eating ginger had worked and yelling, "Well, dog my buttons." Daniels declared after the game that Fulmer had really been sick.

In 1884, the Cincinnati Reds led the St. Louis Browns, 13–1, after eight innings. Daniels correctly called the game due to darkness. However, the St. Louis cranks were rowdy and would not tolerate a called game. They threw objects and cursed Daniels. The umpire allowed the game to continue, but the Reds still won.

In 1885, St. Louis' Arlie Latham began screaming in pain and ran in circles and across the field before finally ending up in the coaches' boxes. Daniels went to inquire about his problem. Latham responded, "Oh, nothing, my foot went to sleep."

In 1888, the New York Giants squared off against the Boston Beaneaters. When a foul ball was hit back out of the stadium, New York attempted to send in weaker practice balls in a box. Daniels noticed the seal was broken and sent the balls back for correct ones.

On October 13, 1888, Chicago's Cap Anson and his team were at the hotel when it started to rain. The rain stopped at 3:30, and Anson felt the game would be called. However, the Philadelphia Phillies park was playable according to Daniels. There were 1,500 cranks in the park. Therefore, Daniels forfeited the game to Philadelphia.

After the Philadelphia Athletics won the 1893 pennant of the American Association, they picked up umpires Charlie Daniels and John Kelly for the victory "celebration parade." For one of the few times in early baseball, the umpires were cheered. About 20,000 people lined the streets of Philadelphia.

Jim "Jumbo" Davis

On July 6, 1891, the Boston Beaneaters went to Sportsman's Park for an exhibition game against the St. Louis Browns. Davis was blocked at third by Billy Joyce, but umpire Jim Davis saw the trick and ruled him safe. Then King Kelly cut third short by six feet and was called out. Captain Kelly went behind the umpire and shouted obscenities. Davis fined him $25.

The *Brooklyn Eagle* (July 6, 1891) stated that "Kelly went into a rage. 'Fire away, make it $100, it's all the same to me.' 'Get out of the game,' shouted Davis. 'If I go, my men go too' and he called them off the field." The president of the St. Louis club, Chris Von der Ahe, got Kelly to return his team to the field to prevent a refund. Kelly challenged Davis to remain after the game to have it out. The cranks hissed Jumbo for five minutes."

Stewart Decker

Umpire Stewart Decker was just incompetent. In a July 2, 1883, game, Decker was chided by the Boston Beaneaters and Providence Grays. The *Providence Press* (July 3, 1883) said, "Stewart's bum judgment on balls and strikes was enough to make an angel weep. He required police protection as he left to a chorus of jeers."

Rule 30 defined a hit batter as a dead ball. Decker was calling a game between the Detroit Wolverines and the Chicago White Stockings. Chief Zimmer of Detroit was hit while swinging at a pitch. Cap Anson argued that Stump Wiedman, who stole second on the play, should be returned to first base. Decker, based on the rule, called a dead ball and said Wiedman could not advance. (The swing at the pitch was ignored.)

Other newspaper comments on Decker's umpiring were as follow:

- *New York Herald* (July 13, 1883): On calling a man out at home when runner was five feet away. If there is an incompetent umpire on the league staff, vhis name is Decker.
- *Cleveland Leader* (June 5, 1883): A bare-faced robber of that burlesque of umpires Decker.
- *Chicago Tribune* (May 3, 1883): He is not a bad umpire; oh no—he is just miserable, that's all. Decker ought to write a book about what he knows about umpiring—it would take a second—and then go and jump into the lake.

In a game that Hoss Radbourn hurled on July 16, Decker put sawdust along the front of the box line. Radbourn walked to the plate and threw the ball down. Decker, for spite, would not call any pitch a strike. Radbourn stomped off to the dressing room.

The Cincinnati Reds' Jack Glasscock pushed Boston's King Kelly off base and tagged him. Decker called Kelly out, to all the cranks' surprise. The *Chicago Tribune* reported, "Decker is demonstrating how many different kinds of idiot it is possible to be."

In 1884, Chicago's George Gore grabbed Buffalo's Hardy Richardson to prevent a double play. Decker ruled interference. Cap Anson was not satisfied and continued kicking the call until Decker awarded a forfeit to Buffalo.

Decker is remembered for his remark on home runs: "my jurisdiction doesn't extend to balls hit over the fence."

Dan Devinney

Devinney was an umpire who could be called honest. The *New York Times* (August 6, 1877) reported that

Umpire Dan Devinney was approached by St. Louis Browns' Manager George McManus and asked to come to his Louisville hotel room. I declined and met him in the lobby. He treated me to a cigar and wanted to give me $250 if I would throw two games with Louisville. If I would do the same two games later he would give me an extra $400. I will give $50 on the grounds and the rest at the hotel. The Louisville people have treated me so kindly that I don't have the heart to give them away, although to a poor man, the temptation in the shape of so much money was very great.

The National League rule called for a home team to submit three umpires' names for each game. The visiting team drew the name from a hat. On June 6, 1877, Chicago's Cal McVey picked out a slip with Devinney's name. McVey grabbed the hat and discovered all the slips had Devinney's name. The White Stockings demanded and received a new umpire for their game on August 6, 1877.

Francis "Red" Donahue

What had he got himself into! "On August 1, 1897, when the assigned umpire failed to show, the captains decided 'Red' would be the substitute umpire. Louisville was ahead 5 to 4 with St. Louis batting in the bottom of the ninth. Sub-umpire 'Red' provided a new ball to Louisville pitcher Bert Cunningham. Cunningham threw the ball down into the dirt. Donahue delivered another new ball and got the same result. Five additional balls received the same results. Cunningham's stubbornness cost his team a victory when Donahue awarded St. Louis a forfeit. The forfeit was upheld by the League office." *Louisville Commercial* (August 2, 1897)

Herm Doscher

Doscher was a colorful umpire. The *Cleveland Herald* (May 2, 1881) reported that on Opening Day in Chicago, "the Blues were in a tie game going into ninth inning. White Stockings' Abner Dalrymple ran directly into Cleveland's shortstop Jack Glasscock preventing him from catching a pop-up. The play allowed the winning runs to score. Umpire Herm Doscher stood in his place without uttering a word."

Several days later, Cleveland's Mike McGeary attempted to trip the elusive King Kelly, to no avail. Doscher saw the play and this time fined McGeary $10 for his effort.

The *New York Times* (March 6, 1883) quoted Doscher saying, "I got to play ring master, school teacher, pop, mom and doctor in every game."

Umpiring in 1887, Doscher caught Philadelphia's Charlie Bastian grabbing Boston's second baseman, King Kelly by the arm, preventing a double play. Doscher called Bastian for interference.

In 1888, Cleveland Blues manager Tom Loftus threw Doscher a beat-up ball when the previous game ball was lost. Doscher, not one for wasting time, allowed the beat-up ball to be used, to Louisville's disgust.

On August 22, 1888, Baltimore's manager, Billy Barnie, called Doscher a "stinker" in the *Baltimore Sun*. Barnie was fined $100 by the league.

On September 22, 1890, Doscher ejected Rochester's Sandy Griffin in the ninth inning. Griffin refused to leave the field, and the game was ruled a forfeit. St. Louis was winning, 10–3.

Pat Dutton

Dutton's only record of umpiring was on his first and only game in which he was knocked out. On September 8, 1884, in the fourth inning, Dutton was knocked unconscious by a foul tip off the bat of Cincinnati's Jack Glasscock. Dr. Frantz, who was attending the game, came immediately from the stands. He recognized that a broken jaw bone was preventing Dutton from breathing. Dr. Frantz moved the bone back in place, and Dutton was able to breathe freely. The game was discontinued. Dutton was not wearing a mask and did not umpire again.

Ben Ellis

This umpire did not have a clue about the game. In 1876, he correctly ruled that Boston Red "Cap" George Wright's catch with his "Cap" was a dead ball. When umpiring the next day, the cranks were ready to harm Umpire Ellis. The cranks yelled "dirty ball" and "Yankee trick." A close play at a base was an obvious call, but would bring all the fury of the cranks. His call was "that nobody's out and batsman must resume his play at bat as though nothing had happened." (In other words, "replay the bat as if nothing had happened.") Four policemen were used to escort Ellis from the field. He was released for incompetence.

Bob "Wig" Emslie

Bob Emslie commented on umpiring in the 19th century by saying, "Tempers rise with the mercury, which turns the northeast into a blast furnace. Hot weather makes players and spectators turn ugly. They take the life out of the umpires and cause miscues. The more the players quarrel, the worse it is for the umpire. He is cursed from the first inning to the last because everybody is out of sorts."

Bob Emslie wore a hair piece. The New York Giants' "Dirty Jack" Doyle, after an out call in 1898, grabbed Emslie's wig and ran with the piece. Doyle was fined $20, but said "it was worth the laughs."

The *New York Evening World* (August 31, 1887) said that "Umpire Bob

Emslie got into a sparring match with Chicago White Stockings' 'Cap' Anson that sounded like a vaudeville act."

"CAP" ANSON: You don't say so.
UMPIRE EMSLIE: I do say so.
OLD MAN "CAP": But I don't.
EMSLIE: How brainy and intellectual.

Bob Emslie umpired the craziest game on August 1, 1889, when the St. Louis Browns played the Philadelphia Athletics. The Browns Jack Stivetts had control problems in which he hit five batters. St. Louis was losing, 9–0. The Browns whittled the deficit to 9–7. The Athletics' captain, Curt Welch, went to the mound to bring in a new pitcher. Emslie would not allow the change since Sadie McMahon was not in the original lineup. Welch sprayed Emslie with curse words.

The St. Louis cranks were in an uproar over the delay. Emslie allowed McMahon to pitch. He shut down the Browns' rally, and Philadelphia won the game. St. Louis manager Charlie Comiskey protested the game to no avail.

In 1892, the Boston Beaneaters' Kid Nichols was caught cutting the ball with his cleats. Emslie ignored the kicking by the Baltimore Orioles players. Orioles pitcher Sadie McMahon solved the problem by throwing the ball in question over the grandstand. Emslie ejected McMahon for his action. Boston still won the game.

After the 1894 season, the National League had a playoff between the top two teams for a prize called the Temple Cup. Two umpires were used for the game. At the Polo Grounds on October 8, 1894, the New York Giants routed the Baltimore Orioles, 16–3. Normally in a lopsided game, the captains are somewhat silent. However, John McGraw used vile language on Emslie. Emslie had enough and called the game due to darkness. Even the cranks did not complain.

On May 9, 1896, Baltimore's Hughie Jennings knocked down Cincinnati Reds third baseman Charlie Irwin, causing the ball to sail into the stands. Jennings jumped up and scored the winning run for the Orioles. Cincinnati's captain, Buck Ewing, argued the call. Emslie allowed the run, and the Cincinnati cranks poured on the field. Emslie was escorted off the League Park grounds by the police.

The *Pittsburg Dispatch* (July 29, 1896) said, "Patsy Donovan [Pittsburg] beat out a bunt if ever a man beat out a bunt in the history of the game. But Umpire Bob Emslie called him out because base coach 'Cap' Anson yelled for the decision."

In 1897, Emslie called the Chicago Colts' Bill Dahlen out for oversliding third base. Dahlen jumped to his feet and attacked Emslie by dragging him by the collar. It was the most vicious attack on an umpire that year.

The *Baltimore American and Commercial Advertiser* (April 27, 1897) said, "The Orioles had forced a 3–3 tie. In the ninth, Brooklyn took the lead. With [the] Orioles losing, Jack Doyle went to Umpire Bob Emslie saying it was too dark and dangerous to continue playing. Doyle was hoping to convert the game to the previous inning. Emslie made the Orioles hit. The game ended with a pop-up by Joe Quinn and a Baltimore loss."

The *Boston Globe* (May 4, 1897) criticized that "Emslie was off on strikes on giving Philadelphia's pitcher Jack Fifield the best of it, while Boston's Fred Klobedanz got the small end. Facts are facts."

The Pittsburg Pirates who had chosen to bat first led the Boston Club 5–4 with one out in the ninth inning. When Hugh Duffy, third base coach, immediately jockeyed with Pirates pitcher Frank Killen. Marty Bergen had singled and used an interference to get to third base with two outs. The last hope was Billy Hamilton, who hit a roller too short. As the ball arrived at first base with Hamilton and Pirates first baseman Harry Davis colliding. Umpire Emslie delayed on his decision that brought both teams to celebrate. Finally, Emslie gave a clear decision that Hamilton was out and neither run counted. The Pirates won 5–4, but that did not stop Captain Duffy from complaining [*Boston Globe* (July 16, 1897)].

On June 3, 1898, at the Polo Grounds, Giants first baseman Bill Joyce received a fist from Cincinnati Red Jake Beckley. Joyce grabbed the ball and hurled it at Beckley, hitting him in the side. The two teams erupted into a brawl. Emslie was screamed at by the Giants. He rebutted them with a forfeiture threat. The game continued without further problems.

On June 26, 1899, Emslie ejected Hughie Jennings when he requested it. It seems Jennings had a sore arm and could not throw. Jennings received no fine.

On September 6, 1899, the Boston Beaneaters were playing at the Brooklyn Bridegrooms. Brooklyn's second baseman, Tom Daly, was thrown out at the plate. The Brooklyn cranks jumped out of the stands and attacked Emslie. The Brooklyn players used their bats to protect Emslie from harm.

The Brooklyn cranks came to Washington Park looking for blood the next day. Emslie brought down the fury of cranks on one call against the Bridegrooms. Two unlikely heroes, in "Bad Bill" Dahlen and Tom Daly, sheltered Emslie from attack while Brooklyn won, 5–0, over Boston. The fickle cranks actually cheered Emslie when he walked off the field.

Bob "Ferg" Ferguson

Bob Ferguson reported that his umpiring method was "Never change a decision. Never stop to talk. Make 'em play ball and keep their mouths shut and don't fear the people and they will be on your side and you'll be called the King of Umpires."

In 1873, after a verbal confrontation between the New York Mutuals' Nat Hicks and Ferguson, the umpire picked up the bat and threw it at Hicks, breaking Hicks' arm. *New York Clipper* (August 2, 1873)

Ferguson did not show for a game in 1888 in Cleveland. Former Blues pitcher Bill Crowell was a substitute umpire.

The *Cleveland Leader* (July 30, 1888) stated, "No one doubts Umpire Ferguson's honesty. It's his eyesight that we complain about. Ferguson, one day will give you a ride in a chariot and the next day, he drives the chariot over you."

This exchange between Ferguson and an umpire is related in *Sporting Life*, September 1889:

Commy stood still as a rock and Fergy beckoned him to come in.

COMMY: What that?

FERGY: You're out, come in.

Commy stalked down the base lines.

COMMY: What that you said, Mr. Ferguson?

FERGY: You're out, Mr. Comiskey. Just please get off the line.

COMMY: I'm out?

FERGY: Yes, you're out. Now get away.

COMMY: Why you poor blind chucklehead, alleged umpire. You have a mission, haven't you, since your second trip on earth?

FERGY: What do you mean?

COMMY: You are here for a purpose, and your purpose seems to be to rob the St. Louis team. You are in combination to assist the Brooklyn take the pennant, and you can't deny it.

FERGY: I do deny it, and I warn you now to shut up. I've had enough of your uncalled abuse. Now go and shut up. If you say one word more, I'll give you a $100 slice.

On August 11, 1889, the St. Louis Browns defeated Brooklyn, 14–4, primarily due to errors made by the Bridegrooms. The controversy arose when manager Comiskey would not allow catcher Bob Clack to leave the game due to an injury. Commy called down doctors in the stands to judge the injury. The Brooklyn owner blamed umpires John Kerin and Ferguson for the spectacle, and the crowd poured onto the field. The game took an extra hour because of the crowd delay.

On August 12, 1889, the Brooklyn cranks jumped on the field and prepared to attack Ferguson. He grabbed a bat and exclaimed, "I'm only one man to your thousand, but if you don't think I can't protect myself, just pitch in and give it a trial."

The World Series of 1889 used two umpires, with John Gaffney and Bob Ferguson selected to work the games. The National League New York Giants pitcher Tim Keefe (normally mild-mannered) was disgusted with Ferguson's calls. Keefe accused Ferguson, who was from Brooklyn and had been rejected by the Giants as being biased. After the first game was won by Brooklyn, 12–10, Tom Lynch was hired to replace Ferguson.

The *Cleveland Plain Dealer* (June 6, 1890) reported a scary day at the ball park

> when an ugly looking mass of clouds had been gathering on the field. When without a warning, sheets of water began pouring down. It rained steady for five minutes and more, and then lightning, approached dangerously near. Bolt after bolt descended. Finally, there was a crash and roar as if a cannon had been fired into the stands. At the same instant a trail of blinding fire flashed down a pillar which supports the stands. Splinters and shingles flew in all directions. When the building was struck, everybody in the stands received a shock, and two gentlemen toppled over in shock. Several ladies fainted. Another flash and a big apple tree over in the left field tipped over. Umpire Robert Ferguson said he would have no part of it and the game was over.

Wally Fessenden

Fessenden umpired 53 games in two years. The *Boston Herald* (June 23, 1889) reported that "Boston's pitcher John Clarkson was sitting on the Beaneater bench in street clothes since he had pitched the first game of the double header. Pittsburg Captain Fred Dunlap noticed that Clarkson was giving Boston pitcher Bill Sowders signals on pitches. Umpire Wally Fessenden fired Clarkson off the bench. Boston's Captain 'King' Kelly wanted all the players on the Pittsburg bench vacated. Amazingly, Fessenden made them go sit in the stands too."

Charlie "Chick" Fulmer

The *Chicago Herald* (October 12, 1886) carried this conversation about Fulmer:

BILLY SUNDAY: Fulmer's umpiring in Philadelphia was the worst I ever saw. He robbed us of two games, clean steals, the worst of every decision.

LEW HARDIE: Fulmer is running for some sort of office—Justice of the Peace. He's after every vote in Philadelphia.

"Charlie Fulmer told 'Cap' Anson he would not be bulldozed. Anson spoke to National League President Nick Young that Fulmer was incompetent. Fulmer replied the Chicago players are the hardest set of men to please in the profession today. It has been a case of bluffing with them all through the season and that is how they stay on top." *New York Herald* (October 4, 1886)

"Umpire Charlie Fulmer called Cleveland Blues' player Fred Dunlap out for not touching third, missing it by 20 feet. Umpire Fulmer told the *Leader* that Boston catcher Charles Snyder pulled his sleeve to alert him of the short-cut. However, Snyder was not near Fulmer on the play." *Cleveland Leader* (May 16, 1881)

"Honest" John Gaffney

Gaffney was one of the three best umpires of the era. Gaffney could recite the rule book, which helped to defuse some kicking. He described his umpiring method as "I have studied the rules thoroughly and keep my eye wide open and follow the ball with all possible dispatch. With the player, I try to keep as even tempered as I can, always speaking to them gentlemanly, yet firmly."

In 1884, King Kelly pulled the trick he had made famous by going from first to third base while skipping second. Kelly actually ran past Gaffney, who was moving from behind home plate to first. Kelly was not used to seeing the umpire on the field. Gaffney called Kelly out at third. Kelly went up to Gaffney and said, "All right. Mr. Umpire I've never been on these grounds before and didn't know where second base was." Two innings later, Kelly ran from second base through the pitcher's box to home plate, never getting within 30 feet of third base. Gaffney did not see Kelly and the run counted.

On August 9, 1884, the New York Gothams' captain,

.0191.— *Gaffney, manager of Washington Club.* COPYRIGHTED, 1887.

GOODWIN & CO., NEW YORK.

John Gaffney

John Ward, requested that Gaffney stop the game due to darkness. Gaffney told Ward he "was the only player who thought it was too dark to play." Ward questioned the umpire's ability, and Gaffney remarked that Ward "wasn't a good player." The normally quiet Ward punched Gaffney in the face. Gaffney got up, and Ward slugged him again. Gaffney had a deep cut on his face. But Ward took Gaffney to a doctor and apologized.

The *Providence Journal* (September 9, 1884) stated that Gaffney's umpiring "demonstrated poor performance when Buffalo's Eggler hit a short ball to right fielder Paul Revere Radford who scooped up the ball and threw to first before Eggler reached first base. Every person who witnessed the play thought it was an out except Umpire John Gaffney who called Dave Eggler safe."

In 1886, the Chicago White Stockings' captain, Cap Anson, and Gaffney went toe to toe. *The Sporting News* (July 5, 1886) described their conversation after the disputed call.

> ANSON (in rage): What?
> GAFFNEY: That will cost you $10.
> ANSON: Yes, and it will cost you your position, you SOB.
> GAFFNEY: Fifty dollars more! That makes it $60.
> ANSON: Why you insignificant little Irish b___, what do you mean?
> GAFFNEY: Fifty more, that makes $110, and I'll stay with you for a week.
> ANSON: If you can stand it, I can.
> (Anson paid the fine.)

In an 1889 series, the St. Louis Browns, in support of suspended player Yank Robinson, lost three straight games to the Kansas City Cowboys. John Gaffney spoke to *Sporting Life* (May 15, 1889) to squelch the talk of dishonesty. "I want it distinctly understood that I would not have been party to any burlesque of throwing games on a ball field. Had I suspected such, I would have left the field. The Browns suffered from the loss of second baseman Robinson, but the grounds were awful and tripped up the men, and Kansas City simply did the most terrific slugging I have seen on the ball field."

1889 WORLD SERIES

Game 1

On October 18, 1889, the New York Giants (NL) and Brooklyn Bridegrooms (AA) were in the eighth inning, with the Giants ahead, 10–8. It was freezing cold and getting dark. The Giants started putting away their equipment after the top of the eighth inning. Plate umpire Gaffney was alerted that the street lights were on. Gaffney cried, "Play on." The bottom of the eighth was so dark that the ball could not be seen to hit or catch. The Bridegrooms took an 11–10 lead, then swung at every pitch to end the affair, winning, 12–10. Gaffney ended the game due to darkness. The Giants felt he had robbed them.

Game 4

On October 22, 1889, more controversy awaited Gaffney. In the sixth inning, the Giants' George Gore was in a rundown between second base and third. The ball struck Gore's arm. Gaffney ruled that Gore deliberately stuck his arm out; therefore, interference was called. Giants captain Buck Ewing exploded with verbal abuse as follows: "Mr. Gaffney, if you decide against us, I'll take my men off the field. You know Gore and Ward should be entitled to score. I don't propose to be a bulldozer any longer. One-sided umpiring has been the cause of this loss." Base umpire Tom Lynch conferred with Gaffney, who changed his decision, allowing Monte Ward's run to count because it occurred before the out. The game was called before the ninth inning due to darkness. Brooklyn won, 10–7. The *New York Herald* "blamed Gaffney for not controlling the game."

On May 27, 1893, the Boston Beaneaters' Hugh Duffy railed against Gaffney when he fined him $25. Duffy yelled, "I'll whip you any time any place."

The *Brooklyn Eagle* (May 9, 1893) "Alluded that grease had gotten on the base ball." Brooklyn Bridegrooms pitcher Ed Stein requested a new ball due to a slippery old ball. However, Gaffney would have no part and "shook his head." Stein rolled it where Giants' hitter George Davis hit a three bagger. Stein rolled another ball on the ground and when it was hit, his Brooklyn infielders did the same thing. When Shorty Fuller smacked a double, Stein was boiling with anger and threw the ball 15 feet over catcher Con Daily's head. Stein finally got the Giants out. But New York's Amos Rusie was also having trouble with the slippery ball. Finally, Brooklyn's Billy Shoch fouled the ball over the bleachers, causing Gaffney to put a new ball into plan. (Brooklyn won the game, 11–10.)

In 1895, the Washington Senators did not start games until 4:30 in order to get the federal workers to attend. The Baltimore Orioles had the lead going into the seventh inning. Orioles pitcher Sadie McMahon knew it was getting dark and just pretended to throw the ball. The catcher, Wilbert Robinson, smacked his glove. Gaffney exclaimed "Strike three, you're out." Washington's batter, Kip Selbach jumped in front of Gaffney, crying, "That ball was two feet outside."

On September 19, 1899, Wilbert Robinson, was fed up with ball and strike calls. After the inning was completed, Robinson threw a ball at Gaffney, hitting him in the leg. Robinson followed up with a series of curses. Gaffney ejected Robinson, who refused to send a substitute catcher into the game. Gaffney forfeited the game to the Brooklyn Superbas.

Bill Gleason

Bill Gleason was quite interested in being popular with the home team. He was a rookie umpire calling balls and strikes on April 8, 1891, in a battle between the Cincinnati Reds and the St. Louis Browns. Reds catcher King Kelly, after several walks, threw down his glove and walked off the field. Kelly came back to the field in the fifth inning. Gleason allowed Kelly to re-enter because the cranks loved him. Gleason reminded Kelly that technically he was not in the game even though he batted and was back catching. Kelly, after a few choice words regarding Gleason's strike zone, exited the premises again. Kelly yelled to the cranks, "He is too strong for my game." By the ninth inning, darkness had arrived. Neither team could see sufficiently, nor the cranks. With a tie score, Captain Kelly ordered his players to stall. Gleason had done the same thing in his playing days, recognized the tactic, and threw up his hands, awarding a forfeit to St. Louis. The American Association fired Gleason and ruled the game be replayed.

Fred "Goldy" Goldsmith

Goldsmith was a better pitcher than an umpire. The *Baltimore American and Commercial Advertiser* (September 9, 1888) reported: "Umpire Goldsmith spied Tommy Tucker wearing a white 'Cap' that matched the umpire's suit. The two agreed to a wrestling match. The pair made a rush for each other and paraphernalia flew in all directions. Each man had a death grip, and they rolled around the ground like two balls. Goldy had the wind and staying quality, however, and in ten seconds had Tucker on his back. The 'Cap' was turned over to Goldy, and to this day the boys have not stopped kidding Tommy."

Sporting Life (June 5, 1889) said, "David Orr argued with Umpire Fred Goldsmith and was ejected. After Orr's continued arguing, Goldsmith declared Brooklyn the winner by forfeit. Brooklyn's owner Byrne intervened and requested the game continue with Brooklyn winning 6–3 over Columbus."

On June 24, 1889, Goldsmith was a no-show for a game between Columbus and Brooklyn. Brooklyn chose Bill Paasch as a substitute. Columbus would not adhere to his umpiring, so Paasch ruled the game a forfeit. An argument ensued which resulted in Columbus playing and winning, 13–7. Brooklyn attempted to claim a victory, declaring the game was a makeup game and counting the forfeit game. The ploy worked when the league's Board of Directors upheld the forfeit.

On July 29, 1889, Goldsmith took away an apparent run from the Baltimore

Orioles due to the "kickin'" of St. Louis manager Charlie Comiskey. The game ended in a tie and a riot. Goldsmith admitted he was influenced by Comiskey.

On September 7, 1889, the St. Louis Browns took on the Brooklyn Trolley Dodgers in Washington Park before 15,000 frenzied cranks. It did not take long before Comiskey verbally abused Goldsmith, calling him a "shuttlecock." At the same time, the Brooklyn cranks threw glasses of beer at the St. Louis players. Brooklyn, with a 2–0 lead in the fifth inning, started to use stalling tactics as early darkness approached. Goldsmith stayed his course and ordered the game to continue. As St. Louis grasped the lead, 3–2, Comiskey sent his players into slow motion. Catcher Milligan visited the mound, followed by the infielders. After this visit, outfielders Tip O'Neill and Tommy McCarthy came into talk with pitcher Ice Box Chamberlain. The Browns even stalled while batting.

Browns owner Chris Von Der Ahe brought candles, and they were lit at the St. Louis bench. The Brooklyn cranks threw beer to put out the candles. A piece of paper caught fire and almost set flames to the wooden stands. Browns outfielder McCarthy doused the game ball in a bucket of water. Goldsmith divulged to Comiskey that the darkness was now an issue, but he dared not bring the Dodgers cranks' hostilities down on him.

At 6:25 p.m., Comiskey pulled his Browns off the field. Brooklyn cranks, as expected, threw beer bottles and fruit at the St. Louis players. Tommy McCarthy was hit in the jaw. The Brooklyn police arrived, only to push the St. Louis players around. Goldsmith awarded a forfeit to Brooklyn. After the game, Von der Ahe wired his disapproval to the league office. The American Association Board voted 6–2 that the Brooklyn forfeit win be overturned. The game was reverted to the eighth inning, with a Browns 3–2 victor. Goldsmith was dismissed.

On August 25, 1898, at St. Louis' Sportsman's Park, it had severely rained the previous night. Goldsmith ordered that the game be played under muddy conditions. He was like a kid throwing mud at the players. The pitchers threw balls on purpose to splash the umpire and catcher. St. Louis won, 10–8, defeating the Washington Nationals.

Tom Gunning

Tom Gunning was a disaster as an umpire. His second game in 1884 was with his old team, the Boston Red Stockings, against the New York Giants. The *New York Times* accused Gunning of "shady calls for his old team."

On August 8, 1884, he called a game due to darkness with the sun still shining for another hour. The Giants' cranks were "uncontrollable." The cranks jumped over the fence and surrounded Gunning. The *New York Times*

(August 9, 1884) reported, "the police ran on the field and used their batons to release Gunning. The police put Gunning into a horse carriage and took him to the railroad station." He was released after three games.

Hardie Henderson

In 1896, the New York Giants' Willie Clark was caught in a rundown between first and second base. As the ball was tossed to the Chicago Colts' Cap Anson, Clark stuck out his hand and knocked the ball into the outfield. He hustled to third base to be greeted by umpire Hardie Henderson, who amazingly called him safe.

Ed Herr

Ed Herr was another bad substitute umpire. On August 11, 1887, the Philadelphia A's played the St. Louis Browns. When the game was tied 5–5, Herr called the game due to darkness. Herr complained he had difficulty seeing because of the mask. He was a substitute umpire.

John Heydler

National League umpire Tim Hurst left a game on September 15, 1896, due to illness. John Heydler was picked from the stands to finish the game.

Heydler became a permanent umpire in 1898. He only lasted one year, but he did have some run-ins with the dirty John McGraw. He described McGraw in McGraw's own book. "The Orioles are mean and vicious, ready at any time to maim an umpire if it helps their cause. The things they say are vile and they attempt to break the spirits of some fine umpires. I've seen umpires bathe their feet by the hour. McGraw spikes them through their shoes. I feel the lot of the umpires never was worse than in the years that the Orioles were flying high."

The *Cincinnati Post* (May 3, 1898) said, "Umpire John Heydler has no backbone and is badly in need of stiffening."

The *Cleveland Leader* (July 9, 1898) recorded the following conversation:

> ANDREW FREEDMAN [owner] New York Giants: If Young doesn't remove the incompetent Heydler.
>
> UMPIRE HEYDLEr: I can stand abuse from crowds and players, but when it comes from a President of a Club in the League, I think it is time for me to retire.

Heydler stated about the Baltimore Orioles:

We hear about the glories and durability of the Orioles, but the truth about the team seldom has been told. They were mean, vicious, ready at any time to main a rival player or an umpire, if it helped their cause. The things they would say to an umpire were unbelievably vile, and they broke the spirits of some fine men. I've seen umpires bathe their feet by the hour after McGraw and others spiked them through their shoes. The Club never was a constructive force in the game. The worst of it was they got by with much of the browbeating and hooliganism.

The *New York Star* (August 8, 1898) reported this incident:

Umpire Heydler ran flush against John McGraw as he entered the park and McGraw blazed at him.

McGRAW: Here I am trying to stir my ball club and make a fight out of the pennant race and I'm suspended three days for criticizing a rotten umpire! You're a rotten umpire and you know it.

Heydler attempted to get in a word but was quite overwhelmed by McGraw. His face flamed with anger. McGraw didn't care who heard him.

Richard "Dick" Higham

Dick Higham was the worst umpire in the National League in 1881. It did not take long for him to get into trouble in 1882. Umpires in the early years were assigned to a particular team. However, it was obvious that the Detroit Wolverines' opponents were getting all the close calls. Detroit owner William Thompson hired a private investigator to look into Higham's activities. The investigator discovered telegrams between gambler Todd Jones and Higham. Jones was winning by betting against Detroit. One telegram read, "Buy all the lumber you can." *Detroit Press* (July 1, 1882) Higham was fired from baseball.

He went on to be a bookmaker in Chicago. His comment: "Base ball is like measles. I had it once and that's enough."

Will Hoagland

Will Hoagland was a former prize fighter, his closest experience to umpiring; however, he did not last long as an umpire.

A Cleveland Spiders crowd in 1894 felt Hoagland was biased to the Pittsburg Pirates. Spider Jack O'Connor's single into left field was called foul by Hoagland. Cleveland's captain, Patsy Tebeau, jumped in the umpire's face and even removed his mask. Hoagland walked to the mound for safety. On the next pitch, O'Connor caught the ball and threw it over the stands. Hoagland fined O'Connor $25 and forfeited the game to Pittsburg. The cranks rushed out of the stands, with Tebeau leading them. Tebeau shouted, "I'll take you in the dressing room and whip you." Hoagland exited the field, leaving his clothes in the dressing room. Tebeau and the other Spiders left for a train.

Billy Holbert

Holbert only umpired one year in the Players' League. He still managed to be controversial. Holbert made the mistake of calling King Kelly out at first base when Harry Stovey interfered on a double play attempt. That wasn't enough; he ruled that Kelly interfered with the throw home. Kelly grabbed the baseball and tossed it over the grandstand, then ran off the field. Kelly returned to his catching position. Amazingly, Holbert did not eject the "King." After the game, the *Boston Globe* reported Kelly as saying, "I won't play another game if Holbert umpires." But he did.

Joe Hornung

He was a rookie umpire who had used trick plays in his playing career. The *New York Telegram* (June 1, 1893), reported a confrontation between the New York Giants and Cincinnati Reds: "Cincy's Captain-Manager Charles Comiskey had pitcher Frank Dwyer give a batter an intentional walk. The action of Comiskey to deliberately send a man to base on balls was signalized by the cranks as an outrage. Umpire Joe Hornung allowed the play."

"Bad" Tim Hurst

Tim Hurst was the meanest umpire in 19th century baseball. In 1887, Hurst called the Boston Beaneaters' George Yeager safe when a throw pulled Nationals first baseman Ed Cartwright off first base. The Nationals questioned the call. Hurst touched Deacon McGuire on the chin. McGuire didn't think the move appropriate and swung at Hurst. Hurst ducked, and McGuire went back to the bench.

In 1889, Hurst and Orator O'Rourke got into a confrontation.

HURST: Mr. O'Rourke, I have a profound respect for you as a ball player. But, I have come to the conclusion you are a loquacious disputer.

O'ROURKE (after hitting a home run on the next pitch): I suppose that was a strike too.

HURST: No. James, that was a home run. But the question will cost you five bucks.

The *Cleveland Plain Dealer* (July 5, 1891) reviewed Hurst's umpiring: "His work was fair, but his judgment of balls and strikes was poor. He allows the catchers to pull the ball over the plate."

In Pittsburg (1891), Chicago's Cap Anson used vulgar language on Hurst. The next day, another vile tirade was given to Hurst, even accusing him of murder. Anson was ejected.

Another problem occurred on April 22, 1891, with Buck Ewing.

HURST: If you don't shut up, I'll have you removed from the field.

EWING: I'm a spectator. I've got a right to get excited and yell as much as anyone.

HURST: I don't care how much you yell if you don't give orders to your men.

On July 24, 1891, Hurst ejected Brooklyn's manager, John Ward, in the first game of a doubleheader. Ward protested to National League President Charlie Byrne, who was attending the game. Byrne yelled to Ward, "If I had my way, you wouldn't play at all."

Arlie Latham disapproved of Hurst by throwing his bat at him. Hurst simply kicked the bat back toward Latham, who threw the bat back. Hurst kicked it back, again saying, "I'll give you one more kick. Get out of here before I tie your shoelaces."

In the same season, Hurst made the following remark about his job as umpire: "You can't beat the hours." That year included Hurst knocking down a crank with his mask.

The *Baltimore American and Commercial Advertiser* (September 7, 1893) reported, "Boston Beaneaters' Tommy McCarthy could not find his bat. He cursed and refused to bat. Umpire Hurst reprimanded Tommy so that it was heard in the grandstand."

On June 30, 1894, two bitter rivals were brought together. The Cleveland Spiders were playing the Baltimore Orioles. In the pregame meeting, Cleveland's captain, Patsy Tebeau, warned Hurst that close calls had better go to the Spiders or he would cut the ropes holding the cranks back. In the second inning, Hurst called Tebeau out at second base and yelled, "Ye may have beat the throw, but I called yez out. Now go and cut the ropes. If yez turn your face to the crowd, I'll kill you right where you stand." The game proceeded to the ninth inning without any more trouble until Jimmy Ryan (Baltimore) hit a ball that appeared foul. Even Ryan did not move until Hurst yelled, "Run Jimmy run. Foul ball." Hurst shook his fist at Tebeau, saying "Cut the ropes." Score: Orioles 5, Spiders 3.

In 1894, Boston's Foghorn Tucker was coaching first base and giving constant abuse to Hurst. By the fifth inning, Hurst had enough and tossed Tucker. (In the 19th century, that meant going to the team bench.) After Hugh Duffy was called out on a close play at first base, the following dialogue ensued:

DUFFY: You are on the level!

HURST: That'll cost you ten dollars!

DUFFY: I'll see you in Boston.

HURST: I will see you here, so go sit on the bench for the rest of the game.

Unbelievably, Tucker replaced Duffy in the field. Since Tucker had only been ejected as a coach, he was still able to play in the field.

The *Baltimore Herald* (March 7, 1895) reported the following statement made by Hurst to Louisville's manager, Billy Barnie, about Pittsburg's Connie Mack.

> You know that trick he has of shoving his glove under the batter's bat and elevating it a few inches so that the ball can glide under it and the umpire can shout strike one. I was onto him. You had two men on base and Mack pushed the bat up. I forgot who was handling it. I told him to quit, and he apologized by saying, "It was an accident. I fight the ball instead of waiting for it." If you fight it again that way, there will be trouble. Yes, that's an old trick. Mack is the cleverest man at it. If a batsman gets onto it he is liable to hit the catcher on the fingers. The gloves are so big, you see, the catcher is protected and you can't hurt him unless by design.

On September 14, 1895, during a game in Baltimore against Brooklyn, a foul tip broke Hurst's wire mask. He was bleeding badly, but stayed in the game.

In 1895, the St. Louis manager, Lou Phelan, confronted Hurst, saying "close calls better be in our favor." Hurst replied, "Any more cracks, and I'll give you a nosebleed." Phelan apologized.

Another Baltimore/Cleveland game in late August brought a fly ball from Baltimore's Hughie Jennings heading to Cleveland's left fielder, Jesse Burkett. The cranks broke through the ropes to prevent the catch. *Sporting Life* (August 29, 1896) said, "Umpire Hurst wisely called the game a tie."

The *Baltimore Sun* (May 31, 1897) had this account:

> Baltimore was leading Chicago 4–2 with Bill Hoffer pitching. Relations between Umpire Tim Hurst and the Orioles were strained even with the lead. Colts Bill Lange's interference on Frank Bowerman allowed Bill Everitt to steal second without any umpire call. Then with Lange on first, Jimmy Ryan swung at a pitch in the dirt. When catcher Bowerman reached to pick up the ball, Ryan hit the ball away, allowing Lange to move to second. Unbelievably Hurst did not see the play and ejected Captain Joe Kelley for arguing. Then Chicago's George Decker hit the ball over centerfielder Jake Stenzel's head. Then a relay throw to "Heinie" Reitz resulted in a tag out at third. However, Umpire Hurst declared the ball had reached the spectators and was a ground rule triple. Then [the] Orioles Hughie Jennings came in to argue and was ejected. The Orioles line-up now had three pitchers. Hoffer had enough and just lobbed the ball, allowing five runs. The Oriole players believed there was a conspiracy to prevent them from winning.

Umpire Hurst was umpiring a Pirates game in 1897. He ruled Orioles pitcher Bill Hoffer safe on a pickoff attempt at first base. The Pirate cranks let him know they didn't agree. Later in the game, he called Pirates Jesse Tannehill out for interference. He used his hand to knock Hoffer's throw out of the glove of Pittsburg's Tom O'Brien (first base). The cranks jumped out of the bleachers. Hurst ran for the Club House, knocking one crank down. He hit another crank with a punch and then kicked him. He stayed in the Club House until the Pittsburg police came to escort him from the field [*Pittsburg Post* (May 26, 1897)].

Hurst not only had trouble with the Orioles, he didn't fare well with the Cincinnati Reds either. In June 1897, after getting behind the Boston Bean-eaters, the Reds attacked Hurst. Boston, in the bottom of the fifth inning, got in the brew when Herman Long was fined $10 for arguing. The *Boston Globe* (June 12, 1897) said, "Mr. Hurst had an off day, but as usual played no favorites."

Sporting Life (August 7, 1897) reported this altercation: "Umpire Hurst and Cincinnati's catcher 'Heinie' Reitz got in a fist fight in the first inning. The Umpire hit Reitz in the chest with his mask. Reitz came back with a stiff right to the chin. Amazingly, Reitz was not ejected or fined and the game resumed."

In 1897, umpiring an Orioles game was "ejection day." Joe Kelley and Jack Doyle were both tossed by Hurst.

On August 4, 1897, a Cincinnati crank hit Hurst with a beer mug. Hurst fired the mug back, cutting a different crank on the head. The Cincinnati police arrested Hurst at the completion of the game and charged him with assault. He was found guilty and fined $500.

In 1898, New York's hot-tempered Kid Elberfeld shoved Hurst, who knocked Elberfeld over the head with his mask. "The Kid" was knocked unconscious.

The *Brooklyn Eagle* (September 2, 1899) reported that

Umpire Tim Hurst called a strike on Brooklyn's Bill Dahlen. He objected by standing on the plate. Hurst warned "Get off the plate or I'll call you out." Hurst then told Philadelphia's pitcher Bill Bernhard to throw a pitch. When he threw the pitch, Bernhard threw the ball right at Dahlen who caught the ball. "Yer out" yelled Hurst. Brooklyn's Joe Kelley and Hughie Jennings came off the bench to argue. "You can't call a man out for that," they shouted. Hurst replied, "Well, I have, and there you are." The players argued a minute and took their seat.

On May 23, 1900, Pittsburg club president Barney Dreyfuss requested that the National League office not assign umpire Tim Hurst to umpire in Pittsburg. The request was refused.

Hurst commented on his approach to umpiring: "Every umpire makes mistakes. I remember that I even made a mistake one time. I called a strike, with no more than a seam of the ball over the edge of the plate. I have been accused of making other mistakes, but that is unjust."

John Hunt

"John McGraw told him he was a 16-string Jack," said the *Boston Globe* (May 4, 1899). On August 13, 1898, Hunt had a confrontation with Chicago Orphans pitcher Clark Griffith about Bill Everitt being called out at third base. Griffith was ejected without throwing another pitch. The Orphans lost to the New York Giants, 9–2.

On October 14, 1899, Baltimore's Jimmy Sheckard was called out on an attempted steal of second base. Sheckard argued the call with Hunt until he was ejected. Hunt asked the Brooklyn catcher, Aleck Smith, to persuade Sheckard to leave. Sheckard would not back down, and Hunt went to Baltimore captain John McGraw, but got no assistance. Hunt looked to Brooklyn manager Ned Hanlon, Sheckard's previous manager, without success. In frustration, Hunt forfeited the game to Brooklyn.

"Umpire Hunt fined Steve Brodie after he shook him. He was fined $50." *Baltimore American and Commercial Advertiser* (August 16, 1895)

The *Cincinnati Commercial Tribune* (September 17, 1898) recorded this unusual situation: "Baltimore's third base coach John McGraw ran on to the diamond to whisper a few pet names into the ear of Cincinnati pitcher Bill Hill. Umpire John Hunt allowed McGraw's actions. Pitcher Hill was not rattled by the ploy."

Al "Alamazoo" Jennings

Jennings was a better fighter than umpire and only lasted one year. In 1884, Jennings attempted to beat up a *Washington Post* sports writer. When Jennings went to the newspaper, the sports editor (unknown) met him and threw a paste pot at him. Then he tossed "Alamazoo" out of the building. Jennings only umpired 27 games that season before being released.

Fred Jevne

His first full season was his last. The *Cleveland Leader* (July 4, 1895) reported, "Pittsburg Pirates first baseman Jake Beckley tripped Cleveland's Jimmy McAleer at first base. Umpire Fred Jevne fined Beckley $25."

Jevne caught Boston Beaneaters ace pitcher Jack Stivetts spiking the ball to gain an advantage. When a new ball was put in play, Stivetts spiked that ball too. This time, Jevne fined Stivetts $10.

The *Pittsburg Chronicle Telegraph* (August 17, 1895) reported "Umpire Red Bittman was substituted for regular Umpire Fred Jevne. Anson said 'I never had the luck or pull to get an umpire changed when I wanted to.'"

"Umpire Fred Jevne called a strike on Willie Keeler. When Keeler objected, the whole Oriole bench opened up on Jevne like a lot of hyenas. Pittsburg's catcher Bill Merritt yelled 'Let's everybody kick.' This remark made the birds wild. Jevne only called them down in a half hearted way." *Pittsburg Chronicle Telegraph* (August 30, 1895)

Charlie Jones

The *Columbus Evening Dispatch* (June 29, 1891) said, "Jones is decidedly the rankest umpire bar none that ever disgraced a diamond."

Charlie Jones was umpiring when a strange tactic was employed. The *New York World* (August 24, 1890) stated that "New York Giants Dan Shannon jumped from the batter's box to in front of the catcher. Cleveland Infants pitcher Henry Gruber failed to throw the ball. Umpire Jones called a balk. Infants' Captain 'Patsy' Tebeau's argument was nonsense."

"Sir" Tim Keefe

Tim Keefe went from future Hall of Fame pitcher to umpiring. The mild-mannered Keefe would be in over his head as an umpire. The *Pittsburg Dispatch* (June 24, 1895) said, "Baltimore's Steve Brodie made a bad throw to home plate and Captain Wilbert Robinson called Brodie down. Orioles Hughie Jennings, always one to remark, chimed in with 'it is not necessary to play good ball when we have a robbing umpire.' Keefe resented the insult and fined Jennings $25, which made him more abusive, resulting in Jennings' ejection."

The Chicago Colts were playing the Philadelphia Phillies on May 8, 1896. In the ninth inning, Phillies captain Billy Nash argued a strike call with Keefe. Nash was in the batter's box, holding a bat. Chicago's pitcher, Clark Griffith, fired a pitch which hit Nash's bat. The ball rolled to Griffith, who started a double play to end the game. Nash and the umpire stood in wonderment. Keefe screamed, "You're out, you're out, game over." The Colts won, 5–3.

Baltimore's catcher, Wilbert Robinson, said, "Umpire Tim Keefe can only see when we interfere. He's blind when Chicago is at bat. Hughie Jennings stepped in front of Malachi Kittridge without touching him, the lynx-eyed Keefe called Jennings out for interference." *Chicago Tribune* (May 16, 1896)

On May 13, 1896, the Boston Beaneaters scored six runs in the top of the 11th inning. The Chicago Colts began stalling tactics, hoping the score would revert back to a tied game. Keefe had seen enough and would not allow it to continue, awarding a forfeit to Boston.

The *Cincinnati Times-Star* (May 20, 1896) reported that "Philadelphia Phillies Ed Delahanty and Tuck Turner complained to Umpire Keefe that it was too sandy in the infield. Other players began to kick the sand away. They brought out a rake and removed a peck of loose sand. Cincinnati Reds groundskeeper John Schwab eventually arrived with a wheelbarrow of sand and poured it back on the field. Keefe ordered the game to continue."

The Cincinnati Reds "worked padded balls into the game with the New York Giants. They had used the trick of soft balls inserted into the ball boxes. A ball was taken out of the box and thrown to Umpire Keefe. Keefe rejected the ball for not being in a sealed box. *New York Herald* (May 22, 1896)

In Pittsburg in June 1896, Baltimore captain John McGraw got in Keefe's face and accused him of having a whiskey before the game. Keefe replied that he had taken a little drink because he was sick. McGraw replied, "Sick. Drunk you mean. You were drunk all last week in Chicago."

Keefe walked off the field in the middle of a game on July 6, 1896, in St. Louis.

Sporting Life (July 7, 1896) carried Keefe's letter of resignation to the National League:

> My sole reason for leaving the field and severing my connection with the National League. Base ball has reached a stage where it is absolutely disgraceful. It is the fashion for every player engaged in a game to froth at the mouth, and emit shrieks of anguish whenever a decision given is adverse to the interest of the Club to which he belongs.
>
> This may not be wearing to the general public, but it is certainly disgusting to umpires, who give decisions disinterestedly and as he sees the plays. The continual senseless and puerile kicking at every decision has been trying to me.

John "Kick" Kelly

Kelly was probably the biggest "homer" umpire of all time. His record indicates the home team won 69 percent of his games. Therefore, he was one of the most popular. He did turn down a $10,000 bribe to fix a pennant deciding series.

Cleveland's third baseman, Dude Esterbrook, approached Kelly. The following conversation was recorded by the *Cleveland Plains Dealer* (May 16, 1882):

> ESTERBROOK: Strange that these asylums don't keep their doors locked. Kind of sad too, for one of these days an umpire will get run over by an ice wagon, and then what'll come of his poor family. But, I suppose there must be good money in it. They say "Prize Fights" are crooked and the referee gets funny money. A shame the James Boys didn't referee.
>
> KELLY: Say, you fresh dude. I won't take any more of your gaff. You are a big baby. If you come in the dressing room after the game, I'll give what's coming.

Kelly was umpiring in an 1883 game between Louisville and the St. Louis. Browns captain Ted Sullivan got into a loud confrontation with Kelly. The noise caused a horse carriage outside the field to race down Grand Avenue. The buggy hit a pole and was torn apart. Never underestimate the voice range of an umpire.

He was called, by some, "Honest" Kelly. However, he decided that the final game of the 1885 World Series would be in Cincinnati. The truth was that the St. Louis Browns had won the Series, four games to two. The seventh game or last game was played to earn money for the players. The two participants, Chicago and St. Louis, agreed to play in Cincinnati, hoping for higher attendance.

The *Pittsburg Post* (May 12, 1886) noted that Pittsburg Alleghenys second baseman Sam Barkley demanded to Kelly that a returned ball be used. Cincinnati's pitcher, Tony Mullane, wanted to use a new ball. Kelly stated, "a new one cannot be used until the previous ball has been lost for five minutes." Kelly yelled, "Continue!"

The *Sporting News* (June 14, 1886) offered this account of St. Louis manager Charlie Comiskey arguing with Kelly:

COMMY: You're no good.

KELLY: That will cost you $25.

COMMY: You're still no good.

KELLY: That will cost you another $25.

COMMY: You're no good if it cost me a million dollars.

KELLY: No, just another $25.

Comiskey decided to shut up.

The *Chicago Daily News* (August 16, 1888) reported that "Umpire John Kelly caught Boston Beaneaters' 'King' Kelly cutting third base short by ten feet. However, he just sent Kelly back to third base as the crowd howled with delight."

Chris Von der Ahe, during the 1888 Dauvray Cup Series between his St. Louis Browns and the New York Giants, accused umpires John Kelly and John Gaffney of betting on the Giants. Gaffney replied, "I don't care about Von der Ahe's opinion of my work. I do object to being called a crook. I will quit the business."

Kelly's statement was, "If Gaffney won't umpire, I won't either."

Von der Ahe, at a press conference at Union Depot, said, he "had been misquoted and Kelly and Gaffney were doing a swell job." Both umpires finished the Series.

In 1888, Kelly's intoxication caught up with him when he attacked Miss Emma Gordon in a saloon. He knocked two of her teeth out and was arrested for assault and battery. He paid a $25 fine and sobered up for the game. He was released from the American Association at the end of the year.

Kelly was rehired for the 1897 season. In St Louis, he was verbally abused by a crank, walked to the stands and spoke with Browns owner Chris Von der Ahe. Von der Ahe, a notorious umpire hater, stepped on the field and told Kelly to do his duty. Just then, a crank yelled, "Put Von der Ahe out." The police grabbed both cranks by their collars and escorted them from the grounds. Von der Ahe, after the game, declared that he "had never before seen a better exhibition of umpiring." One would guess that St. Louis winning the game had an effect on his remark.

Kick Kelly replaced Sandy McDermott. The Philadelphia Phillies were playing the rowdy Baltimore Orioles. Philadelphia's Lave Cross fouled a ball into the press seating area. A reporter threw the ball to Kelly, but it was not usable. He gave Baltimore's pitcher, Joe Corbett, a new ball. Corbett was upset that the Phillies would be swinging at a new ball. Baltimore scored two runs on their next turn at bat. This time Kelly allowed the play to continue. Orioles captain Wilbert Robinson kicked and was ejected. Clarke took up the argument and was also ejected. This forced Manager Hanlon to put in substitute Tom O'Brien. When O'Brien batted, he was called out on strikes by Kelly. O'Brien's objection put him in the clubhouse with the others. The *Baltimore Sun* titled its headline "The Dictator of the Diamond." *Baltimore Sun* (August 13, 1897)

Mike "King" Kelly

King Kelly, one of the great "kickers" of umpires, was behind the plate for seven games. *The Pittsburg Press* (August 20, 1892) reported, "Boston's 'King' Kelly served as a substitute umpire on August 19, 1892. When his teammate Hugh Duffy made an objection over a call in the first inning, Kelly simply pointed his finger looking as if he was going to fire a pistol and said 'Mind your own business.' There were no other remarks that game."

Jack Kerins

Jack Kerins was a no-nonsense umpire in the American Association. In 1891, Baltimore Orioles captain Wilbert Robinson was arguing with Kerins. Kerins declared there would be one more inning. Orioles pitcher John Clarkson threw a lemon, and Kerins called it a strike. Robinson showed Kerins the lemon. Kerins softly said, "Well, I guess that will be enough. Game called due to darkness."

Also, Kerins fined Denny Lyons (St. Louis) for knocking over the Columbus Solons' Jack O'Connor, costing him $25. The same year, Kerins called Louisville's Harry Taylor out for skipping first base by five feet on a double.

John "Bud" Lally

Lally was a substitute umpire who had his problems. Pittsburg Pirates pitcher Frank Killen confronted Lally after a walk. Killen was so upset he struck Lally in the face. Lally did not sit still and got in a few licks on Killen. Killen was arrested and charged with disorderly conduct (not assault?).

St. Louis pitcher Donahue was given a ball in the eighth. He walked up to a puddle at home plate and covered the ball with mud. Baltimore catcher Robinson objected vigorously. Lally presented Donahue a new ball, according to the August 21, 1896, *Baltimore American & Commercial Advertiser*.

Frank Lane

Lane was an umpire with guts. He told Cap Anson to drop his "funny business," per the *Buffalo Courier* (August 14, 1883). The *Detroit News* (August 9, 1883) reported that "in a rundown, Chicago's Tom Burns ran past teammate Ned Williamson on the base path. Umpire Frank Lane called Burns out after Williamson was tagged out. The next day, Umpire Lane said the run should have counted." (There was no rule to penalize passing another runner.)

"Umpire Frank Lane caught Boston Beaneaters' Sam Wise going directly from first base to third. Lane called Wise out and fined him $10 when he complained." *Detroit Post and Tribune* (May 26, 1883)

"Buffalo Bisons and Detroit Wolverines had played to a 5–5 tie in the ninth inning. Detroit complained that it was too dark to play. Umpire Lane went out to shortstop and asked Buffalo Jim O'Rourke to hit him a ball. O'Rourke hit it slowly, but Lane still fumbled the ball. Lane yelled for O'Rourke to hit it harder. This time O'Rourke threw the ball and it hit Lane in the head. Then, Umpire Lane called the game for darkness." *Detroit Free Press* (September 2, 1883)

Arlie Latham

Arlie Latham was called "the freshest man on earth." He was also the last player one would think to don an umpire's blue coat. He had spent a lot of time in the umpire's face during his playing career.

In Pittsburg, Latham was the first umpire to receive a large ovation on first encounter. On July 3, 1899, in Louisville, Cleveland outfielder "Dummy" Hoy objected at a strike three call and shook his fist at Latham. Latham responded to Hoy, who was deaf, "None of your pantomime, 'Dummy,' if you could hear, I would soak you for $10, but seeing your telephones [earphones] are on the bum, I will let you go."

In the *St. Paul Globe* (August 1, 1899), Latham described his role as an umpire. "I should say I like to umpire. I haven't been at it long. The only kick I have was in Cincinnati. Yes, I made a mistake every once in a while, but you can bet they were few."

However, by September the love of umpiring disappeared when a bad call cost his old team, St. Louis, a victory. St. Louis manager Patsy Tebeau and Jack O'Connor shoved Latham. Cranks who had previously cheered him jumped out of the stands and sought to tear him apart. The St. Louis police rescued him and took him to a hotel for safety. He quit the next day.

Tom Lynch

He did such a good job at umpiring that he was later elected president of the National League. In his rookie year of 1888, a ball hit a spectator on a wild pitch. Chicago Colt Tom Daly was stealing second on the play. Lynch ruled a dead ball and returned Daly to first base. Batter Jimmy Ryan argued violently until captain Cap Anson stopped him, saying Lynch ruled correctly. (It was a dumb rule then.)

"Tom Burns on a close inside pitch headed toward first base. When Umpire Lynch didn't make a call, he headed for first base. Lynch solicited his opinion and he returned to the plate." *Chicago Tribune* (August 8, 1888)

In Washington in 1889, the groundskeeper kept two large dogs chained in deep center field. After Lynch made several calls against the Nationals, a Washington outfielder let the dogs out. They tore across the field and leaped on Lynch. The New York Giants players came to his rescue, using bats to drive off the dogs.

Manager Cap Anson was upset over the balls used in Louisville in 1894. Hugh Fullerton, a writer for the *Chicago Tribune*, played a prank on Anson. He sent a fake telegram saying, "Don't play with Barnie's balls. James Hart, National League President." When Anson arrived at the park, he took the telegram to Lynch, who ordered the game be played with Chicago's balls. The Louisville club refused. The situate was a stalemate. Anson pulled the Colts, saying "Get in the carriages boys, Hart will back us." Lynch forfeited the game to Louisville, and Anson never discovered the prank.

The *Baltimore Herald* (April 22, 1894) said, "During the game, Baltimore

Orioles John McGraw twisted away to avoid a pitch, but the ball hit his bat. Instantly, 'Little Mac' clapped his hand to the back of his head, hollering in pain and walking to first base. The bluff was so gigantic that the crowd roared and McGraw smiled as Umpire Tim Lynch called him back to home plate."

The *Chicago Tribune* (June 28, 1894) reported on a game umpired by Tom Lynch. "'Muggsy' McGraw was attempting to steal second base and batter Willie Keeler tried to help him by throwing his bat at the ball. Lynch called a strike; and McGraw left the base and addressed the umpire in such choice and expensive language that Lynch ordered him to get out of the game."

Another confrontation between McGraw and Lynch was described by the *Baltimore Herald* (July 11, 1894): "McGraw threw the ball striking Umpire Lynch in a tender spot. He fined him $25 and wished it was $100."

In 1894, the Cleveland Spiders' Chief Zimmer was hit by a pitch and proceeded to first base. Lynch requested to see Zimmer's injury. Captain Patsy Tebeau ordered his player to first base. When he got to first, Tebeau pinched his arm. Zimmer showed Lynch his arm. Lynch apologized to Zimmer and awarded him first base.

In 1896, Lynch changed a close call, which caused Cleveland manager Tebeau to burst out with profanity. Lynch ejected Tebeau, who refused to leave the field. Lynch and Tebeau got into a fist fight. Lynch refused to continue umpiring the game. Cleveland's Cy Young and Chicago's Bill Dahlen alternated as umpires. Baltimore won, 9–4.

On April 23, 1897, Baltimore defeated Boston because Lynch was not able to catch the Orioles' shortcutting behavior on the bases while he was calling plays on the other side of the diamond.

On May 3, 1897, the New York Giants jumped to an early 7–0 lead over the Washington Nationals. In the second inning, the Nationals had already started stalling tactics with rain clouds overhead. Lynch would not accept the nonsense and declared a forfeit.

On August 6, 1897, Lynch lost his temper and hit Baltimore Oriole Jack Doyle in the face. The Boston police restored order. Lynch wrote the league office, refusing to umpire the rowdy Orioles.

In May 1897, at Union Park in Baltimore, the Orioles were leading when Hughie Jennings scored on a single. Amazingly, Lynch called Jennings out on a play that did not appear close. However, the 3,700 cranks let Lynch know their fury. Despite the bad call, the Orioles won the game, 6–3, over the New York Giants.

Lynch got into an argument with Baltimore Orioles Hughie Jennings and Jack Doyle, along with Boston Beaneaters Fred Tenney and Hugh Duffy, at second base. Tenney said, "You tried to block me off." Jennings replied, "I beg your pardon, but I didn't." Then Duffy shouted, "I saw you." Doyle sauntered over and got in Tenney's face, saying "You are too big a man to light into Jennings." Then Mr. Lynch remarked, "There, that's enough, now get back in the game." And it was all over. *Sporting Life* (May 8, 1897)

The same year, John McGraw told Lynch that Phillies outfielder Sam Thompson could loan him his glasses.

> Ten thousand fans overflowed the seating in Boston where late comers took up spots along the outfield fence. They witnessed the Boston players doing things reminiscent of the Orioles. Fred Tenney stepped in front of a throw. Then he ran out of the baseline to avoid a tag. Then, Hugh Duffy stepped in front of Colts' catcher Tim Donahue, causing a wild throw. Later, Tenney stepped in front of another toss. None of these actions warranted an interference call from Lynch. Further, Duffy grabbed second baseman Jim Connor. Lynch errors were almost as numerous as the Colts" [*Chicago Tribune* (June 1, 1897)].

> The Boston Beaneater game against the Chicago Colts was in a 6–6 tie. Colts George Decker was on third when Danny Friend ran to second with the hope of drawing a throw from Boston's catcher Marty Bergen. Herman Long cut the ball and attempted to run down Friend who was heading back to first base. Decker took the opportunity to break for the plate. Umpire Lynch called Decker safe. The Beaneaters came off the bench protesting that Fred Lake had tagged Decker out. "Cap" Anson came to the plate to protest Chicago's interest. Lake took a swing at Anson hitting him in the chest. "Cap" grabbed Lake and threw him to the side. Lynch broke up the tussle and ordered Anson back to the coaches' box. As Lynch walked away, Anson chased in a vicious tirade. Anson shoved Lynch and drew back his fist but never threw a blow. Lynch fined and ejected "Cap" [*Chicago Tribune* (July 9, 1897)].

On July 17, 1897, New York Giants shortstop George Davis and the Louisville Colonels' Fred Clarke got into a fist fight and both were ejected by Lynch. Lynch refused to umpire the second game of the doubleheader, saying "he had earned his pay."

The next day, Lynch watched sabotage by the New York Giants' Buck Ewing. He was accused of doping the visitors' water keg. The Cincinnati Reds solved the situation by bringing their owner water keg. Lynch did not investigate the original keg.

The *Baltimore Sun* (August 7, 1897) reported, "Baltimore Orioles Manager Ned Hanlon accused Umpire Tom Lynch of throwing the game to the Boston Beaneaters. Orioles Jack Doyle cursed Lynch and head butted him, giving Lynch a blackened eye. Lynch decked Doyle with a left to the neck. Kelley and Joe Corbett separated the combatants."

The *Boston Globe*'s Tim Murnane (August 9, 1897) wrote, "Umpire Lynch was greeted with applause as he entered the field. The tribute was far less about him that it was Jack Doyle. Lynch remarked, 'Ladies and gentlemen, let us forget the trouble on the field here for the last few days and start all over.' The crowd responded, 'Bravo, Mr. Lynch.'"

The *Chicago Tribune* (September 3, 1897) recorded that "Tom Lynch was favoring the Boston Beaneaters with his calls. Malachi Kittridge hit a bounder off the plate. He was tagged by Marty Bergen and was called out by Umpire Lynch. Malachi claimed the ball was fouled. The decision was such that the crowd hissed."

The *Washington Star* (August 31, 1899) reported that Lynch commented, "Unquestionably, the Orioles and the Cleveland Spiders were the worst two teams I ever umpired against. When I umpired a Baltimore game, I thought the Orioles were the worst, but when I worked in Cleveland, I wasn't sure. Maybe, they were tougher and meaner than the Orioles. As for individual players who were toughest on umpires, I'd say it was a tie between McGraw and Pat Tebeau."

Michael "Jerry" Mahoney

On April 20, 1892, at Union Park in Baltimore, the Orioles were ahead, 6–5, after five innings. Baltimore's captain, George Van Haltren, told Mahoney they had to leave to catch a train to Boston. The Giants could not believe what they were hearing. Van Haltren argued that the game started at 3:30 p.m. and should be over at 5:00 p.m. However, Mahoney said they should have scheduled a later train and forfeited the game to the Giants.

"Baltimore's Curt Welch cut third base short by ten feet, but Umpire Mahoney did not see him, yet called him out. Mahoney said 'He had sense enough to know that Welch could not score that fast.'" *Philadelphia Inquirer* (July 24, 1891)

Fergus Malone

Malone was a stubborn umpire. He made a call in 1884 against the Chicago nine. Malone stated, "Anson would walk in first, while 'King' Kelly came up from third. They would meet at the plate. I would take it from both sides, then Boston's Captain John Morrill would stand in front after his interest." He was released after the season.

"On a pitchout, Chicago White Stockings 'Cap' Anson tried to protect 'King' Kelly, who was attempting to steal second base. On the pitchout, Anson stepped out of the batter's box and struck at the ball, thus blocking Boston's catcher Mert Hackett from throwing to second. Umpire Fergy Malone allowed the play." *Boston Globe* (August 31, 1884)

The Sporting News (July 5, 1886) said, "A gentleman of preternatural stupidity surpassed in this respect everything that has been known. Frequent expressions of amusement at Fergy Malone's strenuous exertions to umpire the game intelligently and impartially. Perhaps it would be fair to say that his ignorance equally affected both teams, but it was a sort of catch-as-catch-can operation. Whatever presence were given were unexpected [*sic*], and hence all the more surprising and ludicrous."

Thomas N. "Sandy" McDermott

On April 24, 1890, the New York Giants were in Boston to play the Bean-eaters. The game was tied, 2–2, in the seventh inning. Giants catcher Pat Murphy attempted to pick off Herm Long at third, but Long ran home, racing a relay throw from Jack Glasscock. A close play at the plate was ruled safe by McDermott. The Giants pitcher, Mickey Welch, and Murphy argued vehemently to the point that McDermott fined each $10. Welch threw the ball down and walked off the field. McDermott put captain Glasscock "on the clock." Jack Sharrott was signaled to go to the box. McDermott, after 60 seconds, declared a forfeit to Boston. Glasscock said he did not realize the time limit had been changed from five minutes to a minute.

McDermott was released mid-season in 1890 after being accused of being intimidated by Cap Anson of Chicago.

The *Baltimore Sun* (April 29, 1897) called McDermott "the worst the Orioles have encountered this season."

McDermott was reinstated as an umpire in 1897. On June 1, 1897, the Pittsburg Pirates, leading New York 7–4, refused to continue due to what they felt were biased calls by McDermott. McDermott had no alternative but to award a forfeit to the Giants.

In Philadelphia, "the Cincinnati Reds' players kept arguing about the ball. Every time Umpire 'Sandy' McDermott threw a ball out, there was a howl and one Cincinnati player threw the ball over the grandstand when McDermott wasn't looking. Cincinnati Manager 'Buck' Ewing tried to throw the horsehide out of the lot. He created a laugh when he failed." *Philadelphia Press* (June 8, 1897)

Jim McDonald

Jim McDonald was a silent umpire! He was also an ex-boxer, which came in handy. The *Baltimore American and Commercial Advertiser* (June 12, 1895) said that "Cleveland Spiders pitcher 'Nig' Cuppy before pitching smiled at Umpire Jim McDonald and gave the ball a shampoo of spit and sand before his next effort. McDonald did not issue a word."

The *Boston Herald* (August 30, 1895) said, "Umpire McDonald discarded a ball that Cleveland pitcher 'Nig' Cuppy had mutilated with his spikes."

In 1895, a confrontation occurred between the Baltimore Orioles and McDonald, "Trailing in a game and hoping for rain before the game became official, Orioles' players were mad as wet hens and crackled around McDonald like a convention of barnyard roosters over a grain of corn." *St. Louis Globe Democrat* (May 20, 1895)

The *Chicago Tribune* (July 14, 1897) reported that "John McGraw was arguing while standing on home plate. Chicago Colts Clark Griffith was waiting to pitch. Griffith threw two pitches that hit McGraw, but he still didn't move. Griffith walked up and stepped on his foot. McGraw hit Griffith's foot with his bat. Amazingly, the game continued. McDonald never said a word to either player."

The next day, the *Chicago Tribune* (July 17, 1897) said, "Umpire McDonald ejected McGraw in the third inning." He stated, "No more of your bulldozing tactics. If it happens tomorrow I'll fine the whole team."

A reporter for the *Chicago Tribune* (July 19, 1897) wrote,

> On July 19, 1897, the Chicago Colts were leading 4–3. Centerfielder Bill Lange was batting. "Cap" Anson signaled for a double steal. Orioles catcher "Boileryard" Clarke threw to second, but Lange nudged him, causing an off balance throw to left field. Clarke hollered at Umpire McDonald but denied seeing any interference. Two innings later, McGraw was leading off and attempted to get on base anyway he could. On the first pitch, he eased his knee over the plate causing the ball to bounce off his leg. But Umpire McDonald wouldn't allow him the base and that the pitch didn't count. McDonald got abuse from McGraw and other Orioles Jennings, Kelley and Stenzel. McDonald did get the support of the cranks.

McGraw got back in the box and leaned into another pitch. McDonald signaled "no pitch." Now Chicago's pitcher, Clark Griffith, came in and tried to spike McGraw. McGraw used his bat on Griffith's feet. McDonald called McGraw out on strike three. Orioles manager Hanlon protested the game, saying the two pitches that hit McGraw were balls and McGraw should have gotten a walk. The protest was ignored.

The *Baltimore News* (September 14, 1897) reported another verbal session between McDonald and Chicago's Cap Anson: "Hughie Jennings had three balls and then a strike call by Umpire Jim McDonald. 'Cap' came from first base waving his cap and shouting 'Hooray! Hooray!' Hughie walked on the next pitch but Baltimore's pitcher ambled innocently to the home plate where he was called out by McDonald. 'Cap' yelled another 'Hooray!'"

On September 11, 1897, Louisville and Baltimore had fought to a 3–3 tie after eight innings. John McGraw was called out at the plate and bumped McDonald. To the wonder of all, McDonald did not throw McGraw out of the game.

The *Chicago Tribune* (June 23, 1899) stated, "With the bases loaded, Chicago Orphans' Jimmy Ryan bumped New York Giants third baseman Fred

Hartman, causing him to miss a pickoff throw. When Chicago's Barry McCormick scored, Umpire Jim McDonald declared a 'do over' and everybody returned to their base."

The *Brooklyn Eagle* (May 11, 1899) noted that "Brooklyn's Joe Kelley interfered with Washington third baseman Win Mercer when he was tagged out. He hit Mercer's arm but Umpire Jim McDonald called the runner at second automatically out."

The *Baltimore American and Commercial Advertiser* (July 5, 1899) said, "Jim McDonald called John McGraw out at home plate. Crazy with wrath, McGraw grabbed the brawny umpire's coat, and McDonald squared off to return any impending blow. Instead of blows, McGraw's passions evaporated in torrents of adjectives at which McDonald ejected him."

Horace McFarland

In 1896, Chicago White Stockings President Jim Hart confronted McFarland after a game in Cincinnati. The *Cincinnati Times-Star* (August 14, 1896) reported this conversation: "Hart: I'll say to you, Mr. McFarland that you are the worst I ever saw. No man who lets the players haul him about as you do today is competent to fill the position you are trying to fill. You are simply incompetent. I haven't any doubt you are honest, but you haven't any ability. You missed your calling. You ought to resign, and at once."

McFarland did resign.

McFarland was recruited back in 1897 with the resignation of two umpires during the season. He caught the final game of the St. Louis versus Boston series. The game came down to the final inning. Boston's Fred Tenney, with Billy Hamilton attempting to steal second base, stepped in front of Pirates catcher Morgan Murphy as he threw the ball. As Murphy threw, he shot an elbow to Tenney's jaw, knocking him out. It took a few minutes to revive Tenney.

Jack McGinnity

McGinnity is not even listed as a National League or American League umpire. He was a fill-in umpire on July 24, 1897. The Philadelphia Phillies believed he was a homer, favoring the home team on strike calls. They even threatened to walk out on the game in Cleveland. The Phillies protested a walk to Cleveland's Patsy Tebeau. Chief Zimmer, the next hitter, was also given a walk. The Phillies charged from every position, thinking the game had already been decided. Philadelphia's shortstop took a punch at McGinnity but missed. McGinnity had enough and forfeited the game to the Spiders. The Orioles filed a protest, to no avail.

Bill McLean

McLean was an ex-boxer who became an umpire. If nothing else, he was diligent. When he missed his train, he walked from Boston to Providence.

The Chicago White Stockings squared off against the Cincinnati Reds on July 2, 1879. McLean fined players from both teams after constant bickering. He then walked off the field. Both captains promised there would be no more kicking, and McLean returned to complete the game.

The Providence Grays' Jim O'Rourke was headed for third base, only to discover that teammate John Ward had dislodged the base. So he touched where the base had been. The Buffalo Bisons protested, saying he missed tagging the bag. However, McLean ruled correctly that he was safe.

McLean was cursed in Philadelphia in 1884. He became so upset he grabbed a bat and tossed it into the stands, striking a crank. Police came on the field and arrested him, charging him with assault. He apologized, saying he "forgot his position as an umpire and did what a normal person would do."

The Boston Beaneaters' Joe Horning told McLean he needed glasses. McLean fined him $20, but bought glasses.

"Chicago's George Gore was reprimanded in yesterday's game by Umpire Bill McLean for using his hand to attempt to knock the ball loose from Syracuse first baseman George Adams." *Syracuse Herald* (June 20, 1879)

The *Indianapolis News* reported on May 2, 1878, "Indianapolis' George Shaffer attempted to steal second but was held by Chicago's 'Cap' Anson at first base. The Blue's catcher Bill Harbridge overthrew second. But, instead of being on third base, he was stuck at second. Umpire McLean claimed to have not noticed anything."

On May 12, 1884, McLean was umpiring a game between the top two National League teams, the Chicago White Stockings and the Providence Grays. Chicago's versatile Mike Kelly, who was playing shortstop, jumped into the path of Paul Radford, causing him to retreat to second base. McLean saw the blocking and ordered Radford to third base. The Umpire reprimanded Kelly for his action.

Four days later, in another series against Chicago, Hoss Radbourn confronted McLean and yelled "it is too damn dark to see the mud stained ball." McLean fired back, "shut up and play." Then a heavy rain fell and the umpire called time. After 18 minutes, Cap Anson insisted the game be resumed, and

McLean obliged. There were no tarps put on the field. The Providence Grays' Charlie Sweeney immediately threw a wild pitch. Sweeney then struck out the side. The eighth inning brought more heavy rain and a halt in play. After the eighth inning, again came the rain. The ninth inning was finally started at 6:00 p.m. The Grays scored two runs to take the lead, 7–5. Providence hurler Tommy Corcoran prevented additional scoring for the victory. After the game, King Kelly said, "Water never did agree with Kelly, he preferred whiskey."

June 22, 1884, brought the rival White Stockings and Red Stockings to the diamond. Boston outfielder Jack Manning turned his ankle sliding. He attempted to continue but collapsed on the bench. Manager Harry Wright sent Charlie Buffinton, a sub, to the outfield. Chicago's Cap Anson protested so vigorously that McLean ordered Manning back to his position. Boston's captain, John Morrill, would not allow the hobbled Manning off the bench. McLean gave Manning five minutes to take his position. Boston continued playing with only eight fielders. Chicago was victorious, 11–7.

The results of the game were not over. The *Chicago Herald* quoted a Boston crank, J. M. Allen, as saying, "If McLean steps foot upon the Boston base ball grounds you do at your peril." McLean, the ex-pugilist, replied in the *Cleveland Leader* (July 2, 1884): "Sir, you are a coward. If you are not, write and inform me where you can be found, for in that case I shall find you when I go to Boston again. *Chicago Herald* (June 29, 1884) McLean justified his call, saying "I expect abuse and am prepared for it. I do not count popularity at the expense of justice of fair play."

The *Cincinnati Times-Star* (October 12, 1889) recorded a fight between Cap Anson and McLean. Anson thought "to ridicule the idea, believing I could give him the quiet, without special effort on my part." "McLean ended up beating him so well that he offered to pay him handsomely if he would teach him the trick."

Jack McQuaid

His philosophy of umpiring was "always keep your eye on the ball. No play can be made without the ball. Therefore, it behooves you to follow it with your optics all the time. Once in a while, a player is given to play 'dirty ball,' such as catching hold of a base runner or blocking him, may 'turn a trick' while you are watching the ball and get away with it, but that is the only kind of play that you miss." *Brooklyn Eagle* (April 24, 1894)

The Board of Umpires consisted of Gracie Pierce, Joe Quest, John Kelly, and John McQuaid. Prior to the 1886 World Series, the question of Mark Baldwin's eligibility was questioned by St. Louis owner Chris Von der Ahe.

Pierce did not show. Kelly refused to vote, Quest voted yes and McQuaid voted no. The tie vote was decided by a coin flip. McQuaid won and ruled Baldwin ineligible.

On June 16, 1887, in a game between the St. Louis Browns and Baltimore Orioles, McQuaid was accused of making close decisions against the Orioles. St. Louis' Curt Welch ran out of the baseline and knocked second baseman Bill Greenwood off his feet. McQuaid ruled Welch safe. The Baltimore cranks leaped over the wire fence and overran the field. All order had been destroyed. Welch was arrested for assault. McQuaid was blamed for the debacle for not calling Welch out for obstruction.

On October 3, 1889, the *New York Times* reported that when Boston's Hardy Richardson was called out at the plate, King Kelly decided to act. "With blazing eyes and inflamed face, he told McQuaid that he had come west to rob Boston of the pennant. Kelly took a swing at McQuaid but was stopped by two policemen who used a choke hold on the "King." He was ushered out of the park and was seen smoking and talking to young boys."

On May 23, 1890, McQuaid admitted he made an error in not allowing Billy Grey into the Philadelphia lineup as a substitute. The National League directors overturned the Chicago victory, and the game was replayed.

In 1891, Pittsburg was playing Chicago when Doggie Miller threw his glove, missing Cap Anson as he ran the bases. McQuaid ejected Miller for his toss.

In 1892, Boston was playing in Cleveland. King Kelly was so drunk he sat on the bench wearing an overcoat. He was too drunk to argue with McQuaid. McQuaid was not going to tolerate Kelly's belligerence. He summoned the Cleveland police, who took Kelly out of the park. Kelly, the Boston captain, was outside looking in.

Sporting Life (August 15, 1891) reported,

> Umpire McQuaid gave first base to "Cap" Anson when "Kid" Nichols took over one minute to deliver the pitch. Boston protested the game going to base on balls. The protest is the most absurd I ever heard of. "Kid" Nichols and Charlie Bennett plainly intended to give Anson his base on balls, and McQuaid seeing it, sent him to base to avoid delay. What difference there is between sending Anson to base and having Bennett stand half way up the line towards first base while Nichols tossed four balls to him, is one of the things I cannot understand. It looks like a weak subterfuge on the part of the Beaneater to try and shift the blame of the defeat on McQuaid's shoulders, but it won't do with intelligent people.

The following incident occurred in Brooklyn in 1892. McQuaid called Tom Daly, a utility player, out on a pickoff play at first base. The problem was that no one heard the umpire. So Cap Anson, coaching first for Chicago, yelled "You're out!" Anson told the umpire, "When you make a decision, call it loud. No man on the field heard the umpire's decision." McQuaid smiled and laughed, replying "I'm a little weak," motioning to his throat. "Oh well," Anson answered. "All right," McQuaid returned. A crank then yelled to Anson, "You're right, Pop." Anson stated, "Certainly, I made the decision before he did."

On August 20, 1894, Chicago's Bill Lange secured a 5'10" bat from a New York play. He went to home plate with the bat, and the cranks went wild. McQuaid allowed him to use the bat, and he grounded out to first. The New York Giants won the game, 11–3.

The *Cincinnati Enquirer* (May 16, 1893) said, "Umpire Jack McQuaid fined and ejected Cincinnati's catcher Harry Vaughn for hitting St. Louis Steve Brodie with a bat."

The *Boston Globe* (August 16, 1894) claimed that "Umpire Jack McQuaid, the same umpire who ruled against 'Kid' Nichols three summers earlier, ruled Nichols' hit down the left field line was foul. The homer was good by five feet."

Arlie Latham was upset at the 1894 infield fly rule. Latham stood perfectly still on a pop-up, letting it drop at his feet. He picked up the ball and tossed it to the pitcher to demonstrate the absurdity of the rule. McLean ruled the runner out.

In 1897, McQuaid made several questionable calls. He allowed Boston's Jack Stivetts a base on balls when he struck at the third strike. He gave Tommy McCarthy a hit on a ball which was foul by several feet. Even Stivetts admitted after the game that he swung at the pitch, and a couple of Boston players acknowledged McCarthy's foul ball.

Harry Medart

A St. Louis Browns crank, Harry Medart was pulled from the stands to umpire Game Four when managers could not agree on an umpire. Medart ruled a Chicago base runner Tom Burns out when Arlie Latham tagged him with his empty hand. Cap Anson protested to no avail. Medart remained out of controversy until the ninth inning, when he ruled that St. Louis first baseman Comiskey tagged Jim McCormick out on a pickoff throw, which drew an outburst from the entire Chicago club. Even the religious Billy Sunday charged Medart, yelling "That man was not out!" Medart called Sunday "a liar, if you don't [take it back]. I'll make you." Both combatants took a boxing stance. King Kelly acted as a peacemaker by pulling Sunday away. Chicago's McCormick then moved in with rage. Medart requested assistance from Anson. Kelly again prevented a fight by stepping in front of McCormick. Due to Kelly, the game resumed. The game ended with a 3–2 victory for the Browns. The win was in no small part helped by Medart.

Bobby Mitchell

On July 22, 1887, at Athletic Park in Philadelphia, Athletics Harry Stovey and Lou Bierbauer were on third and first. Bierbauer took a lead to draw a throw. Cleveland Blues pitcher Mike Morrison tried to pick Bierbauer off, which resulted in a rundown between first and second. Cleveland's second baseman, Cub Stricker, saw Stovey breaking for home. The batter, Ted Larkin, seeing Stovey would be an easy out, blocked Charles Snyder's throw, allowing Stovey to run back to third. Mitchell called Stovey out, then changed his mind and called Larkin out for interference. Cleveland argued for the out at third. Suddenly, Mitchell threw up his hands and forfeited the game to Philadelphia. This occurred with Cleveland leading, 6–4. Cleveland's whole team surrounded the umpire in disgust, but to no avail.

Jeremiah "Miah" Murray

Murray called a strike on Baltimore's John McGraw for hitting a foul ball which the umpire deemed he did on purpose. (Foul balls were not counted as strikes in the rule book.) McGraw was so mad that he threw his bat and cap on the field. McGraw was fined $25.

The *Baltimore Herald* (May 13, 1895) reported, "Baltimore was down by one run in the fifth inning and it looked like rain. Muggsy McGraw yelled in pain and fell to the ground. Umpire Murray said, 'If you can show a mark on him, I will give you the base.' McGraw tugged at his sleeve, but all the time inflicting a number of vicious pinches on his upper arm. There was a large red spot and he showed it to Murray who awarded him first base."

Also in 1895, Baltimore's Steve Brodie pulled off Murray's mask and flung it, resulting in his ejection.

Hank O'Day (HOF)

He was a soft-spoken umpire who was a no-nonsense individual. On September 11, 1884, as a substitute umpire for a game in Toledo, he worked his first game.

On August 20, 1895, in Washington, the Nationals were leading, 7–4, in the seventh inning. They began to use stalling tactics. Cleveland was batting last even though they were the visiting team. O'Day allowed Cleveland to bat in the dark. Ed McKean hit a three-run homer to win the game. A large group of older boys rushed at the umpire. Some even threw rocks and coal. A rock hit Nationals pitcher Al Maul, cutting him. A "lady" hit O'Day with her parasol, yelling "robber."

On September 6, 1895, Pittsburg manager Connie Mack objected to a call at second base. O'Day fined Mack $100 and ejected him due to "insulting and abusive language." The New York police were required to make Mack leave the field. This was Mack's lone ejection in his Hall of Fame managerial career.

The *Cincinnati Enquirer* (July 5, 1897) said, "Baltimore Oriole John McGraw was arguing with Umpire Hank O'Day when he dropped his bat and caught the pitch. Umpire O'Day called the pitch a strike.

"Louisville's Fred Clarke detached second base and took the base as he ran to third base. When tagged, he showed the base to Umpire Hank O'Day and claimed as long as he had the base he was safe. The crowd laughed as O'Day ruled Clarke out." *Chicago Inter Ocean* (July 26, 1897)

The *New York Sun* (September 10, 1897) reported that the New York Giants were after a new ball. Giants catcher Jack Warner picked at the seams of the ball with his fingers. When Warner continued picking, O'Day asked, "Why don't you bite it?" Warner tossed the ball to O'Day, who without looking threw it to the pitcher.

"None of the Baltimore Orioles could talk to Umpire O'Day except Joe Kelley as he did in Baltimore. Kelley called him everything, even using profanity, and got away without a word." *Louisville Courier-Journal* (September 12, 1897)

Cap Anson made the following statement about O'Day in 1897: "In the first place, I think that in several of our close games we got the worst of it from the umpires. That is surely true of our first games at Baltimore. The rank decisions O'Day gave in our first game with Baltimore were responsible for the score going 3 to 2 against us, and if had gotten our just desserts we would have won it in a walk."

In 1897, the Cleveland Spiders hosted the St. Louis Browns. Browns owner Chris Von der Ahe was run off the field by Cleveland manager Patsy Tebeau. Von der Ahe complained to O'Day, "Trow dos men oud." O'Day refused, and the contest began. Tebeau, while coaching third base, made faces at Von der Ahe, who would blow a shrill whistle. The cranks were now involved in Von der Ahe's amusement. Cleveland manager's brother, George Tebeau, grabbed Von der Ahe's bodyguard by the throat when he came on the field. O'Day had had enough of the on-field activity by non-players and halted the game, telling Von der Ahe he would be removed. Von der Ahe sat in his seat and was quiet the rest of the game.

The *Baltimore Sun* (July 1, 1898) stated that "Louisville Colonel's Coach Bert Cunningham blocked John McGraw's throw to home plate allowing Claude Richey to score. Umpire Hank O'Day ejected Cunningham and called Richey out."

Sporting Life (September 18, 1897) reported: "In Pittsburg, middle September, Umpire Hank O'Day was ruling a double header. The Pirates won the opener 5–4. Giants Captain Bill Joyce took too much time getting back to the field, so O'Day walked off the field and left the teams to their own devices. New York's sub outfielder Walt Wilmot and Pittsburg's pitcher Jesse Tannehill served as emergency umpire replacements. The Giants won the second game that was stopped after six innings because of darkness."

Chicago Record (June 11, 1898) said: "The Chicago Colts' Clark Griffith used the base ball to jar dirt from his spikes. After players from Cleveland complained, Umpire Hank O'Day deemed the ball to be fine. Cleveland's Manager 'Patsy' Tebeau imitated Griffith's tactic. The ball with Patsy's spike mark was passed around in the crowd."

"Cincinnati Reds batter Harry Stenfeldt struck his bat against the arm of Pittsburg Pirate 'Jiggs' Donahue to make a poor throw. Two runners advanced a base, but Umpire O'Day made them return to their previous base." *Cincinnati Commercial Tribune* (April 22, 1899)

The *Chicago Chronicle* (May 18, 1899 reported that "Chicago Orphans Clark Griffith hid a ball under his foot on the bench, requiring Umpire O'Day to put in a new one."

"The Chicago Orphans outfielder for some unknown reason applied Vaseline to the ball. But Umpire Hank O'Day threw out the ball and replaced it with a new one." *Chicago Tribune* (July 21, 1899)

On June 22, 1900, the Philadelphia Phillies were playing the Brooklyn Superbas. Ed Delahanty was called out on strikes by O'Day. Brooklyn took the lead. Delahanty, who was still fuming, went to stalling techniques by telling the pitcher to walk batters so to revert to the preceding inning. O'Day had seen these tactics before and declared the game a forfeit. The *Philadelphia Inquirer* (June 23, 1900) called the play "inexpressively stupid and tactless, since 45 minutes of sunlight existed."

Later in the season, O'Day was accosted by the Brooklyn club, which charged on the field, throwing their gloves at O'Day. O'Day forfeited the game to New York, 9–0.

Jim "Orator" O'Rourke

His first performance as an umpire was rated by the press as follows: "His umpiring performance was poor and that was a mild term. His rulings on balls, strikes, and base decisions merited the condemnation that he received from the crowd. He gave everything to them and they can thank him for the victory." *New York Times* (April 24, 1894).

On April 30, 1894, the *Philadelphia Enquirer* described his umpiring as:

"Why O'Rourke's a robber. We're taking up a collection to send him home. Scorekeeper, how many assists did Mr. O'Rourke get."

The *Cincinnati Enquirer* (May 16, 1894) stated, "The Cincinnati Club claimed O'Rourke was incompetent and a wretched umpire."

The *Baltimore Sun* (May 17, 1894) wrote about one of O'Rourke's controversial calls: "When Tommy Tucker slid into third, he got up with his nose bleeding and he declared that John McGraw had kicked him in the face. Umpire Jim O'Rourke disagreed that McGraw hit him with his foot."

The *Washington Post* (June 22, 1894) reported that "Louisville Colonels runner John Grim was thrown out at the plate, but Umpire O'Rourke sent him back to third claiming he wasn't ready to watch the play."

National League President George Wright said his problem was nervousness. O'Rourke complained, "umpiring is too tiring." By late June, he had had enough and quit.

Dickey Pearce

After umpiring for one year, he took a three-year vacation. Pearce was umpiring a game between Providence and Cleveland in 1882. The coin flip to decide batting choice was won by Providence, which selected batting first. A missed throw by first baseman Joe Start, which he could not locate, resulted in three runs. The cranks littered the field with 25-cent seat cushions as Cleveland won, 4–1. Pearce was lauded for his calling of balls and strikes.

The *Kansas City Times* (August 18, 1886) said, "the Kansas City Cowboys' Pete Conway ran from first base to second on a passed ball. He turned and asked Chicago's first baseman that day, 'King' Kelly, if it was a foul ball. 'Yes,' said Kelly, and thereupon, Conway walked back to first. On the way, second baseman Fred Pfeffer tagged him out. When Conway kicked, Kelly explained by saying, 'O, I thought you asked if that was a passed ball.'" Kansas City's captain, Dave Rowe, came out to kick with Pearce. The conversation was:

> ROWE: "We won't stand that. You've no right to call that man out on such a play."
>
> PEARCE: "What are you going to do about it? Mr. Conway asked, I didn't tell him it was foul."

He was umpiring a St. Louis Browns' game in late 1886 when a slight drizzle began. Manager Charlie Comiskey, with the first drop, requested that Pearce halt play. Pearce refused, but that did not stop Comiskey from inciting the cranks. Thousands of cranks poured onto the field, which resulted in a delay. By the time the cranks returned to the stands at the urging of the police, the rain had stopped and play resumed.

Pearce umpired Game Six of the 1886 Championship Series. In the ninth inning, Curt Welch was hit by a pitch and awarded first base. Chicago manager Cap Anson protested that Welch did not attempt to avoid the pitch. Pearce changed his call and brought Welch back to the plate. Welch stormed back to the box with anger but managed a sharp single to center. He would eventually score the winning run on a wild pitch by John Clarkson. The play would be called the "$15,000 slide."

In the 1886 Series, Chicago's catcher, King Kelly, complained to Pearce that Arlie Latham was using a flat-head bat. Latham had whittled one side of the bat, which was illegal in 1886. Pearce examined the bat and ruled that Latham must get another bat.

Dave Pearson

The *Cincinnati Enquirer* (October 14, 1877) reported that "Philadelphia Athletics cut first base short and when the ball was wildly thrown from the outfield, Mack ran some more. In running home, he passed ten feet inside of third base, but Umpire Pearson wasn't looking that way and didn't call him out. Mack said an umpire should never let the ball bother himself, but keep his eyes on the base runner." Denny Mack did umpire in the American Association in 1886.

Phil Powers

Phil Powers wore questionable attire when umpiring his first game in 1891, his final season. "He wore a dirty shirt, no coat and hand-me-down pants." He had an uneventful year before quitting.

The *Chicago Herald* (August 19, 1887) said that the Pittsburg Alleghenys' Jim McCormick was alerting his teammate to Chicago's Cap Anson's tricks when the following conversation ensued:

McCORMICK: I'm where you can't play your dirty tricks.
ANSON: What tricks?
McCORMICK: Money tricks.
ANSON: I don't owe you any money.

The two players were so close that their uniforms touched. Powers broke up the reunion and said, "This ends the story."

Powers was one of the better umpires on catching runners who cut bases short. He caught Chicago's Silver Flint and Marty Sullivan in the same week.

On July 27, 1888, Chicago White Stockings pitcher Mark Baldwin took a half-swing which was called a strike by Powers. Cap Anson came to the plate with the pretense of coaching Baldwin. Anson used the excuse to argue the call. Powers paid no attention to Anson's antics. Washington Nationals pitcher Hank O'Day threw the ball, and Powers called strike three with Baldwin and Anson still kicking.

On August 14, 1889, New York's captain, Buck Ewing, convinced Powers that Cleveland's Jimmy McAleer had cut first base short on a double. When Powers ruled McAleer out, the cranks rushed the field. Three policeman and the Cleveland players protected Powers, who took sanctuary under the stands until the physical threat was eliminated.

Per the *New York Herald* (May 13, 1890), in a game pitched by Boston's future Hall of Famer, Kid Nichols, the following event occurred: "When [the] Giants Mike Tierman came to bat, he nipped a foul into the stands. Umpire Powers tossed a new ball into play. Then the old ball was thrown back onto the diamond. Nichols requested to use the old ball. Umpire Powers stated 'the new ball was on the field first.' The next pitch was the last as Tiernan hit a game winning home run."

The *Philadelphia Inquirer* (July 25, 1890) was critical of Powers when it said, "Phil Powers was incompetent and dishonest, according to the cranks. While he is neither of these, he did give a combination of glaring decisions which robbed the Philadelphia Club of the game."

The *Chicago Daily News* (July 7, 1891) reported that Brooklyn's Oyster Burns flied out to right field. Dave Foutz had wandered too far off first base and would have been doubled up, but Burns got in the way, preventing the ball getting to Cap Anson. Powers allowed the play. Anson told Burns, "Just you try a thing of that kind again and see what I'll do to you!" Anson shouted his warning to all who could hear, including Powers.

In 1891, Cincinnati's Arlie Latham grabbed Cleveland's Jimmy McAleer to prevent him from scoring. After Cleveland captain, Patsy Tebeau alerted Powers, he gave McAleer the plate.

On July 30, 1891, the Cincinnati Reds met the Chicago Colts. The Reds felt Powers' calls were one-sided. Cincinnati pitcher Tony Mullane was boiling made when he walked up to Powers and struck him in the face. Powers declared, "I won't rob Chicago and you are fined $100." Mullane exclaimed, "You robbed me bald." Powers fined Mullane an additional $100 and added, "I dare you to strike me again." Mullane was out of control and pushed Powers, costing himself another $50. Mullane's total fine was $250, yet National League President Nick Young reduced the fine to $5. This situation is indicative of how lax the league was on supporting its umpires.

Philadelphia Inquirer (August 10, 1892): "Umpire Powers has been unanimously elected a member of the Society for the Promotion of Riots."

Sporting Life (August 23, 1892) described his umpiring as "a detriment to the game. Mr. Powers is not competent. He doesn't know the rules and his eyesight is certainly impaired."

Joe Quinn

He was a player who was a substitute umpire for one game. The *Boston Journal* (May 31, 1882) saw "Buffalo Bisons outfielder 'Blondie' Purcell cut a ball with a corn knife. He did it to help his team's pitcher 'Pud' Galvin grip the 'punky' ball. Umpire Joe Quinn threw the ball out and fined Purcell $10."

Jack Remsen
(Substitute Umpire for Game Two of the 1884 Championship Series)

Remsen was a one-game umpire in the 1884 Championship Series. What? After the 1884 season, a three-game Series was played between the National League Providence Grays and the American Association New York Metropolitans. The Grays, behind Hoss Radbourn, won the first game. The umpire for the second game was Brooklyn Trolley Dodgers' outfielder Jack Remsen. This was basically an exhibition game, yet when Remsen declared the Grays' Jack Farrell safe, the Polo Grounds' cranks yelled outbursts of disgust. In the top of the eighth inning, Remsen called the game due to darkness at 4:55 p.m. It was not dark, but it was cold, so no one put up a fight. The Grays won the first baseball "World Series" the next day.

Jack Sheridan

He called a game because of sunshine. That's right, on May 16, 1892, as a substitute umpire in a game between the St. Louis Browns and Washington Nationals, he stopped the game after 14 innings. The sun was shining directly in the catcher's and umpire's faces. It was the only time in the history of baseball that a game was called because of sun.

In the season opener in 1896, St. Louis' Arlie Latham accosted new umpire Jack Sheridan in the dressing room. The St. Louis police rescued Sheridan.

He seemed to thrive on controversy and was famous for his boisterous "Y-Y-yo O-O-utt" call. The *Louisville Courier* (April 24, 1892) said, "the Chicago spectators went wild on an out call and threw seat cushions on the field even though their team was up 4–2. Captain Anson grabbed a bat when cranks jumped on the field to fend them back to the stands. The Louisville Club, hoping for a forfeit, grabbed cushions and threw them on the field at their teammates. One Louisville bench player hid in a water barrel. Umpire Jack Sheridan awarded a forfeit for Louisville."

In 1897, Sheridan was given credit for a Cincinnati offensive rally. The

Reds' Dusty Miller hit a ball that appeared foul that Sheridan ruled fair, giving Miller a double. Later, the Baltimore Orioles' Wilbert Robinson hit one that bounced over the fence, which was a ground rule home run. A policeman threw the ball over the fence, but Sheridan missed the action and only gave Robinson a double.

In a *Pittsburg Record* (February 17, 1897) interview, John McGraw stated,

A runner on first started to steal second and he spiked Orioles first baseman Jack Doyle. Doyle retaliated by trying to trip him. When he got to second base, "Heinie" Reitz tried to block him. Hughie Jennings covered the bag and took the throw to tag him out. The runner evaded Reitz and jumped feet first at Jennings to drive him from the bag. Jennings dodged the spikes and threw himself bodily at the runner knocking the breath out of him. In the meantime, the batter hit our catcher "Boileryard" Clarke over the hands with his bat so he couldn't throw, and our catcher stepped on Umpire Sheridan with his spikes and shoved his mitt in his face so he couldn't see the play. Ump Sheridan punched "Boileryard" in the ribs and called it a foul ball, and sent the runner back to first.

The *Baltimore Sun* (May 22, 1897) said, "Cincinnati first baseman 'Farmer' Vaughn had touched third, but was now being strangled. He got out of McGraw's grasp to score. McGraw, in the eighth inning attempted to spike Vaughn. Vaughn cried 'You owe me an apology.' McGraw responded with "I don't owe you anything." Vaughn threw a ball that hit McGraw in the back, who didn't even flinch. Umpire Jack Sheridan then ejected McGraw and a real tirade started."

In a July 10, 1897, game between Brooklyn and St. Louis, the St. Louis cranks tossed eggs at Sheridan. The umpire demanded police protection. St. Louis owner Chris Von der Ahe, a noted umpire abuser, stood in the stands and demanded that the cranks desist. After the game, St. Lois manager Hugh Nicol blamed the 4–3 loss on the umpire. The *St. Louis Dispatch* sided with the manager, resulting in a big crowd for the next game. The Browns lost, 22–4, to Baltimore, and the umpire was not questioned.

One of the umpire calls which would not occur today occurred when Sheridan called a game when too few cranks showed up due to threatening rain. He used the excuse of "wet grounds." The game was rescheduled. Both teams agreed.

The *Baltimore Sun* (July 23, 1897) reported, "Umpire Sheridan was calling balls and strikes behind the pitcher's mound. Hawley verbally abused Sheridan, until Sheridan hit Hawley in the face. The fiery pitcher retaliated with two blows of his own, which knocked Sheridan out. Hawley was ejected and his teammate Charlie Hastings finished umpiring the game. The Orioles won 9–1."

Sheridan had a bad week in Louisville with a game involving the Philadelphia Phillies in 1897. The bleacher cranks poured on the field to attack

Sheridan. He sought shelter in the club's office until the crowd left. He required 16 policemen to escort him to his hotel. Louisville President Henry Pulliam sent a telegram to National League President Nick Young, saying "We will not stand any more of Mr. Sheridan."

Baltimore owner Fred Robinson went to manager Ned Hanlon about Sheridan's umpiring: "Do you propose to play tomorrow with this umpiring! Hanlon, the team is ready to walk." "It was the worst skinning I have had for a long time," reported Hanlon.

In May 1899, Baltimore pitcher Harry Howell cursed Sheridan for a safe call at home. Sheridan ejected Howell along with Ducky Holmes, who hit him in the back with a thrown ball. Orioles manager John McGraw told Howell to return to the mound, which resulted in Sheridan awarding a forfeit to Detroit. McGraw wrote a letter saying Sheridan was an incompetent umpire.

On April 28, 1899, McGraw had to dodge an inside pitch to prevent being hit by Boston pitcher Bill Dinneen. The next pitch hit McGraw, but Sheridan did not allow him to take his base. A loud argument ensued. In McGraw's next at-bat, he simply sat down in the batter's box. Sheridan ejected McGraw for his actions. The Baltimore cranks mobbed Sheridan at the game's conclusion.

Charles "Pop" Snyder

"Pop" Snyder was a catcher for 877 major league games, which should have made him a good umpire. On August 2, 1890, in an extra-inning game, Snyder ejected the Brooklyn Wonders' George Van Haltren for throwing his bat at the pitcher. However, Snyder allowed St. Louis' Charlie Comiskey to stand on home plate after scoring. He ejected Brooklyn manager John Ward, who argued and called him a crook. *The Sporting News* (August 2, 1890) said Snyder was liked as a player, but that wasn't going to help him in his new occupation.

On October 4, 1890, Brooklyn's hot-tempered pitcher, Gus Weyhing accosted Snyder, yelling that he "was on [the] Buffalo Club's pay." His vile language was so offensive, the police escorted Mr. Weyhing to the police station and put him in jail. Weyhing's teammates raised $200 bail money. The *Boston Globe* (October 4, 1890) stated, "The double-umpire system has been tried and found wanting. It has been illustrated that two poor umpires are worse than one."

"Umpire Charlie Snyder when he returned to umpiring wore a tennis shirt without a coat, leaving him no place to put the base balls. He just left them on the ground which resulted in disputes." *Brooklyn Eagle* (May 9, 1893)

The *Baltimore American and Commercial Adventurer* (August 1, 1893) said that "Baltimore's John McGraw smashed home plate with his bat. However, opponent New York Giants' 'Shorty' Fuller threw the bat against the grand stand. When Umpire Snyder reprimanded Fuller, he verbally abused Snyder, resulting in a $30 fine."

The game Snyder is most remembered for umpiring was in 1898, when a torrential downpour occurred. The Cleveland Spiders and Pittsburg Pirates were allowed to play two innings in ankle-deep mud. The *Cleveland Plain Dealer* (June 13, 1898) reported, "Snyder was last seen in full-slog looking for dry land." The game was awarded to Pittsburg after four innings.

On June 16, 1898, before 15,000 spectators in New York, Snyder called Boston's speedy "Sliding Billy" Hamilton safe at third base. The Giants' cranks surged over the rails onto the field. Snyder needed a police escort to vacate the stands and retreat to his hotel.

In 1900, the Brooklyn Bridegrooms' Joe Kelley threw his glove at Snyder, which resulted in his ejection. Also, pitcher Joe McGinnity shoved Snyder. The police prevented the Brooklyn cranks from any additional behavior.

The *Pittsburg Commercial Gazette* (June 1, 1898) reported, "Baltimore's John McGraw and Hughie Jennings chewed on pitcher Bill Hoffer after a loss to the Pirates. McGraw took it out on Umpire Charles Snyder as McGraw flew off the handle with his hollering. Snyder gave him a look and the latter part of the sentence was not much more than a growl."

Ed Steward

He was a substitute umpire brought out from the stands. The *Chicago Tribune* recorded that "'Bad Bill' Dahlen argued a called third strike and Umpire Ed Steward fined him $10. Dahlen continued to argue, saying the ball was too far inside. But, he didn't have the right to throw dust into Steward's eyes to prevent an unfavorable decision at the plate. Steward used his handkerchief vigorously for some seconds, but said nothing."

Dave Sullivan

His time in the spotlight came in the 1885 Championship Series between the Chicago White Stockings (NL) and the St. Louis Browns (AA). Sullivan erroneously called King Kelly out on a steal of second base in Game Two. Unfortunately, Sullivan attempted to make up for the mistake by a series of "make-up" calls for the reminder of the game. He called St. Louis' Sam Barkley out on a pitch "over his head." A foul ball was called fair. St. Louis captain Charlie Comiskey was boiling mad. The St. Louis cranks yelled for a new umpire. Comiskey said, "Your calls are so biased that you should quit umpiring." Sullivan retaliated by threatening a forfeit. Two hundred cranks stormed the field with the White Stockings leading, 5–4. Police escorted Sullivan to the Lindell Hotel. Sullivan called the game a forfeit to the White Stockings from his hotel room. The next day, Sullivan was fired by the National League.

Jerry Sullivan

On August 12, 1887, the Cleveland Blues faced the New York Metropolitans. Blues pitcher Gus Weyhing hit a ball that landed in the "Fall of Babylon" scenery in right field. Sullivan ruled a two-base hit. Captain Harry Stovey argued that the ball hit the heel of right fielder Eddie Hogan's foot and should be ruled a home run. Stovey would not return to the bench, therefore, Sullivan awarded a 9–0 forfeit to New York.

Edward "Big Ed" Swartwood

He was one of the toughest umpires in baseball history, which he proved by throwing John McGraw in a creek.

He fined Arlie Latham $25 when he objected to a strikeout. When Latham continued his outburst, he was ejected. Later that year, the *Brooklyn Eagle* (June 10, 1894) reported, "Only once did Cincinnati Captain Latham address Mr. Swartwood and that was to request the game be hurried so the team could catch the train for Philadelphia."

In 1897, the Orioles' John McGraw was ejected by Swartwood. After the game, McGraw ran into Swartwood on a bridge. McGraw said, "I have a notion to punch you." Swartwood stuck out his jaw. McGraw swung but missed with a punch. The ump picked up McGraw and threw him in the creek. McGraw crawled out soaked but laughing. Swartwood laughed too.

The *Pittsburg Commercial Gazette* (July 30, 1898) recorded that "Umpire Ed Swartwood put a new ball in play, swept off home plate, and turned around to see that Pittsburg Pirates second baseman Dick Padden had the ball and it looked as if it had been dug out of a sewer."

The *New York Sun* (May 16, 1899) stated that Swartwood threw the ball over the grandstand. The Brooklyn players swarmed around the umpire, and captain Joe Kelley said, "You have no right to throw the ball out of the grounds. You ought to be ashamed of yourself. It cost a dollar and quarter, and you ought to be made to pay for it."

In 1899, Ed Delahanty and Nap Lajoie knocked consecutive blasts off the brick wall in center field. The ball was split open and was delivered to Swartwood. He put a new one in play and kept the old one as a souvenir.

Sporting Life (August 11, 1900) called Swartwood "the worst offender in the bunch." The *Philadelphia Inquirer* (September 8, 1900) said Swartwood "was incompetent, always had been incompetent and promised no better for this year than he had in years." One game that supported this claim occurred on July 16, 1900, when Swartwood reversed a game-ending double play call to safe. There were several calls which favored the New York Giants. The Brooklyn Superbas exploded with anger. Swartwood threw a punch at Bill Dahlen. The Giants' Joe McGinnity grabbed Swartwood to prevent any more fisticuffs.

On August 6, 1900, Swartwood became ill during the first game of a doubleheader and was unable to begin the second game. Boston's Kid Nichols, who pitched the first game, and Cincinnati pitcher Ted Breitenstein umpired the game and, as the *Boston Globe* said, "umpired without calling fourth a murmur."

Ben Tuthill

Tuthill was a substitute umpire for two games. The *Baltimore Herald* (June 25, 1895) reported, "McGraw and Joe Kelley tore Tuthill from side to side with their expositions. They pulled his arm and pushed him around now and then. Tuthill fined McGraw $25 but cancelled it after the game because he made an erroneous call."

Jack Valentine

Jack Valentine was an honest umpire. In 1884, he reported a bribery attempt.

In 1884 Valentine had trouble with Louisville pitcher Guy Hecker stepping beyond the pitcher's box. He inserted small, smooth stones at the edge of the box, and Hecker would slip on the stones. Louisville complained about the Cincinnati pitcher starting his delivery outside the box, so Valentine inserted stones on the right side of the box. How long before a hit ball struck a stone?

The Philadelphia Quakers were playing the St. Louis Browns at Sportsman's Park in 1884. The Quakers' Harry Stovey hit a blast to right field. However, there was no foul pole; therefore, Valentine was not sure if it was a fair ball. Stovey circled the bases in a trot. Valentine failed to make an immediate decision. St. Louis owner Chris Von der Ahe jumped over the rail and addressed the umpire: "Look here, Mr. Umpire, vot's knocked is knocked, and vot's over de fence is ofer de fence. Go ahead mit der game." Valentine's compromise was to award Stovey a double.

Valentine resigned because of pressure from managers to influence calls in games. He resigned on June 16, 1895.

The *Louisville Commercial* (July 5, 1886) recorded this encounter: "When New York Metropolitans' 'Chief' Roseman argued with Umpire John Valentine when he refused to wait for a foul ball to be returned, Roseman claimed Valentine had waited for a previous foul ball. Valentine put a new ball in play." (Normally the hitter wants a new ball.)

In 1887, Valentine officiated with his arm in a cast, but eventually had to stop due to the pain. Umpires were not paid when ill or injured.

In May 1888, Billy Sunday was chastised by Valentine for coaching Pittsburg's hitter, Bill Kuehne. Sunday's remark was "If you strike out, run it out."

The *Chicago Times* (April 21, 1888) reported that "Indianapolis' first baseman 'Dude' Esterbrook collided with Chicago's runner Marty Sullivan. When they got up, Esterbrook knocked Sullivan down with is fist. Umpire John Valentine fined each player $25 and the Chicago police arrested both."

Mike Walsh

Walsh was a National League founding umpire noted for his patience. In 1877, a Providence outfielder was given five minutes to locate the original ball. The importance of keeping one ball was demonstrated by Walsh's action. The "five minute rule" held until 1886.

In 1882, Louisville's Pete Browning used a pinch runner who stood behind him, Guy Hecker. When Browning smacked a single, he got excited and beat Hecker running to first base. You cannot have two runners on first base. Walsh ruled Browning out since he was an illegal runner.

In 1882, Walsh felt the outburst of one of the vilest players of the era. In Buffalo, profanity burst forth from "One Arm" Daily after he was called for an illegal pitch. Walsh, a veteran umpire, refrained from ejecting Daily even though the Buffalo cranks called for his removal.

In Baltimore in 1882, spectators came out of the stands and surrounded Walsh after an out call. Walsh ran to the club house. After 15 minutes, he returned to the field and completed the game. Cincinnati beat Baltimore, 1–0.

In 1883, "Pop" Smith hit a foul tip which struck Walsh in the face. There was no face mask. Walsh lay silently on the dirt. A doctor came from the stands and offered Walsh liquor. Walsh went into convulsions. Unbelievably, they took the injured umpire to the Bingham House Hotel. Eventually, he recovered with only a broken nose.

Al Warner

Warner cursed as well as any player. The Philadelphia Phillies protested his calls, and he rebutted by cursing and ejecting them. After continuous bad calls on the next day in May 1899, the players were so upset that Duff Cooley and Elmer Flick signed affidavits attesting to Warner's obscene language and incompetence, and sent them to the league office.

On September 19, 1900, St. Louis Cardinals catcher Wilbert Robinson was called out at home. Robinson walked away and hurled the ball at Warner, who fired his mask at Robinson. After some more words, Robinson was ejected. Cardinals captain John McGraw, the rowdiest player of the 19th century, refused to replace his catcher. Warner forfeited the game to Brooklyn. However, the cranks were not happy with the shortened game, and Brooklyn's president refunded their money to those who requested it.

George "Stump" Weidman

Weidman umpired half a year and received plenty of abuse. On June 25, 1896, Cleveland was playing at Louisville. In the first inning, Jesse Burkett was called out on strikes. According to the *Cleveland Plains Dealer* (June 26, 1896), "Burkett took Weidman by his shoulders and gave him a good shaking." The rookie umpire did not eject Burkett.

Arguing continued the next day between Weidman and various Cleveland players due to questionable calls. Cleveland went up by four runs in the top of the ninth. However, Louisville loaded the bases in the bottom of the ninth, at which point Weidman called the game due to darkness. The *Cleveland Plains Dealer* (June 27, 1896) described what happened next: "The entire Cleveland team surrounded Weidman. The Louisville team also got into the push. The police kept them from attacking. Weidman was so intimidated that his usefulness as an umpire is forever ended."

Weidman was fired as an umpire.

Charlie Wilbur

Wilbur was a rookie umpire who stayed that way. The *Providence Star* (May 12, 1879) reported, "Buffalos' centerfielder Dave Eggler caught a fly ball and then tossed it in the air. Providence's John Ward had tagged up at third base. Umpire Charlie Wilbur only saw the tossed ball being caught and ruled 'Monte' Ward out for leaving early."

In another controversial play, "Providence right fielder Jim O'Rourke caught and dropped a short fly ball in an attempt to get a double play. Umpire Charlie Wilbur ruled the play a catch and only the Troy's batter Ed Caskin was out." *Providence Journal* (May 27, 1879)

William "Chicken" Wolf

Wolf was a substitute umpire for a double header which was played in Louisville on July 16, 1897. Umpire Tom Lynch, after working the first game and ejecting two Giants, refused to work the second game. Louisville got ex–Falls City player "Chicken" Wolf to umpire the second. The game was without incident until the ninth inning, with the Giants leading, 7–2. Wolf was calling nothing but balls on Giants starter Mike Sullivan. The Giants brought in future Hall of Famer Amos Rusie, but the results were the same, walking in the tying run. The Giants had had enough and surrounded Wolf. He was a Louisville favorite, and the crowd poured onto the field to rescue the umpire. The police took several Giants players away. Louisville won, 8–7.

Wolf substituted again in Louisville on August 4, 1897. Cleveland was playing Louisville. Wolf called two strikes on Jesse Burkett, who dropped his bat and went to the dugout, where he picked up a broom and returned to sweep home plate. Burkett was cursing and called Wolf a thief. Wolf quickly ejected Burkett, who refused to leave the batter's box. Wolf told Cleveland manager Patsy Tebeau he had three minutes. Tebeau replied, "He won't leave if you give him thirty minutes." Wolf said, "I'll forfeit the game 9–0 to Louisville."

Wolf went to the pitcher's mound and started a three-minute count. After the three minutes had elapsed, Wolf declared the game a forfeit. Burkett walked up to Wolf and stated, "you're a good fellow" and went to the dugout.

It did not take long for an eruption in the second game. In the first inning, Burkett was tossed again for arguing strikes. A policeman removed him from the game. He sat in the stands with the Louisville cranks, chatting with them.

Ben Young

Young was a rookie umpire who lasted 20 games in 1886–1887. That did not prevent him from some scuffles.

On June 29, 1886, *The Sporting News* reported that Arlie Latham was fined $25 just for walking up to the umpire.

COMISKEY THEN YELLED, "You are no good."
YOUNG SAID, "That will cost you $25 more."
I SAY AGAIN, "You are no good."
YOUNG AGAIN, "That will cost you another $25."
I SAY AGAIN, "You are no good if it cost me my whole salary."
YOUNG RESPONDED, "That will cost you another $25."
(Comiskey said he never called him any name and refused to pay the fines.)

St. Louis was playing Louisville on July 3, 1887. Louisville had an early 5–1 lead when it began to drizzle. Young called a ten-minute delay, then ordered the game resumed. St. Louis manager Charlie Comiskey, a notorious kicker of umpires, wanted the game halted. Young denied the request, and Comiskey took his team off the field even though it was only drizzling. Young called a forfeit. However, Comiskey used his pull to get rid of a good umpire.

7

OTHER ROWDIES

Rowdy Baltimore Orioles Groundskeepers

Not only did Baltimore head groundskeeper Tom "Murph" Murphy do all that Ned Hanlon asked, he thought of ways himself to help the team. He helped "Foxy Ned" make Union Park a major field advantage for the Orioles. Some of the tricks they employed were:

- Buried a concrete block in front of the home plate so chop hits would go higher.
- Built up the ground outside the foul lines so bunts would remain in fair territory.
- Allowed field grass to grow high to help bunts stop.
- Did not water the dirt all summer, which made the playing surface like cement.
- Put soap flakes in the mound dirt to make the ball slippery. Orioles pitchers kept the good dirt in their back pocket.
- The infield dirt was mixed with clay to make the surface hard.
- The outfield grass was left high for concealing extra balls.
- Special mud was used to rub balls before the game; this provided better traction.

Murphy was appreciated by all the Orioles for contributing to the team's success.

Rowdy Philadelphia Phillies "Telegraphy"

On September 7, 1900, Cincinnati Reds shortstop Tommy Corcoran slid into third base, unseating a wire with his spikes. Corcoran pulled the wire that unearthed an electric vault and more wires leading to the Philadelphia Phillies' clubhouse in the outfield. A player would sit in the clubhouse with binoculars and signal the pitch by buzzing the ground under the third base coach. He would then alert the batter. The umpire insisted that the game continue. Corcoran joked that it was a mine laid for opposing coaches. Reserve catcher Morgan Murphy was responsible for the wire system.

Rowdy Cincinnati Reds Cranks

Umpire George Bradley made several close calls against the home team. A crank threw a beer mug, hitting Bradley in the head. Bradley left the field and hid in the director's room. The game was delayed but Bradley returned to finish the game.

Rowdy Cleveland Spiders/Baltimore Orioles Cranks

In the Temple Cup Series of 1895, the Cleveland Spiders played the Baltimore Orioles. The Cleveland cranks tore the boards off the fence to get into the park, eliminating the outfield fence. In Game One, the Spiders cranks threw vegetables to prevent the Orioles from catching fly balls. When the Spiders got to Baltimore, they expected trouble. When they left their hotel, the Spiders' omnibus carriage was pelted with tomatoes and needed a police escort. At the game, the Orioles cranks used boat horns. When the game started, rotten fruit and mud balls were hurled at the Spiders. The game had to be stopped twice. "The park reeked with obscenities and profanity. The worst species of abuse and ruffians ever witnessed," said *Sporting Life* (September 2, 1895).

In the 1886 Championship Series, the St. Louis Browns' cranks threw two Chicago White Stockings cranks onto the field after beating them. The Browns cranks then jumped on the field to continue to hit the White Stockings cranks until the police arrived.

Cleveland Spiders (1899): Worst in Baseball History

The 1899 Spiders had a winning percent of 13 percent. Their top pitcher was Jim Hughey who had a 4–30 record. Therefore, the cranks were not about to attend the games, leaving the average attendance at 147 per game. With such low attendance, owners Frank and Stanley Robinson shifted home games to away games. They only won 20 games for the season and set a record that will never be broken with 101 road losses. The team was dissolved after the season. Stanley Robinson had stated before the season to "operate the team as a side show."

Rowdy Fixes: Louisville

In 1877, the Louisville Grays lost the last seven games of the season, giving the Boston Red Caps the pennant. Four players—pitcher Jimmy Devlin, outfielder George Hall, shortstop Bill Craver and third baseman Al Nichol—were involved in fixing games with poor pitching and sloppy play in the field. The players were sporting expensive jewelry and were frequenting expensive restaurants.

Louisville Courier Journal reporter John Haldeman uncovered telegram traffic to Al Nichol. Team Vice President Charles Chase investigated the charges. The gamblers were betting on the Hartford Dark Blues, who were less talented. A game on August 21 indicated seven errors in a 7–0 loss. National League President William Hulbert banned all four players after reviewing Western Union telegrams.

Rowdy Dog

Man's best friend was also the home team's best friend. On August 22, 1886, Cincinnati visited the Louisville Colonels at Eclipse Park. Chicken Wolf of the Reds hit a ball in the gap. When center fielder Ab Powell ran after the ball, a dog grabbed Powell by the leg and would not let go. Wolf circled the bases with the winning run since Powell was unable to get loose from the dog. The run broke a 3–3 tie in the 11th inning. Louisville won, 5–3.

Rowdy Horse

The *Cincinnati Commercial Tribune* (May 1, 1899) reported,

The Chicago Club had an old horse hitched to a lawn mower. The Club buys one for a dollar, then kills it after the season. One year the old gray had many ailments known to horseflesh. He was lazy. No one could put life in the cripple. But don't spit at the horse because his temper would result in the horse chasing every player.

On one occasion the gate was left open and the old gray horse charged through the gate aiming straight for the players. The horse chased them all over the grounds and then drank from the water keg. The players used the event to stop practice. The players used this trick on more than one instance. The horse would get the last laugh by drinking out of the only water keg.

Rowdy Newspaper Reporters

These reporters' ugly comments spoke for themselves:

Boston Globe (August 12, 1883): "He is not a bad umpire, oh no, he is just miserable that's all. Decker ought to write a book about what he knows about umpiring—it would only take a second—and then go jump in the lake."

The *Chicago Inter-Ocean* (June 6, 1891) criticized Bill Dahlen by commenting, "a stupid play by Bill Dahlen who seemed to be half asleep all day."

The *Boston Globe* (May 31, 1899) said, "'Chief' Zimmer was jogging around the path like a six-day walker with first money in sight."

The *Boston Globe* (August 8, 1889) described Dan Brouthers stealing second against Boston: "Twas no earthquake.... Brouthers slid to second, that's all."

Brooklyn Eagle (October 12, 1892):

Farewell, ye Brooklyn wonders
Tis not hard to say farewell,
Ye have made full many blunders,
Ignobly ye fought and fell.

Chicago Tribune (September 27, 1884): "The Chicago ball team is made up largely of cripples, bums and big heads."

Chicago Tribune (August 15, 1886):

Mother May I Slug the Umpire?
Let me clasp his throat, dear mother
In a dear, delightful grip
With one hand and with the other
Bat him several on the lip.
Let me climb his frame, dear mother
While the happy people shout.
I'll not kill him, dearest mother
I will only knock him out.
Let me mop the ground up, Mother,
With his person, dearest do.
If the ground can stand it, mother,
Don't see why you can't too.

The *Cincinnati Enquirer* (May 13, 1899) reported that "Selback's strongest point is making his toilet [dressing] while standing at the plate."

The *Cleveland Plain Dealer* (June 24, 1899) described Charlie Knepper's running by saying, "a hay wagon drawn by lame horses could have reached third, but Knepper is no hay wagon and had no lame horses to assist him."

Louisville Courier-Journal (July 23, 1883): "If Gerhardt will lead the club out into the woods and lose them, he will confer a favor upon many base ball admirers in this city."

New York Times (August 18, 1884): "There seems to be a screw lose in New York; the Club is without a head."

New York Times (October 12, 1885): "The Giants have lost games with comparatively insignificant nines while using exceedingly bad judgment in certain quarters." (The Giants had an 85–27 record that season.)

Sporting Life (April 7, 1894) said, "'Big Dan' Brouthers cannot be expected to work into shape as soon as some others, for when he has an ache, it must certainly be an immense one. Just think of an elephant having a pain."

The *Troy Daily Times* (July 20, 1880) reported, "The left handed batters of the home team played a child's game after the second inning and tried to hit right handed. They could not hit the side of a meeting house batting right handed."

The *Troy Daily Times* (May 17, 1882) said Troy, "won the game by the 'funny fumbling' of Carpenter, the poor pitching of Richmond, and the accidental hit of Megatherian [an elephant-sized prehistoric sloth] Connor."

Appendix: Rowdy Ball Player Awards

Smartest King Kelly—Used every trick not in the Rule Book, such as an extra ball in his uniform for phantom catches, catching a ball while sitting on the bench by yelling "substitution for the catcher."

Dirtiest "Noisy Tommy" Tucker committed over 50 dirty tricks on other players.

Biggest Clown Arlie Latham—He would bat with his cap over one eye and legs crossed while leaning on his bat in the box. He jumped over Cap Anson while running to first base.

Best Looking Win Mercer—His ejection from the game on Ladies Day created a riot.

Saloon Patron "Budweiser" Gore—His drinking resulted in his suspension. Gore was eventually released from Chicago for excessive drinking.

Best Wrestler "Dirty Jack" Doyle—Head-butted umpire Tom Lynch, and put a headlock on umpire Bob Emslie. He even hip-checked "Muggsy" McGraw.

Best Pugilist Muggsy McGraw—Punched pitcher Frank Dwyer and catcher Heinie Reitz. Slapped a minor league Chattanooga player. Kicked Tommy Tucker. Fought "Wee Willie" Keeler in the shower.

Fastest Lip Pike—Beat a horse called Clarence in a race before a game.

Second Fastest Billy Sunday—Ran like a deer.

Toughest "Black Jack" Burdock—Knocked unconscious five times and still played.

Loudest Oyster Burns—He had the most irritating voice and was dubbed the "disturber."

Craziest Marty Bergen—Walked sideways and thought balls were knives. Believed his own players were trying to poison him.

Foulest Mouth   "One Arm" Daily—Screamed curse words at the batter while pitching.

Most Underhanded   George Bechtel—Threw baseball games for cash and enlisted others to do the same.

Biggest Gambler   John McGraw—He bet on horses, pool shooting and prize fighting. He was suspended for betting $500 on his own team.

Biggest Trouble Maker   "Gladiator" Browning—Said he could not hit without a drink, and was known for frequenting prostitutes.

Most Prejudiced   Cap Anson—Refused to play against black players and did everything to keep them out of the National League. He called their mascot "little coon."

Stingiest   Arthur Soden—Boston owner who charged players $20 for the use of their uniform.

Best Fisherman   Rube Waddell—Missed games to go fishing and even wrestled an alligator.

Worst Family Man   Arthur Irwin—He was a bigamist who had two wives and families at the same time.

Worst Deed   Owner Chris von der Ahe—Paid a burglar to rob his own player of a watch and $19 cash.

Biggest Ego   Only Nolan—Thought he didn't need teammates and could win with just his pitching.

BIBLIOGRAPHY

Achorn, Edward. *Fifty-Nine in '84: Old Hoss Radbourn*. New York: Harper Perennial, 2011.
_____. *The Summer of Beer and Whiskey*. New York: Public Affairs, 2013.
Alexander, Charles. *Turbulent Seasons*. Dallas: Southern Methodist Press, 2011.
_____. *John McGraw*. New York: Penguin, 1988.
Allen, Lee. *The American League Story*. New York: Hill & Wang, 1962.
Anson, Adrian. *A Ballplayer's Career*. Chicago: Era, 1900.
Appel, Marty. *Slide, Kelly, Slide*. Norwalk, CT: Easton, 1996.
Axelson, G. W. *Commy*. Jefferson, NC: McFarland, 2003.
Bak, Richard. *New York Giants: A Baseball Album*. Mt. Pleasant, SC: Arcadia, 1999.
Bogovich, Richard. *Kid Nichols: A Biography of the Hall of Fame Pitcher*. Jefferson, NC: McFarland, 2008.
Bready, James H. *Baseball in Baltimore: The First 100 Years*. Baltimore: Johns Hopkins University Press, 1998.
Browning, Reed. *Cy Young: A Baseball Life*. Boston: University of Massachusetts Press, 2000.
Cash, Jon David. *Before They Were Cardinals*. St. Louis: University of Missouri Press, 2002.
Casway, Jerrold. *Ed Delahanty in the Emerald Age of Baseball*. South Bend, IN: University of Notre Dame Press, 2006.
Chadwick, Bruce, and David M. Spindel. *The Baltimore Orioles: Memories and Memorabilia of the Lords of Baltimore*. New York: Abbeville Press, 1995.
Charlton, James. *The Baseball Chronology*. New York: Macmillan, 1991.
Deford, Frank. *The Old Ball Game: How John McGraw, Christy Mathewson and the New York Giants Created Modern Baseball*. New York: Grove Press, 2001.
DeValeria, Dennis, and Jeanne Burke DeValeria. *Honus Wagner: A Biography*. New York: Henry Holt, 1996.
Doxsie, Don. *Iron Man McGinnity: A Baseball Biography*. Jefferson, NC: McFarland, 2009.
Egan, James M. *Base Ball on the Western Reserve*. Jefferson, NC: McFarland, 2008.
Felber, Bill. *A Game of Brawl: The Orioles, the Beaneaters and the Battle for the 1897 Pennant*. Lincoln: University of Nebraska Press, 2007.
_____. *Inventing Baseball: The 100 Greatest Games of the Nineteenth Century*. Phoenix: Society for American Baseball Research, 2013.
Fleitz, David. *Cap Anson: The Grand Old Man of Baseball*. Jefferson, NC: McFarland, 2005.
_____. *Ghosts in the Gallery at Cooperstown: Sixteen Little-Known Members of the Hall of Fame*. Jefferson, NC: McFarland, 2004.
_____. *The Irish in Baseball: An Early History*. Jefferson, NC: McFarland, 2009.
_____. *Napoleon Lajoie: King of Ballplayers*. Jefferson, NC: McFarland, 2013.
_____. *Rowdy Pasty Tebeau and the Cleveland Spiders*. Jefferson, NC: McFarland, 2017.

Frommer, Harvey. *Old Time Baseball: America's Pastime in the Gilded Age*. Lanham, MD: Taylor Trade, 2005.

Hardy, James D., Jr. *The New York Giants Base Ball Club: The Growth of a Team and a Sport, 1870 to 1900*. Jefferson, NC: McFarland, 2006.

Hetrick, J. Thomas. *Chris Von der Ahe and the St. Louis Browns*. Lanham, MD: Scarecrow, 1999.

Hubbard, Donald. *Heavenly Twins of Boston Baseball: A Dual Biography of Hugh Duffy and Tommy McCarthy*. Jefferson, NC: McFarland, 2008.

Ivor-Campbell, Frederick, ed. *Baseball's First Stars: Cleveland: Society for American Baseball Research, 1996*.

James, Bill. *Bill James Historical Baseball Abstract*. New York: Villard, 1986.

_____. *The New Bill James Historical Abstract*. New York: Free Press, 2003.

Jones, David, ed. *Deadball Stars of the American League*. Dulles, VA: Potomac, 2006.

Kavanagh, Jack. *Uncle Robbie*. Cleveland: Society for American Baseball Research, 1999.

Kelly, Mike "King." *"Play Ball": Stories of the Diamond Field and Other Historical Writings About the 19th Century Hall of Famer*. Jefferson, NC: McFarland, 2006.

Kerr, Roy. *Big Dan Brouthers: Baseball's First Great Slugger*. Jefferson, NC: McFarland, 2013.

_____. *Roger Connor: Home Run King of 19th Century Baseball*. Jefferson, NC: McFarland, 2013.

_____. *Sliding Billy Hamilton: The Life and Times of Baseball's First Great Leadoff Hitter*. Jefferson, NC: McFarland, 2010.

Laing, Jeffrey Michael. *The Haymakers, Unions and Trojans of Troy, New York: Big-Time Baseball in the Collar City, 1860–1883*. Jefferson, NC: McFarland, 2015.

Leavengood, Ted. *Clark Griffith: The Old Fox of Washington Baseball*. Jefferson, NC: McFarland, 2011.

Levine, Peter. *A. G. Spalding and the Rise of Baseball: The Promise of American Sport*. New York: Oxford University Press, 1985.

Lieb, Fred. *The Baltimore Orioles: The History of a Colorful Team in Baltimore and St. Louis*. Carbondale: Southern Illinois University Press, 2005.

_____. *The Baseball Story*. New York: Putnam, 1950.

Macht, Norman L. *Connie Mack and the Early Years of Baseball*. Lincoln: University of Nebraska Press, 2007.

McKenna, Brian. *Early Exits: The Premature Endings of Baseball Careers*. Lanham, MD: Scarecrow, 2007.

Morris, Peter. *Baseball Fever: Early Baseball in Michigan*. Ann Arbor: University of Michigan Press, 2003.

_____. *Game of Inches: The Stories Behind the Innovations That Shaped Baseball*. Revised and expanded edition. Chicago: Ivan R. Dee, 2010.

_____. *Level Playing Fields: How the Groundskeeping Murphy Brothers Shaped Baseball*. Lincoln: University of Nebraska Press, 2007.

Names, Larry D. *Bury My Heart on Wrigley Field: The History of the Chicago Cubs*. Neshkoro, WI: Sportsbook, 1990.

Nemec, David, and Eric Miklich. *Forfeits and Successfully Protested Games in Major League Baseball: A Complete Record, 1871–2013*. Jefferson, NC: McFarland, 2014.

_____. *The Great Encyclopedia of 19th-Century Baseball*. New York: David I. Fine, 1996.

_____. *The Official Rules of Baseball Illustrated*. Guilford, CT: Lyons Press, 2006.

Okrent, Daniel, and Steve Wulf. *Baseball Anecdotes*. New York: Harper & Row, 1990.

Pearson, Daniel Merle. *Base-Ball in 1889: Players vs. Owners*. Bowling Green, OH: Popular Press, 1993.

Phillips, John. *Chief Sockalexis and the 1897 Cleveland Indians*. Cabin John, MD: Capital, 1991.

Roer, Mike. *Orator O'Rourke: The Life of a Baseball Radical*. Jefferson, NC: McFarland, 2005.

Rosenberg, Howard W. *Cap Anson 1: When Captaining a Team Meant Something: Leadership in Baseball's Early Years*. Arlington, VA: Tile Books, 2003.

_____. *Cap Anson 2: The Theatrical and Kingly Mike Kelly: U.S. Team Sport's First Media Sensation and Baseball's Original Casey at the Bat*. Arlington, VA: Tile Books, 2004.

_____. *Cap Anson 3: Mugsy John McGraw and the Tricksters: Baseball's Fun Age of Rule Bend-ing.* Arlington, VA: Tile Books, 2005.
_____. *Cap Anson 4: Bigger Than Babe Ruth: Captain Anson of Chicago.* Arlington, VA: Tile Books, 2006.
Ryczek, William J. *When Johnny Came Sliding Home: The Post-Civil War Baseball Boom, 1865–1870.* Jefferson, NC: McFarland, 1998.
Seymour, Harold, and Dorothy Seymour Mills. *Baseball: The Early Years.* New York: Oxford University Press, 1960.
Smiles, Jack. *"EE-YAH": The Life and Times of Hughie Jennings, Baseball Hall of Famer.* Jefferson, NC: McFarland, 2005.
Solomon, Burt. *Where They Ain't: The Fabled Life and Untimely Death of the Original Balti-more Orioles, the Team That Gave Birth to Modern Baseball.* New York: Free Press, 1999.
Spalding, *American's National Game: Historic Facts Concerning the Beginning, Evolution, Development and Popularity of Base Ball; with Personal Reminiscences of Its Vicissitudes, Its Victories and Its Votaries.* Lincoln: University of Nebraska Press, 1992.
Spatz, Lyle. *Bad Bill Dahlen: The Rollicking Life and Times of an Early Baseball Star.* Jefferson, NC: McFarland, 2004.
Stern, Bill. *Bill Stern's Favorite Baseball Stories.* Garden City, NY: Doubleday, 1950.
Sullivan, *Early Innings: A Documentary History of Baseball, 1825–1908.* Lincoln: University of Nebraska Press, 1995.
Sutter, L. M. *Arlie Latham: The Freshest Man on Earth.* Jefferson, NC: McFarland, 2013.
Tiemann, Robert, ed. *Nineteenth Century Stars.* Phoenix: Society for American Baseball Research, 2012.
Turbow, Jason, with Michael Duca. *The Baseball Codes: Beanballs, Sign Stealing, and Bench-Clearing Brawls.* New York: Pantheon, 2010.
Voight, David Q. *American Baseball: From Gentlemen Sport to the Commissioner.* Norman: University of Oklahoma Press, 1966.
von Bories, Phillip. *American Gladiator: The Life of Pete Browning.* Bradenton, FL: Booklocker, 2007.
Zumstree, Derek. *The Cheater's Guide to Baseball.* Boston: Mariner Books, 2007.

Newspapers

Baltimore American & Commercial Adventurer
Baltimore Daily News
Baltimore Morning Herald
Baltimore Sun
Boston Daily Advertiser
Boston Daily Journal
Boston Globe
Boston Herald
Boston Post
Boston Record
Brooklyn Eagle
Brooklyn News
Brooklyn Times
Buffalo Express
Buffalo Times
Chicago Daily News
Chicago Defender
Chicago Herald
Chicago Inter-Ocean
Chicago Mail
Chicago News
Chicago Record
Chicago Sportsman's Reference
Chicago Times Herald
Chicago Tribune
Cincinnati Commercial
Cincinnati Commercial Times
Cincinnati Enquirer
Cincinnati Post
Cincinnati Times Star
Cleveland Plain Dealer
Cleveland Press
Columbus Evening Dispatch
Daily Inner Ocean
Detroit Free Press
Detroit News
Detroit Post and Tribune
Grand Rapids World
Holyoke Transcript

Kansas City Times
Louisville Courier Journal
Louisville Times
New York Clipper
New York Daily Mirror
New York Daily Tribune
New York Evening World
New York Herald
New York Journal
New York Press
New York Sun
New York Sunday Morning Telegram
New York Times
New York World
New York World Telegram
Pentagraph, The
Philadelphia Evening Bulletin
Philadelphia Inquirer
Philadelphia Inquirer Journal
Philadelphia Item
Philadelphia Press
Philadelphia Record
Philadelphia Sunday Dispatch
Philadelphia Times
Pittsburg Chronicle Telegraph
Pittsburg Commercial Gazette

Pittsburg Dispatch
Pittsburg Post
Pittsburg Post Gazette
Pittsburg Press
Pittsburg Referee
Pittsburg Times
Providence Journal
Providence Press
Providence Star
Providence Telegram
St. Paul Globe
St. Louis Commercial
St. Louis Dispatch
St. Louis Globe Democrat
St. Louis Post Dispatch
St. Louis Republic
Sandusky Star
Sporting Life
The Sporting News
Toledo News-Bee
Troy Daily Times
Troy Press
Washington Herald
Washington Post
Washington Star
Washington Times

INDEX